29-50

The National Institute of Economic and Social Research

POLICYMAKING WITH MACROECONOMIC MODELS

2 Dean Trench Street, Smith Square, London, SW1P 3HE

The National Institute of Economic and Social Research is an independent, non-profit-making body, founded in 1938. It has as its aim the promotion of realistic research, particularly in the field of economics. It conducts research by its own research staff and in cooperation with the universities and other academic bodies. The results of the work done under the Institute's auspices are published in several series, and a list of its recent publications will be found at the end of this volume.

National Institute of Economic and Social Research

POLICYMAKING WITH MACROECONOMIC MODELS

Edited by
ANDREW BRITTON

Gower

Aldershot · Brookfield USA · Hong Kong · Singapore · Sydney

Published by
Gower Publishing Company Limited
Gower House
Croft Road
Aldershot
Hants GU11 3HR
England

Gower Publishing Company
Old Post Road
Brookfield
Vermont 05036
USA

British Library Cataloguing in Publication Data

Policymaking with macroeconomic models.
1. Great Britain. Macroeconomic policies.
Formulation. Mathematical models
I. Britton, Andrew, *1940–*
339′.0724

ISBN 0 566 05748 4

Printed and bound in Great Britain at
The Camelot Press plc, Southampton

Contents

Contributors

Professor M.J. Artis, Department of Economics, University of Manchester

A. Blake, Department of Applied Economics, University of Cambridge

A.J.C. Britton, Director, National Institute of Economic and Social Research

Professor A.P. Budd, Department of Economics, London Graduate School of Business Studies

N. Christodoulakis, Athens School of Economics and Business Studies

Professor D. Currie, Department of Economics, Queen Mary College, University of London

A. Gurney, Research Officer, National Institute of Economic and Social Research

S.G. Hall, Economics Division, Bank of England

S.G.B. Henry, Economics Division, Bank of England

S. Holly, Centre for Economic Forecasting, London Graduate School of Business Studies

P. Levine, Centre for Economic Forecasting, London Graduate School of Business Studies

D. Mackie, Economics Division, Bank of England

D. Miles, Economics Division, Bank of England

Professor A.P.L. Minford, Department of Applied Economics, University of Liverpool

J. Odling-Smee, Under Secretary, HM Treasury

B. Pesaran, Senior Research Officer, National Institute of Economic and Social Research

A. Rastogi, Department of Applied Economics, University of Liverpool

C. Taylor, Economics Division, Bank of England

D.S. Turner, ESRC Macroeconomic Modelling Bureau, University of Warwick

Professor D. Vines, Department of Political Economics, University of Glasgow

Professor K.F. Wallis, Department of Econometrics, University of Warwick

M. Weale, Department of Applied Economics, Cambridge; Clare College, Cambridge and Bank of England

J.D. Whitley, ESRC Macroeconomic Modelling Bureau, University of Warwick

S.J.Q. Wren-Lewis, Senior Research Fellow, National Institute of Economic and Social Research

1 Introduction

Andrew Britton

The use of estimated econometric models in the discussion of macroeconomic policy is now very well established in the United Kingdom, although still not altogether unchallenged. It has been discussed in numerous publications over the past two decades and has been the subject of several conferences before the one out of which this volume arises. Some of the leading references are listed at the end of the book.[1]

Ten years ago the National Institute organised a conference on a closely related theme and published the papers with the title 'Demand Management' (edited by Michael Posner, 1978). It is also about ten years since the publication of the Report of the Ball Committee on Policy Optimisation (1978), which was a milestone in the development of macroeconomic modelbuilding and policy analysis at the Treasury. In introducing the present volume it is natural to ask how the events of the last decade have changed the way macroeconomic policy questions are addressed, and the role that econometric models play.

The empirical base of modelbuilding

The relationships that make up macroeconomic models are quantified and have been estimated, in the main, using the techniques developed by econometricians. This distinguishes them from purely algebraic representations of the workings of economics. The estimated models are often also relatively large and complex, but that is not their distinguishing characteristic. The point of modelling is to make quantified statements about policy: by *how much* output will fall, for example, if interest rates are raised by one percentage point; *how long* it will take for the balance of payments to respond to exchange depreciation. It is also of the essence of modelbuilding that these estimates are based, as far as possible, on empirical evidence. That evidence consists largely of the time-series behaviour of macroeconomic variables in this country over the past twenty or thirty years.

Many of the relationships used in macroeconomic models are well established and have changed little over the last ten years. We can be relatively confident, for example, of the direction and the broad magnitude of the effect of real personal disposable income on consumer spending and the effect of domestic demand on imports. These have changed little over the last decade or more. The passage of time and accumulation of further experience has also confirmed some research findings which were still quite tentative ten years ago. We can, for example, be more confident now that changes in international competitiveness have a predictable effect on export performance and that a higher rate of inflation will increase the personal sector savings ratio. There is also a growing conviction (although it is not shared by all modelbuilders) that employment in the manufacturing sector at least suffers when wage growth accelerates. It is now almost universally accepted, as it was not ten years ago, that wage inflation does respond to the pressure of demand in the labour market, but the precise specification of the relationship and the size of its parameters are still much in dispute.

Negative conclusions are also important. In the last ten years it has been established that movements in the broad monetary aggregates do not have a consistent, measurable effect on economic activity or on inflation. It has also been established that the so-called 'law of one price' (by which the prices of traded goods are equalised in an international market) does not hold in the face of rapid cost inflation or a sharp rise in the exchange rate.

Knowledge of the structure of the economy, based on time-series analysis, necessarily advances slowly, but it is clear that in many areas important gains are being made. Other fields, however, to which research resources have been devoted over the last ten years, have not proved very fruitful. We still lack a satisfactory data-based model of financial flows. We are still very uncertain as to the magnitude of interest rate effects on either consumption or investment. We cannot explain exchange rate movements at all well, let alone predict them. In all these cases a major obstacle to empirical work has been the changes of regime and regulation: the abolition of exchange control for example, which make our data sets discontinuous. Substantial advances may only come after a long period of institutional stability.

The difficulty of modelling the exchange rate is of particular significance, as it undoubtedly plays a key role in the interaction of prices and quantities at a macroeconomic level in this country. That is one reason for the prominence given to it in Chapter 2. Brian Henry and his colleagues at the National Institute seek an empirical model of the exchange rate, not one based on theory alone. For reasons they explain, their search has been only partly successful. The principle of consistent expectations, which has been adopted by most modelbuilders over the last ten years, requires that the expectations attributed to agents by the model should not be systematically different from the predictions of the model itself. But a numerical model can only be solved over a finite period, so the expectations held by agents at the end of the solution period must be based on something other than a model prediction. In the case of the exchange rate it seems that the setting of appropriate 'terminal conditions' is of some importance in determining how the model behaves even in the short run. There is therefore a danger that a non-empirical treatment of the terminal condition in a model with consistent expectations will undermine the claim of the model as a whole to be based on data rather than on theoretical presupposition alone.

It is sometimes said that theoretical reasoning should determine our view of the long-run behaviour of the economy, whilst empirical investigation helps quantify the dynamics of short-term adjustment. (This question is raised by John Odling-Smee in his comment on page 32.) If this is true then a shift of policy concern from short-run 'fine-tuning' to medium-term strategy design might justify a shift of attention by policymakers from econometrics to economic theory. But it is not necessarily the case that theory on its own has much to say even about the long term. We all now accept, for example, that 'money illusion' should not be a long-run property of relationships in a macroeconomic model, but we accept this, partly at least, because the experience of rapid inflation in the 1970s demonstrated that it was empirically valid. Other propositions advanced on theoretical grounds, such as the existence of a 'natural' rate of unemployment independent of the rate of inflation, which are more difficult to demonstrate from the data, must still be regarded as controversial. Moreover, it is not always the case that the long-run properties of estimated equations are less well determined statistically than the short-run. The relative degrees of uncertainty will depend in quite a complicated way on the behaviour of the variables concerned over the sample period. Cointegration techniques, now being used by macroeconomic modellers, mean that some theories of long-run economic behaviour can be submitted to new empirical tests.

Policy analysis with macroeconomic models

One of the most widespread uses of models, ever since their first construction in the 1950s, has been in the analysis of alternative policies over the horizon of a short or medium-term forecast. There was another upsurge in this kind of activity in 1986 and 1987 as the General Election approached. The major political parties all made more or less clear quantified policy proposals, some of them based on work by groups of economists using the various macroeconomic models available to them. There was considerable public interest in the implications of these alternatives for the behaviour of the economy during the lifetime of the next Parliament and the models were extensively used in the public debate that followed. The chapter by Ken Wallis and his colleagues at Warwick (Chapter 5) was no doubt partly provoked by the problems they and others faced in making use of the models available to them to evaluate the policy proposals.

Users of models sometimes complain that policy simulations give very different answers according to the assumptions on which they are carried out. For example, the assumption that interest rates vary to keep the money supply constant may change the whole character of a fiscal policy simulation. This is, however, one of the great advantages of model simulations, not a 'problem' with them. Models require the user to be precise about the question he is addressing, as indeed he must be if he is to give it a coherent answer at all.

Thus a 'change' in fiscal policy may be characterised either as a unique departure from an established rule, or as the establishment of a new rule. The effect of the policy action will be different in the two cases, because expectations will be differently affected. In either case it is necessary, moreover, to specify what rule is being followed for other policy instruments, in particular for monetary policy. Ten years ago it was already getting difficult to say what was meant by 'unchanged' or 'neutral' monetary policy. Sometimes it meant unchanged interest rates (nominal or real), sometimes unchanged money supply. Nowadays we think increasingly of monetary policy in terms of predetermined responses (or feedback rules) – rather than predetermined settings of actual policy instruments such as nominal interest rates or inflexible targets for monetary aggregates or nominal exchange rates. The more clearly these rules are specified, the less the danger of misunderstanding. This is true when describing policy analysis with a macroeconomic model; and it is true also of policy pronouncements by the authorities in the real world.

In many of the chapters here, policy is analysed explicitly as a choice between alternative feedback rules. This is a useful way of describing regimes as different as the monetarism of 1979, the fixed exchange rate rule of the EMS, the proposals of the New Keynesians and even the fine-tuning of real output growth in some legendary epoch of the more remote past.

In devising feedback rules three sorts of decisions must be taken. The first concerns the variables to be included. This might seem to be the most important issue: yet it is given surprisingly little attention in the work presented here. An informal case in favour of simplicity is made in Chapter 3 by Alan Budd and his colleagues at the London Business School (and in the papers they cite), but what simplicity means in this context needs more explicit treatment. A complex rule might be made simple merely by a redefinition of variables: indicators, such as domestic credit expansion, have been invented for this very reason. But simplicity has its price. If the set of variables in the feedback rule is limited, it becomes very important that they contain most of the information relevant to the attainment of the policymaker's final objectives. This is not easy to establish. The 'welfare loss' from a simple rule that took no account of movements in oil prices might have been small in the 1960s, but in the 1970s it would have become much larger. How can one know beforehand which indicators are going to become important? Simplicity has its dangers as well as its attractions.

The second decision concerns the target values for the variables in the feedback rule. If the rule relates fiscal policy, for example, to deviations of nominal income from some target path, how is that target path calculated? In principle this choice should be made (as Stephen Hall says in his comment on page 234) by reference to the macroeconomic model itself. In common practice, however, the targets are often extraneous to the model and chosen in a quite informal, if not arbitrary, way. For many years money supply targets were set as quite simply last year's target minus 1 per cent. Finally the coefficients of the feedback rule have to be quantified, and here a more formal optimisation procedure can quite readily be introduced. Numerous examples of the techniques available will be found in this volume (see Chapters 3, 7 and 8).

This characterisation of policymaking, and the limited role of optimisation in it, contrasts with the discussion of related issues in the Ball Committee Report. Full optimisation is equivalent to a very complicated feedback rule and will always produce better results, in a given model of the economy, than will any rule that is less complicated. It is, naturally, more difficult to judge how full optimisation will compare with a simple rule when both are calculated using imperfect models. It is sometimes asserted that simple rules are more robust, which would be a very appealing property, but we lack a full understanding of which rules are robust in which circumstances. The advantages of full optimisation were recognised at the conference, although it is not in fact adopted on this occasion in any of the chapters here.

If the choice had been debated more fully we would probably

have been drawn further into discussion of the advantages of different kinds of precommitment. Precommitment to a feedback rule requires that response parameters be announced in advance. But when the model changes, as we know from experience it must (and as with the accumulation of knowledge we must hope it will), then the same parameters will no longer be appropriate. A precommitment to full optimisation, on the other hand, requires a statement of the Government's priorities amongst objectives. These would be political value judgements, not empirical judgements as to how the world works. They would not need to change as new empirical evidence accumulated. But the 'realist' may well argue that there are good political reasons for *not* making value judgements explicit. The cost which the Government is prepared to pay in unemployment in order to reduce inflation by one percentage point is not the kind of figure most governments would wish to state in public. It is not something politicians often discuss, even in private. Perhaps it would be better if they did, but this may be a question which we should leave the political theorists to sort out.

Policymaking in practice

This book provides ample evidence that policy analysis with macroeconomic models is a lively and progressive field of research amongst academic economists. But is it also of practical help to those actually making policy in the Treasury and the Bank of England? I write as an outside observer, and my views should be checked against those expressed by insiders in this volume, John Odling-Smee from the Treasury and Chris Taylor and his colleagues from the Bank. My impression is that analysis using estimated models is very important to policymaking, probably as important now as it ever has been.

Ten years ago, as now, ministers and senior officials were sceptical of all quantified estimates of policy effects presented to them, as indeed they should be. Nevertheless there is an inescapable need for quantification in the conduct of macroeconomic policy. The alternative to numbers that are based on sophisticated models is in fact numbers that are based on crude and unsophisticated models. Macroeconomic models can embody any view of the way the economy works which finds empirical support and can be quantified. The model developed by Patrick Minford, for example, is of particular interest as it embodies a new classical or monetarist view of the world.

There was a time during the last ten years when it seemed possible that the authorities would adopt a position of active hostility to the use of models and quantified predictions based on them in the conduct of policy. But that time, immediately after the change of government in 1979, soon passed. The Treasury and the Bank continue to prepare economic forecasts and to construct and maintain macroeconomic models. They would not, in this cost conscious age, do so if they did not find them useful. Economists from the Bank and the Treasury have played a significant part in the advance of empirical knowledge about the workings of the British economy in the last ten years. They continue to participate, as this volume demonstrates, in debate about the analysis of macroeconomic policy with their fellow professionals, if sometimes in somewhat muted tones. Long may this continue.

The title of the conference volume published by the Institute with a similar theme ten years ago was 'Demand Management'. On this occasion we have chosen a less controversial wording. Nevertheless, there is more continuity in the conduct of policy over the last ten years than many readers of press reports or ministerial speeches would probably realise. Ten years ago the conduct of policy could not reasonably be characterised as demand management, if that means that it was guided solely by objectives for the level of economic activity or employment in the domestic economy. At least as much attention was being paid to the growth of monetary aggregates, the level of public sector borrowing, the real incomes of trade union members and the current account of the balance of payments.

So it is today. But there is also today at least as much concern as there was ten years ago about the need to manage demand, to prevent 'overheating' or to avoid another recession. Admittedly some prefer to discuss policy in terms of nominal rather than real expenditure growth, but they too are engaged in the business of demand management, even if they are reluctant to use the terminology. They require quantitative guidance as to the effects of the policy instruments at their disposal, for this or for other purposes.

Increasingly the problems of economic policy have become international. The last ten years have seen growing interest in the problem of policy coordination and a related interest in the development of estimated world macroeconomic models. It is right therefore that this volume should include one chapter, that by David Currie and Simon Wren-Lewis (Chapter 8), devoted to this set of issues.

The intellectual challenge now is to find a way of conducting and describing macroeconomic policy which is consistent, which is relevant to the conditions of the late 1980s and which uses the empirical knowledge that has accumulated, as well as new theoretical insights. It will probably not be the approach commonly described as 'traditional' Keynesianism, nor the monetarist approach with which the authorities experimented briefly about seven or eight years ago. It may well be characterised as a feedback rule of the sort described in several of the chapters in this volume. If so, there is need for careful attention to the precise way such rules are devised, how they might be changed if they proved inappropriate and the way that a commitment to follow them would be expressed. I hope that this book will contribute to further debate along these lines.

Note

1 See HM Treasury (1978), Hilton and Heathfield (1970), Holly *et al.* (1979), Ormerod (1979), Posner (1978), Renton (1975), Worswick and Blackaby (1974) and Wallis *et al.* (1984, 1985, 1986 and 1987).

2 The Exchange Rate and External Trade*

Andrew Gurney, Brian Henry and Bahram Pesaran

Introduction

Since the publication of *Demand Management* (Posner, 1978), the twin themes of expectation formation and dynamic modelling have become pre-eminent in macroeconomic modelling. Over the last few years a continuous programme of work has been undertaken at the National Institute, directed explicitly at these two themes, in a large-scale enquiry into the presence of forward-looking expectation formation in macroeconometric models. Three distinct aspects of this work are particularly important: econometric issues raised by expectation modelling, especially when the hypothesis of rational expectations is invoked: computational problems when model-consistent expectations are used in a large-scale non-linear model: and the performance of the model in forecasting and simulation modes when consistent or rational expectations are assumed. The motivation for the move to the rational expectations modelling was an attempt to explain the large changes in behaviour which appeared to occur in the early 1980s. These presented macro modellers with a new set of problems, not only those arising within the new policy framework, but also those caused by the speed and scale of the collapse in output and employment in 1979–81, which was unparalleled in the post-war period, and provided a new challenge to anyone attempting a quantitative explanation of the behaviour of the economy. These problems in turn raised a large number of econometric issues, and work at the National Institute over the last few years has tried to provide econometrically satisfactory equations, which arguably outperformed orthodox lagged models of behaviour, and which introduced the sort of volatility in employment, stock-building and so on that had been observed. Much of this material is surveyed in *National Institute Economic Reviews* (nos 114 and

* We would like to express our thanks to the ESRC for their financial support for this work. At the time of writing Brian Henry was employed at the National Institute of Economic and Social Research.

115) and need not be recounted here. Some of this work proved to be quite successful, especially that for the labour market, company sector expenditures, the exchange rate and the demand for money. This strongly contrasts with the experiences of other modellers, who have often had recourse to large-scale imposition in model equations where these were supposed nonetheless to embody rational expectations. On the computational aspects of solving these estimated models, considerable progress was also made, especially in the work by Hall (1985a), who developed computational techniques which enabled the full model, involving some 46 future expected variables, to be solved within minutes.

This is not to say substantial problems do not exist. Our claim is only that this work lays the basis for one important macroeconometric development: the incorporation of *fully estimated* equations with rational expectations into a macroeconometric model which may be readily used for forecasting and policy analysis. One area where much further work is obviously called for is in the modelling of financial and foreign exchange markets. Much of the theoretical and econometric discussion of the exchange rate is based on the assumption of rational expectations. In this chapter we will be describing some of the issues that have arisen in work aimed at an econometric explanation of the exchange rate. This is not just a technical issue, however, as much of this work leads to important policy implications, given the central role the exchange rate plays in influencing output and inflation.

The exchange rate

We will provide here some analysis of the real exchange rate, building upon the approach described in Hall (1987a) (see also Currie and Hall, 1986a and 1986b). The basic reason for electing to start from this point is largely a matter of empirical evidence. This model appears to be supported by a variety of statistical tests, and thus seems a counter example to the view that empirical exchange rates do not appear statistically robust.

Some preliminaries

For some considerable time attention has focussed on the question of exchange rate volatility. In an extreme case it may be that exchange rate behaviour is subject to self-fulfilling speculative behaviour, shifting the exchange rate away from its fundamental determinants. Testing for the presence of such behaviour is difficult because any test must be a joint one of the presence of bubble behaviour and the postulated model of exchange rates used. Speculative bubbles could well be interpreted as omitted variables in the model of exchange rates used in the test, so that the finding of a speculative bubble could equally be regarded as confirming a misspecification in the exchange rate model. Here, and in the following section, we discuss some alternative exchange rate models which figure in our later empirical testing and relate them to this question of exchange rate dynamics.

Before describing the models, one empirical matter should be established concerning the relevancy of the regular finding of a unit root in the time series for the real exchange rate. This leads some economists to state the exchange rate model in first differences, effectively inducing stationarity in the model before estimating it (see, for example, Meese, 1986). Recent developments in the cointegration approach to modelling non-stationary variables show that it may be possible to identify vectors of these variables which nonetheless yield stationary error processes. First-differencing as a prelude to estimation is thus unnecessary.

Some dynamic models of the exchange rate are now described, and these will be used in the empirical section which follows.

The first model we use is based on the present National Institute model. This is a dynamic model of the real exchange rate, assuming costly adjustment due, for example, to government attempts to smooth out short-run fluctuations in the exchange rate by intervention. (See Hall, 1987a, and for a related model based on adjustment costs incurred by international investors, see Currie and Hall, 1986b.) The model supposes exchange rate movements arise from minimisation of

$$C = \sum_t D^t \, [a/2 \, (E_t - E_t^\star)^2 + d/2 \, (\Delta E_t)^2] \qquad (1)$$

where $E^\star$ is some long-run exchange rate to be described later and D is a discount factor, $D < 1$. Then the relevant first-order condition is

$$\left(L - \frac{a + d(1 + D)}{d} + DL^{-1}\right) E_t = -\frac{a}{d} E^\star(\cdot) \qquad (2)$$

In the present National Institute model, the undiscounted case of (1) is taken, where $E^\star$, the target exchange rate, is given by

$$E^\star = a_1 \, (rd - rf) + a_2 \, (rd - rf)_{-1} + \phi \, E_{+1} \qquad (2')$$

where $(rd - rf)$ is the real interest rate differential.

This equation nests a number of alternatives about international asset behaviour. In the case when $a_2 = 0$, $\phi = 1$, the equation gives the open arbitrage condition (the real exchange rate is in logs). When a_1 and a_2 are equal and opposite in sign, $a_1 > 0$, then it is changes in the interest differential which produce asset movements, and then $\phi = 1$ is consistent with a stock view of asset behaviour where asset adjustment is completed within the unit time period. Substituting (2′) in (2) gives the equation

$$\left[\frac{d}{a + d(1+D)}\right] E_{t-1} - E_t + \left[\frac{dD + a\phi}{a + d(1+D)}\right] E_{t+1}$$

$$= \frac{-a}{a + d(1+D)} [a_1 (rd - rf)_t + a_2 (rd - rf)_{t-1}] \qquad (3)$$

The present version of the model used by the National Institute assumes no discounting. In the case when $\phi = 1$ in (2′) above then the weights on E_{t-1} and E_{t+1} sum to unity. (Only if the left-hand side of (3) is symmetric are the roots reciprocal and unity, ruling out a recursive forward solution. See Sargent, 1979. Otherwise in such a model a forward solution will exist.)

We now discuss alternatives to (3) which involve a forward recursive form of equation. There are two parts to this alternative which distinguish it from the present National Institute model. The first is that we will be assuming that a forward recursive solution to an equation like (but not identical to, for reasons we give next) equation (3) may exist. Hence we will assume that discounting is sufficiently heavy or, since these assumptions are not identifiably different in the models we estimate, that ϕ is sufficiently below unity for such a solution to occur. Next we will in effect be enlarging the set of variables incorporated in the right-hand side of (3). We will add other trade effects (proxying the current account, see below). Currie and Hall (1986a) report evidence favouring the inclusion of this variable. We also experiment with oil variables directly affecting the real exchange rate.

We can write the right-hand side of (3) as $\tilde{E}$, where this is related to a set of observable variables Z. $\tilde{E}_t = \delta' Z_t + \epsilon_t$ where ϵ_t is an error term and Z includes terms in interest rates, trade and oil effects. Returning to the first point we will thus be using the familiar decomposition of the Euler equation using the stable root. This may be expressed as

$$(1-\lambda_1 L)E_t = \frac{a}{(dD+a\phi)\lambda_2} \sum_j [\frac{1}{\lambda_2}]^j \widetilde{E}_{t+j}$$

$$= \frac{a}{(dD+a\phi)\lambda_2} \sum_j [\lambda_1 (D+\frac{a\phi}{d})]^j \widetilde{E}_{t+j} \quad (4)$$

where λ_1 is the stable root. Given a representation of $\widetilde{E}(\cdot)$, we will discuss alternative ways of estimating (4) in the next section.

Finally, we will also be considering purely lagged or backward-looking versions of the real exchange rate, which use similar determinants of the real exchange rate as we do. The most notable example here is the work by Meese and Rogoff (1986) who estimate lagged models of the real exchange rate which depend, among other things, upon real interest differentials and trade balances. In the cointegration material we present in the next section, we will build upon these results, and will also provide an example of a lagged model of the real exchange rate for comparative purposes.

Before moving to describe empirical results, we note some of the variables we have used as influences on the real exchange rate. As already noted, these are based on the relatively successful empirical results reported in Hall (1987a), Meese and Rogoff (1985) and in Currie and Hall (1986b). The emphasis will be upon the determination of the exchange rate via asset flows, with trade effects (proxying current account effects) also playing a role (see Hall *op cit.*). The use of the real exchange rate may be justified by assuming that agents make decisions upon relative nominal interest rates and rates of return, conditional upon expected inflation, but that they do not make significant forecast errors in predicting inflation.

In the empirical work which follows we will invariably use the balance of goods and services as a potential determinant of the exchange rate. The current account is the variable suggested by theory. Use of the trade balance may be interpreted as proxying the current account. The underlying reason for using a proxy lies in the well-known problems in identifying structurally stable equations for interest profits and dividends (IPD), the other main element in the current account.

Furthermore, we allow for the possibility that the discovery of oil reserves and variations in the real price of oil have effects upon the real exchange rate. Much of the analysis of the effects of oil is couched in terms of macroeconomic linkages between, say, oil reserves and the exchange rate. Oil discoveries are akin to an endowment of wealth, which produces changes in the structure of the economy, especially the proportion of tradeable to non-tradeable goods, which will be consistent with an appreciation in the real exchange rate. We will be concerned with evidence for a *direct* effect upon the real exchange rate. The interpretation of the oil discovery is that it encourages capital inflows, tending to directly raise the real exchange rate. A similar argument holds for an increase in the real price of oil, benefiting an oil exporting country. Others have found such effects in empirical work. The Treasury model, for example, assumes that the equilibrium exchange rate is determined in part by the real value of oil reserves.

In all the cases we consider, the technique is to let data considerations determine the chosen specification. Thus whether stock or flow factors are crucial is an empirical matter of the evidence favouring levels or rates of change terms in interest rate differentials and the current account. In turn, the evidence may favour trade effects rather than current account effects. Finally, on the question of oil effects, we take a particularly catholic approach. Theory suggests the value of disclosed reserves, though given the nature of the reserves variable, we also test for oil production as an alternative.

Exchange rate models

In this section we provide cointegration or time-series analysis of the level of the real exchange rate and later describe estimation results for exchange rate models under the rational expectations hypothesis (REH).

(i) Time-series analysis

The two tables below give preliminary evidence on real exchange rate movements. In Table 2.1, the Dickey Fuller (DF) and augmented Dicky Fuller (ADF) statistics are used to establish the order of integration of the variables we will be using as potential influences upon the level of the exchange rate.

The table shows that the variables in levels are non stationary, though the evidence on the real interest differential is borderline, the DF being significant, but the ADF not so at the 5 per cent level. If the set of variables are differenced once, the table shows that the hypothesis of a unit root is readily rejected (the ADFs are unclear in the case of the oil variables however). The evidence then is that the variables are I(1) (integrated of order 1), and are *prima facie* candidates for inclusion in a cointegrating vector.

(ii) Cointegration tests

The results show that the variables in table 2.1 (including possibly *DIFF*) are not stationary. Obviously our aim is to take a fairly generous interpretation of the long-run determinants of the exchange

Table 2.1 Univariate analysis

Variable	DF	ADF
REFF	−1.272	−1.547
DIFF	−2.90	−1.985
TB	−1.933	−1.783
OILRES	−2.816	−2.675
QOIL	−2.44	−2.36
PEXOIL	−1.767	−2.514
Δ*REFF*	−6.20	−3.48
Δ*TB*	−8.64	−3.78
Δ*DIFF*	−6.457	−4.168
Δ*OILRES*	−5.235	−1.98
Δ*QOIL*	−5.704	−1.720
Δ*PEXOIL*	−6.00	−2.99

Note: In this table, the definitions of the variables are as follows (variables in logs unless denoted *):

REFF = The real effective exchange rate
*DIFF** = The real interest rate differential
TB = The trade balance (the ratio of exports of goods and services to imports)
OILRES = Real value of disclosed oil reserves
QOIL = Real value of output of the oil sector
PEXOIL = Real export price of oil
Δ indicates the first difference of the relevant variable.

rate. We allow it to be determined by, first, the interest rate differential; second, the trade balance (proxying the more theoretically acceptable current balance, or cumulated current balance) and third, the value of oil reserves, oil production, or real oil prices. Note that the value of oil reserves is essentially the oil price, since disclosed reserves have remained almost constant from 1975.

To obtain a vector of variables determining the level of the real exchange rate we use cointegration methods. This can be interpreted as representing average behaviour of the exchange rate, and it can be assumed to be known to rational agents.

Our results show that the variables above do not quite cointegrate. The three-variable case for example, needs a CRDW of 0.38, a DF of −3.37 and an ADF of −3.17 to satisfy cointegration criteria. In table 2.2 the oil variables can be easily discounted, as they do not appear to help in the explanation of the real exchange

Table 2.2 Tests for cointegrating vectors[a]

	(1)	(2)	(3)
Constant	4.41	4.3	4.3
	(360.1)	(129.4)	(87.5)
TB	1.302	1.17	1.17
	(9.92)	(6.39)	(6.34)
DIFF	0.005	0.006	0.006
	(2.01)	(2.11)	(2.10)
RVO		0.005	
		(1.05)	
RPOIL			0.01
			(0.42)
R^2	0.636	0.64	0.64
CRDW	0.519	0.48	0.48
DF	−2.94	−2.8	−2.89
ADF	−2.02	2.07	−2.06

[a] Dependent variable *REFF*, sample 197201–198604.

rate. Equation (1) gives a simple, and probably the best (that is, nearest to cointegrating) version. This equation depends only on the real interest differential and the trade balance. These results are perhaps more encouraging than those reported by Meese and Rogoff (1985) for example, who report a DF of −1.0 for the sterling–dollar real exchange rate–real interest rate differential. However, our equations do not cointegrate, and this would clearly be a problem if we were to implement two-stage estimation of an error-correction model. (Other variants were attempted, including using the cumulative trade balance, but these did not improve on the results quoted above.) These results may then be regarded as descriptive information, and, for the alternatives we have considered, these are marginally in favour of non-stationary error.

(iii) Estimating rational models

Estimating an equation like (2), we use the errors in variables method. That is, rewrite the equation as

$$E_t = a_0 E_{t-1} + a_1 E^e_{t+1} + BZ_t + e_t \tag{5}$$

where $a_0 = d/(a + d(1 + D))$, $a_1 = a_0D$, and $B = aa_0/d$, and Z is the vector of determinants of the target exchange rate.

Assuming expectations of E_{t+1} are formed in an unbiased way, we replace the expected forward exchange rate by the actual forward rate, and estimate the equation by instrumental variables.

An alternative method used to estimate equation (3) is based on FIML. (This is the procedure used in Hall, 1987a.) As with equation (5), the actual future exchange rate replaces the expected future exchange rate. But with this alternative method, the exchange rate equation is augmented by an equation for the future rate, that is, $E_{t+1} = \theta \tilde{\chi}_t + \epsilon_t$ where $\tilde{\chi}_t$ is a set of exogenous variables (including any exogenous variables entering the E_t equations). Estimating the two equations, the exchange rate and future exchange rate, by FIML will produce consistent estimates. Also, as RHS variables in the exchange-rate equation will typically *not* all be exogenous (for example, the real interest rate differential and the real trade balance are clearly jointly determined), then consistent estimation requires the joint estimation of equations for these variables also.

Estimating equation (4) consistently may similarly be achieved by replacing forward expected terms by actual future values, or by using predictions for the determinants of $\tilde{E}(\cdot)$ based on a VAR model and instrumenting. In these estimates the forward weights are dependent upon the backward weight although in the case of a non-symmetric Euler equation, this dependence will not be straightforward.

(iv) Estimation results

Our first equation estimates of (3) included weighted future convolutions of all the expected determinants of the equilibrium real exchange rate identified earlier (but proxying the current balance of trade). They were quite encouraging, except for the sign on the forward convolution of the real interest rate differential $DIFF^e$. This proved incorrectly signed and insignificant, a feature which remained for a number of alternative specifications of the equation. To further investigate this question, we concentrated upon equation (3) with current interest differentials only. In terms of the underlying behavioural assumptions in this alternative, the current interest differential is assumed to have a dominant influence in agents' plans; because they do not look ahead in forming a view of monetary conditions, or because current values of interest rates provide sufficient information on which to base future ones.

$$E_t = \underset{(3.66)}{0.88} + \underset{(14.69)}{0.80}\, E_{t-1} + \underset{(4.15)}{0.396}\, (TB)^e + \underset{(2.45)}{0.005}\, DIFF_t \quad (6)$$

$$R^2 = 0.91,\ SE = 0.04,\ DW = 1.85$$

This estimate uses forward predictions for the expected variables derived from a vector autoregressive model (VAR). The details of the VAR model are given in an appendix. The estimate in (6) is thus of the two-stage variety, where forward expected terms are replaced by predictions, which are then treated as data, implying that the equation may be estimated by allowing for the restriction between backward and forward weights. An alternative approach is to estimate the equation by using non-linear instrumental variables, as follows.

$$E_t = \underset{(3.2)}{1.03} + \underset{(10.9)}{0.77}\, E_{t-1} + \underset{(2.15)}{0.225}\, (TB)^e + \underset{(2.43)}{0.005}\, DIFF_t \quad (6')$$

$$R^2 = 0.91,\ SE = 0.04,\ DW = 1.8$$

where $(TB)^e = \sum_{j}^{M} (\lambda)^j\, TB_{t+j}$

As is obvious, there is little to choose in practical terms between these rival methods of estimating the equation, and we will generally use non-linear IV in what follows.

This appears fairly successful, and the results indicate important influences from the level of future trade terms and the current real interest differential. A number of comments may be made about the result. Firstly, unlike the equation currently used in the National Institute model, the present one implies a long-run relationship between the real exchange rate, the real interest rate differential and the trade balance. The orders of magnitude for this long-run relationship for equation (6) are $\overline{E} = 1.98\ \overline{TB} + 0.025\ \overline{DIFF}$.

Unlike the current version of the National Institute exchange rate model (for an update see (7) below), this one is not interpretable in terms of international portfolio behaviour. The present model implies the long-run relationship $\Delta DIFF = -0.4\ \Delta TB$ which in turn implies a trade-off between the external deficit and interest rates. In round numbers this suggests that a one percentage point rise in the interest rate differential is required to finance an increase in the external deficit of approximately 1 per cent of GDP.

As well as having a different interpretation in terms of portfolio behaviour, the example given in (6) gives a large weight to the lagged dependent variable, yielding a much more sluggish view of real exchange rate movements than the present National Institute model (again, this is illustrated by equation (7) which attaches preponderant weight on the forward expected real exchange rate).

A further estimate of this version of the real exchange rate equation was made over a smaller sample period to evaluate the structural stability of the estimates shown in (6′), which was estimated up to 1985Q4. The alternative shown below was estimated over a sample ending in 1983Q4.

$$E_t = \underset{(3.03)}{1.03} + \underset{(9.98)}{0.77}\, E_{t-1} + \underset{(1.96)}{0.212}\, TB^e + \underset{(1.92)}{0.005}\, DIFF_t \qquad (6'')$$

$$R^2 = 0.93,\ SE = 0.04,\ DW = 1.9$$

Although the effects on the determinants of the exchange rate target are not as well determined in this equation as compared with (6′), the parameter estimates are little changed in this re-estimate.

Our next illustration is an estimate of the Euler equation, based on (5). This illustration re-estimates Hall's original model (1987a), which comprises equation (5), and an equation for the actual future real exchange rate E_{t+1}, and, since it is an element in the Z vector, an equation for the real interest differential. This gave the following results for the exchange rate and interest rate equations (estimated by FIML)

$$E_t = \underset{(10.84)}{0.259}\, E_{t-1} + (1 - 0.259)\, E_{t+1} + \underset{(3.648)}{0.006}\, \Delta DIFF_t + \underset{(8.122)}{0.24}\, \Delta TB_t \qquad (7)$$

$$\Sigma e^2 = 0.0848,\ DW = 1.919$$

$$DIFF_t = \underset{(0.645)}{0.234} + \underset{(57.08)}{0.98}\, DIFF_{t-1} - \underset{(16.91)}{33.5}\, \Delta E_t + \underset{(0.632)}{0.0109}\, DIFF_{t-2} - \underset{(2.023)}{4.297}\, P_t + \underset{(1.787)}{3.318}\, P_{t-1}$$

$$\Sigma e^2 = 409.3,\ DW = 1.635.$$

These results are remarkably similar to the original ones obtained by Currie and Hall (we use an extra two years data), except for the coefficient on ΔE in the interest rate equation. The negative sign we obtain is more consistent with the interpretation of the interest rate equation as a policy reaction function.

We will discuss the relation of this result to a version of the forward recursive solution later. Before that we briefly note the results of estimating a backward-looking version of the model. This is similar to the model discussed in Meese and Rogoff (1985). Estimating a model dependent upon current and lagged trade balance and interest rate differentials, we were not able to obtain a well-defined version dependent on lagged trade and interest rate effects. A version depending upon current and lagged values was more successful, and this is shown below. This does not, of course, have the reduced form interpretation of the original Meese and Rogoff model, and is shown for illustrative purposes as a model which does not incorporate explicit forward-looking terms.

$$\begin{aligned} E_t = \underset{(2.68)}{0.86} + \underset{(11.09)}{0.806}\, E_{t-1} + \underset{(3.97)}{0.57}\, TB_t - \underset{(1.78)}{0.28}\, TB_{t-1} \\ + \underset{(2.31)}{0.005}\, DIFF_t \end{aligned} \tag{8}$$

$$R^2 = 0.91,\ SE = 0.04,\ DW = 1.79$$

This equation also appears quite successful. The terms in the trade balance may easily be reparameterised into levels and rate of change form, to yield a long-run relationship between the real exchange rate, real interest rate differential and trade balance. Our cointegration results earlier show that there is apparently no long-run relationship in the levels of these variables, so the lagged dependent variable is crucial in producing a stationary error process in (8). (Testing for serial correlation and heteroscedasticity gave an LM(4) of 1.9 and ARCH test of 0.2 for this equation.)

(v) Some assessment of the alternatives

On the issue of volatility three lines of enquiry are possible: variance bounds tests; cointegration; and explicit tests of volatility based on (7) and (6) (see Meese, 1986, and Wadhwani, 1984). We will not comment on variance bounds tests beyond noting that these discuss the issue of volatility in a rather different sense to that used in Meese. (In Wadhwani, 1984, the test is between the variance of actual real exchange rates and that from a rather poorly fitting model based on the Dornbusch overshooting model. That the data exhibits more variability than the model is hardly surprising therefore.) We will briefly discuss only the latter interpretation.

Here the comparison is between the recursive forward solution which of course embodies the transversality condition and is a stable RE solution (a fundamental solution in Meese's terminology). The Euler equation, not being subject to a transversality condition, is compatible with non-transitory movement away from a fundamental solution.

Tests for the presence of bubbles centre on the full RE solution in contrast with the Euler equation (in our case equations (3) and (4) above, with the latter suitably extended to include the time-series model representing the $\widetilde{E}_t$ variables). A full information method estimates (4) and the time-series representation of $\widetilde{E}_t$ jointly. Under the *null* hypothesis that there are no self-fulfilling bubbles, this method provides efficient estimates. The alternative is the McCallum procedure of estimating (3) by replacing E^e_{t+1} by the actual future variable, E_{t+1}, creating an MA(1) error in the process. This may be consistently estimated by instrumental variables (but is not efficient). Under the alternative hypothesis that a bubble exists however, the FIML estimate will be inconsistent, whereas the estimate using the McCallum procedure will still be consistent. Intuitively the reason FIML is inconsistent is because the transversality condition excludes an unstable solution. In effect, the solution in this case is $E_t = E^F_t + d_t$ where E^F is the fundamental solution and E_t satisfies the Euler equation.

The tests provided by Meese use the first difference of the exchange rate given the unit root in the data. We are not able to provide a full information version of the forward model given the number of observations we have, so a misspecification test as described earlier is not possible. We have however an estimate of the forward recursive solution for the real exchange rate in difference form, and this is shown next.

$$\Delta E_t = \underset{(0.12)}{0.00} + \underset{(0.65)}{0.10}\, \Delta E_{t-1} + \underset{(0.87)}{0.01}\, \Delta DIFF_t + \underset{(1.4)}{0.42}\, \Delta TB^e_t \qquad (9)$$

$$R^2 = 0.03,\ SE = 0.04,\ DW = 1.81$$

This result could be compared with that of (7) (which can be rewritten as an equation entirely in first differences). We do not suggest this as a formal test in any way but the comparison does suggest evidence against (9) in favour of (7). This evidence is then some confirmation of real exchange rate volatility, given a real exchange rate model based upon trade effects and interest rate differentials.

The next section will illustrate the properties of both versions of the real exchange rate (6) and (7). Judged as single equations, their dynamic properties are evidently different, and we will now investigate the quantitative nature of these differences in complete macro model solutions.

Complete model properties

The dynamics of the trade sector and the exchange rate are obviously problematic, especially when assuming forward-looking expectation formation. In their empirical analysis, Currie and Hall (1986a) raise the problem of the presence of forward-looking expectations in foreign exchange markets together with a J curve, implying that for exchange rate stability, international investors must be assumed to see through the adverse side of the J curve, to the long-run balance of payments position.

In what follows we will be considering two things which bear on this issue; the dynamic properties of the National Institute model assuming different exchange rate equations and end-point conditions for the solution, and the relation between exchange rate movements and the trade balance when the model is subjected to policy shocks.

(i) Model solutions with different exchange rate equations

Before proceeding to the results, we first discuss the role of end-point conditions in model-consistent solutions. An important problem arises in obtaining consistent solutions when a model equation includes a unit root. In effect this is the same as having the equation in differences, with no levels terms so that there is not a solution for the level of the variable. The exchange rate equation currently used in the National Institute model has a unit root and, as equation (7) shows, this is also a feature of the re-estimated equation. The problem this produces may be described as the practical one of obtaining model solutions which are 'relatively' insensitive to the end-point condition used. By this it is meant that the early part of the solution is unaffected by extensions to the solution period (as is the case in Fair's extended solution method), and that the form of the end-point condition does not significantly affect the nature of the model solution. The present exchange rate equation used in the National Institute model does not satisfy these requirements. The equation is of the same form as (7), and the model is solved using as the end-point condition for the exchange rate the equation,

$$E_{T+1} = E_0 + 1.76 \left[\left(\frac{X}{M}\right)_T - \left(\frac{X}{M}\right)_0 \right] \qquad (10)$$

where T is the solution interval. Firstly this represents an extra-model relationship between the exchange rate and the trade balance, which is at variance with the estimated exchange rate equation. This gives a long-run relationship between interest rates and the trade balance (at given exchange rates). Secondly, an extended solution procedure would not work in this case, simply because the effect of the terminal value on the early part of the solution will not decline, however far ahead the solution is pushed, given the unit root in the equation (see Hall and Henry, 1988).

Although an end-point condition in rate of change form must have some effect on solution values, it is widely recognised as being a fairly neutral assumption to make. It may be interpreted as saying that the model is on some long-term growth solution at the terminal date. Also, solutions using this end-point condition may employ the extended solution procedure, so ensuring that early parts of the solution remain invariant to the terminal conditions.

Next, we illustrate the effects of the exchange rate in whole model solutions. For the purposes of illustration, we take the fiscal policy package reported in Britton (1986), which aimed to take one million unemployed off the unemployment register. Given that this was computed using an equation similar to (7) and end-point condition (10) above, it is natural to question whether the implications of that simulation were significantly affected by the nature of the end-point condition used. Before moving to an analysis of that question, we note other changes in the macro model which also have a bearing upon the implications of a fiscal stimulus.

The results reported use NIESR model 10 (1987b) which, among other things, incorporated evidence of stronger competitiveness effects than its predecessors. For comparative purposes, we show the effects of the package described by Britton (1986), conducted on model 8, with the effects of the same package on model 10.

What is evident in this comparison is that the stimulation is much more effective on the real side in the case of model 10. There are three reasons for this: the stronger competitiveness effects in trade, nominal interest rate effects on manufacturing investment and durable consumption and, finally, weaker inflationary influences in model 10 compared with 8.

The change which is of particular importance for present purposes is the estimated decrease in the effect of unemployment in influencing wage inflation. As compared with model 8, subsequent vintages of the model have almost halved the size of the long-run effect of unemployment on wages. Thus any simulation changing unemployment produces noticeably smaller effects upon wage inflation. Secondly, subsequent models also decreased the

Table 2.3 A comparison of model 8 with model 10 using an expansionary fiscal package

Fourth quarter figures

Year	1	2	3	4
GDP (%)	1.1 (2.3)	2.1 (3.7)	2.9 (4.7)	3.3 (5.1)
Inflation % (CPI annual rate)	−4.7(−4.0)	−3.6(−3.4)	−1.4(−2.1)	0.9(−0.9)
Unemployment (000s)	−288(−294)	−526(−576)	−708(−836)	−819(−1050)
PSBR (£bn, annual rate)	5.5 (5.5)	1.9 (1.6)	0.4(−1.9)	−0.8(−4.2)
Trade balance (£bn, annual rate)	−2.3(−4.1)	−3.9(−6.4)	−4.8(−7.9)	−5.1(−8.2)
Effective exchange rate (%)	−1.4(−2.1)	0.6 (0.2)	1.8 (1.8)	1.9 (2.2)
Real effective exchange rate (%)	−2.9(−4.7)	−3.7(−5.2)	−4.2(−6.0)	−4.5(−6.5)

Note: Figures for model 8 taken from Britton (1986), table 2.2; for model 10 the figures are shown in brackets. The package is an increase in public consumption of £1.6 bn (annual rate, at 1980 prices), employers' contributions and national insurance contributions reduced by the equivalent of 6 per cent of wages and salaries, and an offsetting increase in the standard rate of income tax to produce a change in the tax yield of approximately 11 per cent. In both simulations the real interest rate differential is held constant.

effect of import price changes upon domestic price changes. In the model used for the original simulation shown in table 2.3, the CPI included a direct effect from import prices. Later versions of the model abandoned this in favour of a data preferred version which excluded this direct influence.

The effect of the package in the case of model 10 is something of an overkill, given the aim of one million off the unemployment register. In this and subsequent runs, we will generally quote the trade balance as our index of the overseas sector. This reflects our empirical result for the exchange rate above, which used the balance of goods and services.

The problems with these solutions are similar in nature, and concern the size of the emerging trade deficits and their relation to the size of the real depreciations. In both cases large increases are projected for the deficit and the real depreciations of the exchange rate do little to ameliorate these. The essential question then is, are these outcomes for the current deficit and the real exchange rate

Table 2.4 An unanticipated increase in government current expenditure of £1.6 billion per annum (solution period modified by one year)

	1	2	3	4
GDP (%)	0.68(0.68)	0.58(0.58)	0.67(0.67)	0.69(0.69)
Inflation (CPI %)	0.3 (0.3)	0.5 (0.5)	0.5 (0.5)	0.4 (0.4)
Unemployment (000s)	−70(−70)	−60(−60)	−70(−68)	−80(−78)
PSBR (£bn annual)	−1.7(−1.7)	−2.3(−2.3)	−2.5(2.5)	−2.5(−2.5)
Visible balance	−0.6(−0.6)	−1.0(−1.0)	−0.9(−0.9)	−0.5(−0.5)
Effective exchange rate (%)	−1.1(−1.1)	−1.8(−1.8)	−2.2(−1.6)	−2.4(−2.0)
Real exchange rate	−0.9(−0.9)	−1.0(−1.0)	−1.0(−1.0)	−1.0(−1.0)

realistic? Bear in mind that two further points arise in the case of both these versions of the model. The first is that of the terminal condition used in solving the model. As noted above, for both these versions of the model the terminal condition is given by (10), which introduces a degree of *extra-model* behaviour into the movement of the real exchange rate, so the table illustrates the joint result of the estimated model and the (*ad hoc*) end-point condition, in some unknown combination. The second point is one stressed by Currie and Hall (1986b) which is that alternative models of the exchange rate will alter this picture. Table 2.3 for example uses the flow version of their exchange rate model, a stock version of the model is rather more pessimistic in its implications according to their results (see Currie and Hall, Table 2). The estimation we reported above however, bears on both issues. In the rest of this section we discuss the issue of the terminal conditions. In the next we will return to the problem of the sustainability of the external deficit.

Firstly we conduct a simple experiment on the variant model, using the exchange rate equation given by (6) with rates of change end-point conditions on all expected variables. This illustrates the dependance of a simulation upon the length of the solution period, following a fiscal shock, produced by an increase in government current expenditure (table 2.4).

In this table, the solution shown in brackets is carried out for an additional four quarters compared with the other solution. As can be seen, there is almost no difference between the solutions, except in the final year. This suggests that the model properties are little affected by variations in the solution period.

Table 2.5 Policy package: model 10 compared with variant

Year	1	2	3	4
GDP (%)	2.3 (2.3)	3.7 (3.9)	4.7 (4.8)	5.1 (5.3)
Inflation (%)	−4.0(−4.2)	−3.4(−2.9)	−2.1(−1.2)	−0.9 (0.5)
Unemployment (000s)	−294(−294)	−576(−590)	−836(−867)	−1050(−1112)
PSBR (£ bn annual rate	5.5 (5.7)	1.6 (1.9)	−1.9(−1.1)	−4.2(−3.7)
Trade balance (£ bn annual rate)	−4.1(−5.0)	−6.4(−7.8)	−7.9(−7.6)	−8.2(−7.5)
Effective exchange rate (%)	−2.1(−2.4)	0.2(−3.6)	1.8(−2.9)	2.2(−2.1)
Real exchange rate (%)	−4.7(−5.3)	−5.2(−8.4)	−6.0(−9.0)	−6.5(−8.8)

Note: For details of the package see table 2.3. Variant model shown in parentheses.

We next compare the implications of the two models we have been discussing using a fiscal package run on model 10 with the exchange rate equation similar in form to (7) together with the end-point condition (10), compared with the variant model (equation (6)). The variant uses the alternative exchange rate equation, and a rate of change end-point condition for all expected variables as before. The results for this comparison are shown in table 2.5 where model 10 is the version with equation (7) plus (10) as the end-point condition.

In this comparison the results from these two model solutions differ only in the exchange rate/price nexus. The variant produces a larger fall in the real exchange rate. This appears to have little effect upon the level of output, given the long lags with which trade responds to competitiveness changes. It takes some time before the net trade balance improves as the package also stimulates domestic consumption directly and hence worsens trade. Otherwise the results of the package appear similar between the models, both implying that a boost to growth can be made with an expansion in demand. Though this produces a worsening in trade, our empirical evidence suggests that the resulting exchange rate movements do not produce offsetting increases to inflation. This is confirmed in the variant model, which embodies levels effects from the balance of goods and services proxying movements in the current account.

What we observe is that although the real exchange rate does depreciate more than implied by model 10 (plus its end-point condition), the sluggishness with which import price changes influence domestic prices in the model implies that the different nominal exchange rate profile in the variant is not noticeably more pessimistic about inflation.

It should be emphasised that our illustration indicates that a fiscal package would not imply noticeably higher inflation as between the two variant exchange rates and model solution methods. This observation is consistent with the view that the end-point condition and the exchange rate equation combined produce very similar results to the variant model *for this fiscal shock* in model 10.

What is also evident is the large deficit on external trade which accompanies the package, under both forms of the exchange rate equation and attendant terminal condition. The next section discusses some of the issues involved.

(ii) The exchange rate and external deficits

The previous exercise was directed at identifying the dependence of the results of a fiscal stimulus upon the form of exchange rate and end-point condition used in the model. The variant model for the exchange rate produces a broadly similar picture, with significant deficits accompanied by little additional inflation. The empirical results earlier indicated a long-run relationship for the real exchange rate of the form $E^\star = 1.98\ TB^\star + 0.025\ r^\star$ implying a trade-off between the external deficit (proxied by TB) and real interest rates. This suggests as orders of magnitude that a 1 per cent increase in the level of the ratio of imports to exports implies a 0.8 per cent point rise in real interest rates.

Other questions arise however. Due to the difficulty in obtaining robust equations for IPDs and transfers, we have modelled the exchange rate as a function of the balance of goods and services, rather than the current account balance as a whole. Nonetheless, some orders of magnitude may be given for current account effects. The total effect on the current balance consists of the effect on the balance of goods and services plus any changes arising from net interest, profits and dividends (hereafter IPD). Net IPDs depend on the rates of return earned on United Kingdom assets and liabilities, the level of the exchange rate, and the current account balance (since a current account deficit represents a drawing-down of net United Kingdom assets). Using changes in United Kingdom and foreign interest rates as a proxy for changes in the rate of return, rules of thumb may be used for calculating IPD effects. These suggest that at 1987 levels of assets, liabilities and interest rates, a 5 per cent depreciation in the nominal exchange rate improves net IPD by £0.9 billion a year, and that for each billion on the annual current account deficit, the IPD balance deteriorates by £0.08 billion a year.

Two other questions then concern the possibility of a monetary response to an unsustainable deficit, and the estimated size of the trade effects themselves. Since we have consistently avoided the issue of policy design in this chapter, and concentrated on questions of econometric evidence, it is the latter of these two questions which occupies the remainder of this section, which discusses some additional evidence on competitiveness effects in trade in manufactures.

Recently, two questions on Britain's trade performance have been debated extensively; the possibility of hysteresis, particularly in exports, and the possibility that as nominal exchange rates have fluctuated more substantially over the last few years agents have increasingly tended to discount the transitory component in exchange rate movements. These concerns appear contradictory, but the former may have a bearing on the explanation of United Kingdom exporting performance since 1980, following the over-appreciation in sterling (see Bean, 1987). More recently, the rapid rise in United Kingdom exports of manufactures appears to suggest either a stronger response to changes in competitiveness or possibly a change in the long-term trend of Britain's share in world trade of manufactures. A full assessment of these questions is beyond the scope of this chapter, but we will provide tests that forward-looking prices influence trade behaviour. In our empirical tests we were able to identify these in exports equations, but not in imports, so what follows describes the results for exports of manufactures. (For a fuller account of this study, see Anderton and Henry, 1987.) These equations are demand equations for exports, of the general form

$$x^d = a_0 + a_1 c + a_2 w + \epsilon \qquad (11)$$

where x^d is export demand, c is a measure of price competitiveness and w is an index of world demand. Recently, increasing attention has been paid to export supply, and the potential this may have in explaining recent behaviour (see Holly and Wade, 1986, and Bean, 1987). Again these are matters that we will not be pursuing here. In the econometric equations we assume that agents consider expected prices up to four quarters ahead only. Strictly, as world trade is a determinant of equilibrium demand for exports, it should also enter in a forward-looking way with similar weights. However, we assume here that current and lagged world trade is sufficient to predict world trade movements for a year ahead. Also our interest is in testing for price responsiveness, at a time of price volatility. To estimate the equation with future expected actual prices, we use an errors in variables method, replacing the expected by the actual future value, instrumenting the equation to deal with the resulting correlation between actual future values and the error term as described in the second section. The results of this exercise are shown next (equation is in logs)

$$\Delta x^d_t = \underset{(3.0)}{1.4} - \underset{(4.6)}{0.3}\,\Delta x^d_{t-1} + \underset{(3.5)}{0.4}\,\Delta w_t + \underset{(3.4)}{0.47}\,\Delta w_{t-1} \quad (12)$$

$$- \underset{(3.2)}{0.23}\, x^d_{t-1} + \underset{(3.3)}{0.14}\, w_{t-1} - \underset{(3.3)}{0.22} \sum_{i=1}^{4} (\lambda)^i (c)_{t+i}$$

$$R^2 = 0.81,\ LM(4) = 2.4 \text{ SAMPLE 1966Q2–1986Q1}$$

Compared with the equation used in model 10, which is an orthodox lagged version, the present one shows a long-run competitiveness elasticity of 0.94, which is substantially higher than the lagged model (0.58). According to the forward-looking model, agents rationally predict relative price movements. In a period of volatile relative price movements due, for example, to rapid exchange rate changes, they tend to discount short-run movements in prices, and according to this argument, equations which do not allow for this will tend to underestimate the size of the competitiveness effect.

Using this equation for exports of manufactures, we reran the same policy package from the earlier exercise. The comparative results for the trade balance and exchange rates (real and nominal) are shown below (the differences in output and inflation are too small to warrant inclusion in the table). The results for the version of the model using equation (12) are shown in brackets.

Table 2.6 Variant model compared with new exports of manufactures

	1	2	3	4
Trade balance £bn	−5.0(−4.6)	−7.8(−7.3)	−7.6(−7.1)	−7.5(−6.9)
Effective exchange rate %	−2.4(−1.9)	−3.6(−3.0)	−2.9(−2.2)	−2.1(−1.2)
Real effective exchange rate %	−5.3(−4.9)	−8.4(−7.8)	−9.0(−8.4)	−8.8(−8.2)

The figures for the variant model with the forward-looking exports equation show that, as expected, there is an improvement in the trade balance coupled with somewhat smaller real depreciations, though the quantitative effects are small. Obviously, these effects could be different if forward-looking price formation had been identified in all importing/exporting categories in the model. The size of these may only be speculated on. It is hard to see, however, that they would be responsible for a radical change in the combination of relatively small real depreciations coupled with significant worsening in the trade balance common in these policy simulations.

Conclusions

There are two types of conclusion which we think are implied here, one involving the likely behaviour of the economy following fiscal shocks, the other concerned with modelling. Regarding the first, the results presented here largely confirm the general conclusion in Britton (1986) of the effects of a fiscal package aimed at substantial decreases in unemployment. What we have illustrated, however, is that these results follow in a model where all equations are estimated and generally satisfy conventional statistical criteria. While this was also true of the earlier simulation results, the problem produced there by the *ad hoc* nature of the end-point conditions used meant that those results were inevitably the combination, in an unknown way, of the properties of estimated equations and end-point conditions. Our new results show that with exchange rate equations of a similar genesis to that used earlier, but operated with neutral end-point conditions, the general effects of the fiscal package remain the same.

This brings us to the second point; the significance of the estimation results for the exchange rates we have reported. Here we have been at pains to establish two further things. One is that forward recursive forms for the exchange rates may be estimated with a considerable degree of empirical success. This form of implementing the REH has been used successfully by researchers at the National Institute on other sectors of the model. Our results show, we hope, that similar success is possible in exchange rate modelling. Our second point on exchange rate modelling concerns the original work reported in Hall (1987a) and Currie and Hall (1986a, 1986b), to which we have frequently alluded, and the comparative work we have reported here. In all these works the hallmark is a considerable degree of success in deriving models of the real exchange rate which fit the data, and appear relatively parameter stable. Our comparisons have been based on models which are thus serious contenders for acceptable representations of exchange rate behaviour, a feature noticeably absent in many similar exercises both here and in the United States. There has been a general supposition that the exchange rate is not amenable to modelling. Work on this at the National Institute over the last few years suggests that this supposition may be unfounded.

Appendix

VAR Model

Equation for the trade balance (TB)

Lag	Constant	*TB*	*RM*1
1	0.82**	0.76**	−0.14**

$SE = 0.037$, $DW = 2.28$

Equation for real interest differential (DIFF)

Lag	Constant	*DIFF*
1	−0.82**	0.99**
2		−0.34**

$SE = 2.52$, DW 1.96

Equation for real money supply M1 definition ($\Delta RM1$)

Lag	Constant	ΔTB	ΔRVO	*DIFF*	$\Delta RM1$
1	−0.002	0.16**	−0.03**	−0.003**	0.35**
2					
3					
4		0.16**			0.22*

SE 0.021, $DW = 1.75$

Equation for real value of oil production (ΔRVO)

Lag	Constant	*TB*	*RM*1
1	4.81**	−1.96**	−0.79**

$SE = 0.269$, $DW = 1.81$

Comment on Chapter 2

John Odling-Smee

As the Treasury is the only major modelling group not contributing a main chapter to this book, a few general observations about the use of models in policymaking will be made here, commenting in particular on how thinking in the Treasury about the role of models has evolved over the last decade or so. These comments are grouped under two headings: modelling, and the policy context.

On models, we are now less confident than we were ten or fifteen years ago that models can provide the answers to all the questions of interest to policymakers. This is mainly because the margins of error surrounding numbers generated by models tend to be rather big, at least in relation to the orders of magnitude of policy changes which may be contemplated. The evidence on margins of error comes from a variety of sources, which all point in the same direction.

Firstly, there are changes in model properties over time. Although in the Treasury we have a deliberate policy of trying to avoid sharp changes in model properties, nevertheless properties often change significantly when we alter only one or two of the more important equations. Secondly, there are large differences, which have been well documented by the Warwick Bureau, between the properties of different models. Ten or twenty years ago we might have hoped that the data would enable us to discriminate between rival models. While this might eventually be possible, and it may be the case in respect to specific equations now, in general one cannot say that one model is clearly superior in terms of empirical content and coherence to another. Choices between models have to be based mainly on theoretical preferences and other *a priori* considerations. Thirdly, changes in models over time and differences between models are, of course, mainly a reflection of the parameter and specification uncertainty which modellers are all too conscious of. There is often little to choose, in terms of econometric tests, between two alternative equations, yet they may have rather different implications in a whole model context.

However, the increased awareness of the margins of error has been accompanied by many improvements in the Treasury model as in other models, and in the way we use it. In particular we have filled what were gaping holes in, for example, the financial sector and the treatment of forward-looking expectations in the foreign exchange and gilts markets. Even so there are still many gaps. For example, the Treasury model provides a less than comprehensive explanation of supply-side behaviour. Productivity growth is still largely explained by an exogenous time trend, although there is now an endogenous element in the form of productivity changes in response to changes in factor prices.

Another area where we have advanced is in simulation design. We now pay close attention to how simulations are set up and, in particular, to the assumptions about the macroeconomic policy that is being pursued and to the assumptions about what forward-looking financial markets think is going to happen to policy in future. Our ability to vary assumptions about expectations of future policy changes enables us to model different degrees of credibility in announced policy changes: credibility in the sense of expectations about whether the policy change will be sustained or not. While I would not vouch for the precise quantitative results of such exercises, qualitatively they illustrate the kinds of jumps in the exchange rate and gilts prices that feature in both the theoretical literature and more popular discussion of market reactions.

Turning to the policy context, the main change here over the last decade has been the shift towards emphasising the medium-term effects of policy and its sustainability, and away from an emphasis on the short-term effects. This has affected us as modellers in that we have therefore put more effort into trying to answer questions about the longer-term consequences of policies.

It is too early to say whether cointegration techniques will improve the reliability of our estimates of long-term relationships. It will probably still be necessary to rely to a considerable extent on theoretical considerations and a general view of how the world works in assessing the long-term effects of policy changes.

Our general view in the Treasury is that macroeconomic policy has little effect on output, employment and other real variables in the long run unless there is an impact through changes in supply. Moreover, the model does not include some of the possible routes by which supply might be affected, such as the effects of changes in public or private investment on the capital stock and hence productivity, or the effects of fluctuations in inflation on efficiency, confidence and investment. Thus we would not expect simulations of policy changes on the Treasury model to indicate sustained changes in output. When they do, it is often a signal that the simulation has been set up in the wrong way.

There can be, of course, short-run effects on output from policy changes. We do not subscribe to the new classical macroeconomics doctrine of policy ineffectiveness in the short term. These real effects are attributable largely to differing speeds of adjustment in different markets and hence to changes in relative prices. When we assume forward-looking expectations in financial markets we effectively speed up the adjustment of some relative prices and as a result alter the estimates of the real effects of macroeconomic policy in the short term.

One aspect of the greater emphasis on the medium and long term is that we pay attention to a slightly different set of variables when looking at simulation results than we would if the short term were the main consideration. Whereas a decade or so ago the emphasis might have been entirely on output and employment, supplemented increasingly by inflation, we now look also at variables which might be signalling the build-up of unsustainable disequilibria of one kind or another. Inflation is obviously of central interest in this respect. So also are changes in net overseas assets, financial balances of domestic sectors, and the balance between consumption and investment.

The reduced emphasis on short-term effects means that we do not search for changes in the policy mix that might optimise some welfare function over the first few years but at the expense of difficulties later on. Examples of these would be a loosening of fiscal policy accompanied by a tightening of monetary policy (as pursued in the United States), or a tax switch from employers' national insurance contributions to income tax. In some cases, such as the fiscal–monetary policy switch, we handle the long-term problems by assuming that they are anticipated by financial markets, who therefore assume that they will be reversed. This in turn means that the short-term impact of these policies is less than it would otherwise have been.

To sum up, it might seem at first sight that modelling has a less important role in policymaking in the Treasury than it used to have. It is certainly true that we serve up fewer numbers from policy simulations straight to Ministers. That in itself does not, of course, mean that such work is less influential. Economists in the Treasury still comment on the whole range of macroeconomic policy issues, and provide quantification where necessary. The Treasury model is vital in this process because, first, it is essential when numbers are needed; and second, it is an invaluable aid to clear thinking, especially since the interactions are usually too complex to work through in one's head or in a simple analytical model. We could not operate at all effectively in policy analysis without the model, even if we never showed Ministers a single number.

This chapter is essentially about the specification and estimation of a forward-looking exchange rate equation and its effects on overall model properties. Although a particular policy proposal is simulated, the comment on the results is primarily from a modelling point of view. Comments here are therefore mainly about modelling.

The model of the exchange rate in terms of the current account and interest rate differentials, in either stock or flow terms, is very interesting. Moreover, the forward-looking nature of the specification means that in simulations the exchange rate at the beginning depends on what the model says would happen to the current account and interest rates over the whole period of the simulation. This seems to be the right way of specifying the behaviour of the exchange rate.

The authors conclude that they have been successful in fitting this model of the exchange rate to the data. This may be so, but it is difficult to judge without more information about the results which were discarded. It would be interesting to know, for example, the extent to which levels of the trade balance and the interest rate differential were superior to changes in them in some equations, and vice versa in others.

Where information is provided it might have been interpreted slightly differently. For example, the non-stationary nature of the variables in levels form suggested by the Dickey-Fuller statistics in table 2.1 might lead one to prefer an exchange rate equation in stock terms (that is, $\Delta E = f(\Delta r$ and so on)). But that has not been taken into account in the estimation. Secondly, in interpreting the cointegration tests in table 2.2 one might be less inclined than the authors to be encouraged by results which do not fully satisfy cointegration criteria. Thirdly, many of the equations contain a high weight for E_{-1}, which is worrying because of the implication that they do not explain sharp movements in the rate.

The test for the presence of bubbles is difficult to comprehend and leaves the impression that it is not a very strong one. However, to the extent that it points to evidence of bubbles, presumably one should interpret simulations based on an exchange rate equation which excludes bubbles with some caution.

In discussing the export equation the authors suggest that the higher coefficient on future relative export prices than on past relative export prices suggests that exporters tend to discount short-run movements in prices. This may be the correct conclusion, but it would be helpful to see the two equations tested against each other, using the same data set and sample period. It might also be interesting to use relative export prices for an average of some past quarters and some future ones.

Finally, although this chapter is not really about policy analysis, an observation on the policy simulations in the third section may be made here. In the light of earlier comment about the longer-term consequences of policy changes, one should ask whether rising output, rising inflation and a large current account deficit on this scale really are sustainable and will be perceived by financial markets to be sustainable. If the answer is no, then it might be necessary to reconsider the design of the simulation or perhaps it provides some evidence that the exchange rate is not performing in the way that one thinks it should.

Comment on Chapter 2

Sean Holly

The authors began by placing their work within the context of a broader study of work at the National Institute on forward-looking expectations in macroeconometric models. Three sub-themes were identified: first, econometric estimation; second, computational aspects of imposing consistent expectations on a model; and third, the performance of the model for forecasting and simulation when expectations are consistent.

The approach taken by the National Institute demonstrates how far matters have developed in ten years. The use of 'rational' or 'consistent' expectations has now become part of the mainstream of macromodelling, at least in the United Kingdom. Indeed, practically none of the publicly funded modelling groups in the United Kingdom has managed to avoid its embrace, in one form or another, the Growth Project at Cambridge being the only honourable exception. However, an advocate of rational expectations ten years ago might have difficulty recognising the particular hybrid form which is prevalent today. What has allowed many macromodellers to accept the importance of forward-looking behaviour for understanding how the economy works is the distinction now made between forward-looking behaviour and perfectly-flexible, market clearing price behaviour. We require both of these properties in order to be able to obtain the super-neutrality results of Sargent and Wallace.

It may be that matters have gone too far in watering down the effective role of forward-looking expectations. In terms of the speed with which prices adjust we can distinguish between prices in financial markets which adjust 'instantaneously' to news, and prices in the goods and labour markets which adjust more slowly. Jumps in asset prices, and in particular the exchange rate, together with sluggish adjustment in domestic prices, are key features of the Dornbusch/Buiter/Miller model of the small open economy.

If we turn to how the National Institute has approached the modelling of expectations, we find that forward-looking expectations are predominantly concerned with quantities. Employment is dependent on expectations of output (as well as real wages). Inventories depend on expected sales. In this chapter exports of manufactures depend on expectations of world demand and competitiveness, though here a much more powerful role for prices is detected.

The authors provide a model of the real exchange rate. It is assumed that movements in the real exchange rate arise from the minimisation of a quadratic loss function, given as equation (1) here. At this point it would have been useful to have a precise definition of which real exchange rate this is. Is it the GDP deflator or the traded goods deflator which is being used? There is also a question about why the real exchange rate is considered appropriate. Which group of economic agents is it that can be assumed to suffer losses from the real exchange rate being away from its equilibrium in the sense that they can adjust the real exchange rate towards equilibrium? Of course individual agents may suffer as a consequence of the real exchange rate being out of equilibrium, but there is nothing they can do about it. There is some evidence to suggest that the costs of adjusting nominal exchange rates are negligible. If this is the case then equation (1) could be interpreted as a model of the adjustment of domestic prices.

After appropriate manipulation and use of the calculus, the authors end up with a dynamic equation for the real exchange rate (equation (3) in the chapter), which, it is claimed, nests a number of alternatives above international asset behaviour. I feel very uncomfortable with the notion that relatively loosely parameterised reduced-form equations are supposed to nest alternative theories. Surely we require a theory of the exchange rate which is less restrictive than alternatives and which is empirically superior to others.

Consider a highly stylised, linearised representation of a financial sector shown below.

$$B_t^d = p_t + a_1\, rd_t + a_2\, w_t$$
$$B_t^{df} = p_t - a_3\, rd_t + a_4\, w_t$$
$$M_t^d = p_t - a_5\, r_t + a_6\, w_t$$
$$B_t^\star = p_t^\star - a_7\, rd_t + a_8\, w_t^\star$$
$$B_t^{\star d} = p_t^\star + a_9\, rd_t + a_{10}\, w_t^\star$$
$$M_t^\star = p_t^\star - a_{11}\, r_t^\star + a_{12}\, w_t^\star$$

where $rd_t = r_t - r_t^\star + e_{t+1}^e - e_t$. B_t^d is the domestic demand for domestic bonds. B_t^{df} is the domestic demand for foreign bonds. M_t^d is the demand for money, and an asterisk indicates the equivalent demands by foreign residents. r_t is the domestic rate of interest, w_t is wealth. e_t is the exchange rate, and e_{t+1}^e is the one period ahead expected exchange rate.

Under floating exchange rates the market for foreign exchange is cleared such that the current account is financed by flows on the capital account. So the change in $(B_t^{df} - B_t^{\star d})$ is equal to the negative of the current account.

$$- B_t^{df} + B_{t-1}^{df} + B_t^{\star d} - B_{t-1}^{\star d} \cong -BAL_t$$

We can solve for the nominal exchange rate to give:

$$e_t = e^e{}_{t+1} + r_t - r_t^\star + \psi \Big[- a_4 w_t - a_{10} w_t^\star + p_t$$

$$- p_t^\star - \Sigma_{i=0}^{\infty} BAL_{t-i} \Big]$$

where $\psi = [1/(a_3 - a_9)]$. The terms $a_3 + a_9$ measure the interest elasticity of capital flows. When domestic and foreign bonds are perfect substitutes $\psi = 0$, so we end up with the *uncovered interest parity condition*. This kind of model is a more suitable, though by no means the only, basis for a model of the exchange rate.

3 Stabilisation Policy in Britain*

Alan Budd, Nicos Christodoulakis, Sean Holly and Paul Levine

Introduction

Since the conference out of which this book arose marked the tenth anniversary of the previous demand management conference, we have taken the opportunity to re-examine the condition of the economy and the role of macroeconomic models in analysing it ten years ago. Somewhat parochially we concentrate in particular on the LBS model and on the paper presented to the 1977 conference by Ball and Burns. March 1978 saw the publication of the Report of the Committee on Policy Optimisation (the Ball Report). Since the major contribution of this chapter is the application of control techniques to policymaking we recall briefly the views expressed in the Ball Report and the technical developments since it was written.

The LBS model ten years ago

It seems appropriate to start by looking back at the paper presented by Ball and Burns to the 1977 Demand Management conference. In that paper they reported the main properties of the LBS model at that date and used the model to analyse two previous periods (September 1964–September 1969 and July 1970–July 1975) and to recommend policy for a future period (early 1977 to December 1981).

At that time the LBS model was undergoing important changes, partly in response to the events of the early and mid-1970s, and partly in response to developments in macroeconomic theory and in modelling. An important source of influence was the work of the Cambridge Economic Policy Group, with its emphasis on the link between changes in the public sector deficit and changes in the balance of payments. By 1977 the LBS model incorporated the sectoral flow of funds. Another important issue, which has been discussed in Ball, Burns and Laury (1977) was the effect on the balance of payments of changes in the nominal exchange rate. By 1977 the LBS model had the properties that: (a) under a fixed

* This research was financed by the Economic and Social Research Council.

exchange rate system the rate of inflation will ultimately depend on the world inflation rate; and (b) the effect of an exchange rate change on the balance of payments depends on the fiscal policies pursued after the exchange rate change. Another important change was the incorporation of inflation effects into the consumption function with the result that a rise in the inflation rate *ceteris paribus* raised the savings ratio.

At that stage the LBS model could not incorporate freely floating exchange rates because, as the authors stated, such a system would require a fully specified capital account. The model used a reduced-form exchange rate equation in which the exchange rate was related to the relative money stock and relative output movements. The computed values from this relationship were described as the 'normal' exchange rate. The gap between the actual exchange rate and the normal rate was then related to its own lagged values, flows of sterling balances held by the OPEC countries and the cumulative current account level.

Ball and Burns (1978) reported, in general terms, the properties of the model in terms of its reaction to external shocks and changes in exogenous variables. Under fixed exchange rates a change in real government current spending produced a long-run multiplier close to unity. The effects of the same change under flexible exchange rates were markedly different. It produced more inflation and a smaller rise in output. The crowding out occurred mainly because of the effect of higher inflation on consumption. In each case there was some cut in capital expenditure since the authorities were assumed to raise interest rates in response to the fall in the balance of payments. The authors argued that the model exaggerated the output gain since they were sceptical about the relatively slow elimination of the gain in competitiveness associated with the fall in the nominal exchange rate.

Cuts in income tax had smaller effects on output, mainly because of the leakage to imports. In the fixed exchange rate case the long-run multiplier was about 0.5; under a flexible exchange rate the multiplier was even lower.

Ball and Burns produced a counter-factual version of the two earlier periods by setting policy at 'neutral' levels. For the period 1964–9, comparison of the counter-factual base run with the actual outturn showed that, according to the LBS model, policy changes reduced output in 1969 by over 5 per cent and raised prices by over 8 per cent. Ball and Burns' assessment of this period was that the government was forced into excessive deflation because of a failure to act early enough to remedy the balance of payments problem. The balance of payments problem itself had been partly caused by excessive expansion of demand before 1964.

Policy changes during the period 1970–75 had had relatively little effect on GDP. By 1975 GDP was 0.7 per cent higher than it would have been under neutral policies. Consumer prices were 5 per cent higher and the exchange rate was 26 per cent lower than in the neutral policy case. Ball and Burns concluded that fiscal policy could have been more expansionary in 1970 and that it should have been tighter in 1973 (accompanied by a revaluation of the currency) to offset the acceleration in world inflation in that year.

Although the details of their proposed policies for the two historical periods are extremely interesting, there is not space to describe them fully here. The spirit of their approach is, however, well captured by the following passage which describes the effects of their proposed policies on the period 1970–75:

> The major financial improvement was achieved by maintaining control of the price level and monetary aggregates. The key to this was the maintenance of an appropriate fiscal policy. Expansion at the outset not only raised personal incomes but also prevented interest rates falling to the extent they did. Combined with the removal of the effects of Competition and Credit Control, money supply in 1972 was then 10 per cent below outturn. This enabled us to hold the exchange rate and keep the current account roughly in balance. The cumulative spiral of exchange rate depreciation, inflation, a soaring budget deficit and monetary disorder was avoided. We were able to maintain lower interest rates, control the borrowing requirement and again avoid the problems associated with incomes policy, which produces a solid financial background with a reduced incidence of crisis and conflict. And our calculations suggest that this strategy would have been consistent with higher spending levels and lower unemployment. Within the framework, it has not been possible to avoid the recession of 1975. It is not possible to move significantly away from the behaviour of the rest of the world without significant effects on external stability and the financial framework, with the inevitable consequences for the exchange rate, for inflation and the resulting repetitive crises, when the world is subject to major synchronising shocks. (Ball and Burns, 1978.)

In the light of subsequent events, we may emphasise the following four points from that passage. First, monetary restraint is an essential element of counter-inflationary policy. Second, monetary policy must be supported by an appropriate fiscal policy. Third, movements in the nominal exchange rate are a crucial part of the transmission mechanism from fiscal/monetary policy to inflation. Fourth, it is not possible to insulate the United Kingdom completely from the behaviour of the rest of the world economy.

Policy proposals for 1977–81

Ball and Burns applied the lessons from the past in setting their proposals for the following years. Table 3.1 shows their forecasts of developments on unchanged policy. Table 3.2 shows their forecasts on the basis of their policy proposals. Table 3.3 shows what actually happened.

At the time that the paper was being prepared (mid-1977) it was clear that the British government was deliberately holding down the exchange rate in the hope that it would provide a competitive advantage for United Kingdom exporters. Evidence that this was happening was provided by the rapid fall in short-term interest rates and the accumulation of foreign reserves. (The policy was criticised in Budd and Burns, 1977.) Ball and Burns assumed that the effective exchange rate would be allowed to rise by about 8 per cent from its (then) current level and would be held at that rate thereafter. They forecast that world inflation would slow down in 1979–80 and that a stable exchange rate would bring inflation down sharply. Support of the higher exchange rate required a slower growth of the money supply and a lower PSBR. The growth of government spending was smoothed compared with the Government's announced plans. Taxes were raised by 5 per cent in 1980 to offset the effects of the acceleration of world growth.

As tables 3.1 and 3.2 show, the expected outcome was not greatly different from the base run. Average annual growth of GDP was 2.1 per cent compared with 2.3 per cent in the base run. The annual growth of consumer spending was 2.2 per cent compared with 2.5 per cent in the base run. Inflation fell to 9 per cent by 1978 compared with 13.7 per cent. By the end of the period it was 6.4 per cent compared with 6.8 per cent. As table 3.3 shows, the outturn was considerably different from the base run or the proposed policy run (called the final run hereafter), particularly in the final years, when the United Kingdom experienced a deep recession. If we compare the final run with the outturn, the two most important developments as far as external developments were concerned were first, that the world economy grew strongly in 1979 and then slowed down sharply in 1980; and second, that oil prices doubled in 1979–80.

As far as policy is concerned we can distinguish between events before and after the Conservative victory of May 1979. Fiscal policy was expansionary in 1978 with cuts in taxes and increases in government current expenditure. The changes contributed to a rapid growth of consumer spending in 1978 and 1979 and to a faster growth of GDP in 1979. The public sector financial deficit was larger in 1978 and 1979 than in the final run and the balance of payments deteriorated by about 1 per cent of GDP between the two years. Inflation in 1978 was close to the final run. The Conservative government in 1979, and even more so after 1980, conducted its policies along the *general* lines proposed by Ball and Burns. There was an emphasis on the role of monetary policy in controlling inflation and on the need for consistency between fiscal and monetary policy. Ball and Burns anticipated the longer-term approach to fiscal and monetary policy which was later to be embodied in the medium term financial strategy. Their final words also anticipate Mr. Lawson's Mais Lecture of 1984:

> Viewed in this way, stabilisation policy has only a limited role in long-term full employment policy. Employment is a problem associated with the long-run development of productive potential, real wages and competitiveness which belong in the world of micro rather than macroeconomics. Stabilisation policy can create the appropriate stable financial framework, but an exaggerated belief in our capacity to create full employment through fiscal and monetary means is only likely to destroy financial stability, in much the same way as we have experienced in the last ten years.

Although the general lines of policy were consistent with the Ball and Burns proposals, there were important differences. In particular the Conservative government raised indirect taxes sharply in its first budget, a move which had not been proposed by Ball and Burns. (Some of the potential dangers of this move were described in Budd and Burns, 1977.) Finally, although Ball and Burns recommended a rise in the exchange rate at the beginning of the period, they did not anticipate the rise that actually occurred in 1979 and 1980.

It is important to recall that the 1977 paper was written against a background of considerable disenchantment with fine-tuning. This disenchantment was based on the consequences of a seemingly reckless over-expansion of demand in 1972 and 1973 and the high frequency of budgets and mini-budgets after 1974. After the collapse of sterling in the autumn of 1976, the IMF had imposed longer-term constraints on fiscal policy through its requirements on the PSBR and DCE. By late 1977 the effects seemed to be highly favourable, despite (or perhaps because of) a sharp reduction in the PSBR–GDP ratio.

Ball and Burns argued for a stable approach to fiscal and monetary policy which foreshadowed the medium term financial strategy. The difficult choice, as we now recognise, is that between the need to establish a reputation, which in a sense implies an inflexible approach (that is, *precommitment*) and the need to respond to shocks, which requires a flexible approach to policymaking. In

Table 3.1 Unchanged policy

	1977
Percentage change (at 1970) prices	
GDP	1.0
Consumers' expenditure	−0.4
Public current expenditure	−0.3
Exports of goods and services	6.9
Imports of goods and services	4.2
Factor cost adjustment	−2.1
Stockbuilding	0.3
Public non-dwelling investment	−8.0
Public dwelling investment	−25.7
Private non-dwelling investment	0.4
Private dwelling investment	−17.2
Private manufacturing investment P&M	9.6
Deflator for consumption (1970 = 1)	13.6
Deflator for GDP (1970 = 1)	12.0
Average earnings (1970 = 100)	10.7
Stock of M_3 (£m)	4.8
Real disposable income	−2.1
Personal disposable income (£m)	11.2
Public current grants (£m)	17.5
Level	
Net acquisition of financial assets:[a]	
company sector	−47
personal sector	2,116
public sector	−1,878
overseas sector	−705
private sector as % of GDP	6.8
public sector as % of GDP	−6.2
Public sector borrowing requirement	2,116
Balance of payments as % of GDP	0.6
Bank rate/MLR (%)	10.0
DCE as % of money stock	11.3
Effective exchange rate (1970 = 100)	62.1

[a] Quarterly rate

1978	1979	1980	1981
2.0	2.3	3.7	2.7
1.3	3.9	4.7	3.1
-1.1	1.4	2.3	2.9
4.9	3.1	5.5	5.8
4.4	8.6	10.1	7.2
1.1	4.2	5.1	3.4
0.3	0.9	1.3	1.0
-1.4	8.1	12.0	7.7
-8.2	9.7	8.1	13.6
11.7	2.8	6.8	2.4
19.9	7.5	2.7	7.0
14.6	6.0	10.0	0.9
13.7	12.1	6.2	6.8
15.2	14.4	7.6	7.7
15.1	15.2	9.3	9.2
11.4	13.6	15.9	15.1
2.9	3.1	3.1	2.7
16.9	15.5	9.5	9.6
20.2	16.9	6.4	7.3
-467	-383	-948	-891
2,633	2,896	2,721	2,829
-1,421	-1,902	-1,584	-1,842
-705	-571	-150	-56
6.1	6.0	3.9	3.8
-4.0	-4.6	-3.4	-3.6
2,095	2,193	1,804	2,070
2.0	1.4	0.3	0.1
7.6	7.5	6.4	6.6
8.5	15.3	17.7	17.7
62.1	62.1	62.1	62.1

Table 3.2 Final run

	1977
Percentage change (at 1970 prices)	
GDP	1.1
Consumers' expenditure	−0.1
Public current expenditure	−0.3
Exports of goods and services	6.9
Imports of goods and services	4.4
Factor cost adjustment	−1.8
Stockbuilding	0.3
Public non-dwelling investment	−8.0
Public dwelling investment	−25.7
Private non-dwelling investment	0.7
Private dwelling investment	−17.2
Private manufacturing investment P&M	9.7
Deflator for consumption (1970 = 1)	13.1
Deflator for GDP (1970 = 1)	11.8
Average earnings (1970 = 100)	10.4
Stock of M_3 (£m.)	4.8
Real disposable income	−2.1
Personal disposable income (£m.)	10.8
Public current grants (£m.)	16.9
Level	
Net acquisition of financial assets:[a]	
company sector	−26
personal sector	2,079
public sector	−1,844
overseas sector	−222
private sector as % of GDP	6.8
public sector as % of GDP	−6.1
Public sector borrowing requirement[a]	1,984
Balance of payments as % of GDP	0.7
Bank rate/MLR (%)	9.6
DCE as % of money stock	11.3
Effective exchange rate (1970 = 100)	63.9

[a] Quarterly rate

1978	1979	1980	1981
3.5	1.7	2.3	1.9
3.1	3.2	2.9	1.8
-1.1	1.4	2.3	2.9
4.5	7.3	5.4	5.6
7.6	7.0	6.9	5.5
3.1	3.5	3.1	1.9
0.8	0.8	0.8	0.5
7.2	1.8	5.2	7.2
12.6	2.6	0	2.6
15.0	3.5	4.0	-2.1
23.8	9.3	-1.6	7.5
18.6	7.5	7.7	-4.4
9.1	10.8	6.1	6.4
10.4	12.9	6.2	7.2
10.9	13.2	7.7	8.3
12.4	12.9	9.9	6.9
3.7	2.9	0.3	1.8
13.2	14.0	6.7	8.3
15.3	15.7	6.2	6.9
-544	-468	-1,061	-715
2,237	2,526	2,097	2,237
-1,415	-1,792	-807	-1,139
-238	-226	-189	-334
4.9	5.2	2.4	3.2
-4.1	-4.5	-1.9	-2.4
1,786	2,150	1,166	1,539
0.7	0.6	0.4	0.7
6.4	7.4	6.3	6.3
14.3	15.7	9.6	10.4
67.5	67.5	67.5	67.5

Table 3.3 Actual

	1977
Percentage change (at 1980 prices)	
GDP	2.8
Consumers' expenditure	−0.5
Public current expenditure	−1.7
Exports of goods and services	6.6
Imports of goods and services	1.2
Factor cost adjustment	0.4
Stockbuilding	−0.2
Public non-dwelling investment	−14.0
Public dwelling investment	−10.1
Private non-dwelling investment	8.2
Private dwelling investment	−0.8
Private manufacturing investment P&M	4.6
Deflator for consumption (1970 = 1)	14.9
Deflator for GDP (1970 = 1)	12.3
Average earnings (1970 = 100)	10.2
Stock of M_3 (£m.)	7.7
Real disposable income	−2.2
Personal disposable income (£m.)	12.3
Public current grants (£m.)	19.2
Level	
Net acquisition of financial assets:[a]	
company sector	492
personal sector	938
public sector	−1,531
overseas sector	34
private sector as % of GDP	3.9
public sector as % of GDP	−4.2
Public sector borrowing requirement[a]	1,365
Balance of payments as % of GDP	−0.1
Bank rate/MLR (%)	8.9
DCE as % of money stock	2.7
Effective exchange rate (1970 = 100)	63.1

[a] Quarterly rate

1978	1979	1980	1981
3.4	3.0	−2.8	−1.6
5.6	4.2	−0.0	−0.1
2.3	2.2	1.6	0.2
1.9	4.0	−0.1	−0.7
3.9	10.5	−3.2	−2.6
10.0	3.0	−2.9	−2.5
−0.1	−0.1	−0.9	0.6
−9.9	−0.8	−7.1	−12.4
−7.9	−7.1	−11.5	−32.8
11.1	4.1	−3.8	−5.6
6.7	9.0	−5.5	−10.8
6.6	3.6	−13.8	−13.4
9.2	13.6	16.2	11.4
12.1	12.7	18.9	10.1
14.5	15.5	17.9	13.3
15.5	13.4	16.3	19.1
7.2	5.6	1.4	−1.4
17.1	19.9	17.8	9.9
21.2	17.3	19.1	20.3
378	−16	13	509
1,693	2,140	3,330	3,274
−2,095	−2,162	−2,697	−2,050
−242	−165	−729	1,578
4.9	4.3	5.8	6.0
−5.0	−4.4	−4.7	−3.2
2,109	3,170	2,956	2,647
0.6	−0.3	1.3	2.5
9.1	13.7	16.3	13.2
1.7	19.1	24.8	18.8
63.3	67.8	74.6	73.7

the final part of this chapter we discuss this issue in detail. We propose an approach which maintains the policymaker's reputation at the same time as it allows for predetermined responses to shocks. This takes the form of precommitment to both an open-loop strategy and a feedback rule which stabilises the economy in the face of unanticipated shocks.

Subsequent development of the LBS model

The current version of the LBS model still retains many of the key features which were identifiable ten years ago. Also there have been a number of important changes to other parts of the model in addition to those which Ball and Burns introduced. These changes, like those of ten years ago, are partly a response to the events of the recent past, especially the 1979–82 period. Very briefly, the LBS model now has the following features.

(a) The exchange rate is determined within a market-clearing, rational expectations model of the financial sector (Keating, 1985). This approach to the exchange rate represents a *generalisation* of the monetary model of the exchange rate in which wider portfolio considerations matter as well (Budd *et al.*, 1984). In the model foreign and domestic assets are not perfect substitutes, and the balance of payments therefore has a significant effect on the exchange rate.
(b) The rate of inflation still affects consumption, and thus the savings ratio, but there is also a role for real financial wealth (plus the real value of the housing stock). After tax nominal interest rates also affect the savings ratio.
(c) The labour market is modelled in terms of a bargaining model of wage negotiations (Holly and Smith, 1987). Employers and trades unions bargain about the real wage, while employers set the level of employment once the real wage is known. Real wages depend on the level of unemployment, and on taxes and benefits. A distinction is drawn, also, between the effects on real wages of those who have been unemployed for less than one year and those who have been unemployed for more than a year. This is part of an explanation of the rise in unemployment since 1979 in terms of possible *hysteresis* effects (Budd, Levine and Smith, 1986). The supply of labour by females is also determined within the model (the supply of labour by males is exogenous). Female participation depends upon the absolute level of wages, the wage for females relative to males and the level of unemployment.
(d) Factor prices play a much more prominent role in the model. We have already pointed to the effect of after-tax interest rates on

savings. The level of inventories depends on the financial cost of holding inventories, where this cost includes the effects of the corporation tax system (Holly and Markose, 1986). The demand for labour depends upon the real tax-adjusted product wage.
(e) Asset prices in the LBS model are now forward looking, so that expectations of future policies affect the equity and gilts price and the price of overseas assets (the inverse of the exchange rate). Financial markets respond instantaneously to any 'news' while both the market for goods and labour respond adaptively.

The exchange rate is still the main route by which changes in fiscal and monetary policy are transmitted to the rate of inflation, though there are also direct demand effects on wages via unemployment and on prices via a capacity effect on manufacturing output prices. The sectoral flow of funds is fully integrated with holdings of stocks of financial assets by the private, public and overseas sectors.

The Ball Report ten years on

It is almost ten years since the Report of the Committee on Policy Optimisation (the Ball Report) appeared. The terms of reference given to the Committee were: "To consider the present state of development of optimal control techniques as applied to macroeconomic policy. To make recommendations concerning the feasibility and value of applying these techniques within Her Majesty's Treasury". The Committee concluded at an early stage that it could not confine itself to discussing technical issues. It was also necessary to examine more broadly the process of economic policymaking in the United Kingdom. This meant that the report provided an illuminating insight into the processes of economic policymaking in Britain, at least at the end of the 1970s. In comparison, the discussion of optimal control techniques is more limited. This is a fair reflection of how far research and application of optimal control in economics had progressed by 1977.

The Committee identified three main objections to the use of optimal control in macroeconomics. First, doubts had been expressed about the specification of the economic models which had to provide the basis for the application of optimal control. Secondly, there were difficulties in defining the preferences which were to govern the choice of economic policy, as well as the form of the objective function, especially if it was quadratic. Finally, the Report considered a more fundamental objection to the concept of optimal macroeconomic policy making.

> Optimal control theory, and indeed demand management, is not the appropriate tool for economic planning, even if there were a well-defined and agreed-upon social welfare function and policymakers knew the timing and magnitude of the effects of their actions. Economic planning . . . is not a game against a single agent, say nature, but, rather, a game against rational economic agents. These economic agents take decisions which depend in part upon their *rational expectations* of future policy actions.

The Committee did not necessarily endorse these three objections to optimal control. In its conclusions a distinction was drawn between the *direct* and *indirect* benefits of the application of optimal control methods. Indirect benefits arise if optimal control helps to improve the specification of the economic models used in policy analysis. Direct benefits arise if policies are suggested which would not otherwise be considered and the results of optimal control are brought immediately to the policymaker. The Committee felt that in the present state of knowledge the best application of optimal control lay in the specification and examination of the models themselves, and as a way of improving on simple simulation methods. Thus optimal control techniques were best seen as part of the total procedure of model building, testing and use, and they should not take precedence over improvements to the specification and estimation of macro models.

Developments since the Ball Report

Much has changed since the Ball Report appeared. In 1977 there was only one research group in the United Kingdom devoted to economic applications of optimal control theory (the PREM Group at Imperial College), while some work on the targets–instruments approach of Tinbergen had begun at Cambridge (Barker, 1979). By 1987 the use of optimal control techniques by users and builders of macroeconomic modellers has become commonplace.

Formal cooperation between the Imperial College group and the London Business School began in 1979.[1] The Program of Research into Small Macromodels (PRISM), under David Currie at Queen Mary College, started in 1981. The control exercise in the next section draws particularly on the work of this group. Work on the use of classical control techniques, and their application, in combination with the linearisation techniques of Maciejowski, to large-scale models (Maciejowski and Vines, 1982) began at Cambridge University at about the same time. Studies using the LBS model as a testbed can be found in Holly, Zarrop and Westcott (1978), Zarrop *et al.* (1979a and b), Rustem and Zarrop (1979), and Holly and Corker (1984). Work using optimal control methods has also been carried out at the National Institute (Hall, 1985), and at the Treasury.

This is far from being an exhaustive account of the work in this area over the last ten years. But we can identify a number of themes running through this activity which illustrate the major issues for researchers. The direction of research in the United Kingdom has been influenced most by two major events. First, the development of the rational expectations hypothesis, and secondly, the down-grading of demand management by the Conservative government and the adoption of the medium term financial strategy.

Alongside these developments there are a number of more technical issues which have always been central to attempts to apply control theory to macroeconomic policymaking. There has always been a tension between the use of small (linear) models and the large (non-linear) models which are used in most cases for forecasting and policy analysis. There have also been disputes about the appropriate technique to use. The LQG (linear model, quadratic cost function, Gaussian noise) framework is an attractive theoretical structure which provides explicit, closed-loop solutions (at least when disturbances are additive) in the form of a feedback rule.[2] In contrast, optimisation techniques based on mathematical programming can be applied directly to models whether they are linear or non-linear, large or small.[3] However, while direct optimisation approaches can be made closed loop by sequential optimisation they do not provide an explicit feedback rule. One way in which some of the advantages of the LQG framework can be retained while also using large non-linear models is by linearising the non-linear model,[4] applying linear techniques to the linear model and then re-applying the results, in the form of a closed or open loop policy, back to the non-linear model.[5]

Disputes about the size of economic models or the usefulness of explicit as opposed to implicit feedback rules, and the relative merits of classical versus modern control techniques, or the LQG framework relative to mathematical programming approaches are essentially technical. The rational expectations hypothesis, by contrast, provides a challenge both to the whole concept of optimal macroeconomic policy and to each type of technique used if optimal policies are still to be formulated in a rational expectations world.

The effects of the rational expectations revolution

Lucas (1976), drawing on the work of Muth (1961), was the first to raise doubts about the usefulness of macroeconomic models for policymaking when economic agents formed expectations which were forward looking. Sargent and Wallace (1975) went further than this and showed in one particular model that the presence of rational expectations implied that the behaviour of real output was independent of monetary policy. This super-neutrality proposition meant that an optimal economic policy would not enable the policymaker to have any effect on the behaviour of real output. But more significantly, there was no need for an optimal policy since the performance of the economy was already optimal (Buiter, 1981).

It is now widely agreed that the result of Sargent and Wallace is a particular property of a particular model. A number of counterexamples have since appeared in the literature to show that in rational expectations models there is, in principle, scope for macro policies to affect output (in the short run), and so, in principle, there should be a role for optimal control. However, this conclusion has been upset by the seminal paper of Kydland and Prescott (1977). They argued that there is no way control theory can be made applicable to economic planning when expectations are rational. Much of the subsequent literature in the area of optimal economic policy formulation has been directed at refuting this claim.

Kydland and Prescott were able to show that dynamic programming, the most widely used technique of stochastic optimal theory, is not appropriate when expectations are forward looking, since its use leads to consistent but sub-optimal outcomes. Holly and Zarrop (1979, 1983) were able to show that there is a class of non-recursive methods which are appropriate when expectations are rational. Later Driffill (1982), Miller and Salmon (1985) and Currie and Levine (1985a) showed how existing methods could be modified to take account of forward-looking expectations. However, this is not the end of the matter since these alternative methods produce optimal policies which are time inconsistent, that is, a policy for period $t+1$ which is optimal from the point of view of period t, may not be optimal in period $t+1$. There may be incentives for the policymaker to renege.

This observation has triggered two main developments. First, time inconsistency is something which has also been observed in dynamic game theory when one of the players acts as a Stackelberg leader. Thus a number of the concepts of game theory have been applied to the analysis of economic policy. In particular the notion of a 'punishment' mechanism which can sustain time-inconsistent policies, taken from Barro and Gordon (1983), is developed in the next section. Another fruitful area has been international policy coordination. This is now the subject of considerable research activity, though we do not consider it here.

Optimal control and the LBS model

The design strategy

We now describe the type of policy exercises we have carried out. The policy exercise is carried out in terms of deviations about a baseline forecast which for this exercise is the October 1987 forecast (see London Business School *Economic Outlook*, October 1987 and Appendix 1). The period which is used is 1987(4) and 1995(4). The following notation is employed:

GDP	real gross domestic product
GDP£	nominal GDP
PC	consumer price index
U	unemployment rate (%)
INF	annual inflation of consumer prices (%)
PSBR	public sector borrowing requirement
BAL	current account BOP surplus
GOV	real government spending on goods and services
R	short-term interest rates (%)
TAX	standard rate of income tax (%)
ER	exchange rate ($ per £)

(The precise LBS model variables used are given in Appendix 1). Let $\overline{GDP}$, $\overline{INF}$ and so on be the baseline values and define the targets and instruments in deviation form as

$$
\begin{aligned}
y &= (GDP - \overline{GDP})/\overline{GDP} * 100 \\
\pi &= INF - \overline{INF} \\
psbr &= (PSBR - \overline{PSBR})/\overline{GDP£} \times 100 \\
bal &= (BAL - \overline{BAL})/\overline{GDP£} * 100 \\
g &= (GOV - \overline{GOV})/\overline{GOV} * 100 \\
r &= R - \overline{R} \\
\tau &= T - \overline{T} \\
u &= U - \overline{U} \\
pc &= (PC - \overline{PC})/\overline{PC} * 100 \\
er &= (ER - \overline{ER})/\overline{ER} * 100
\end{aligned}
$$

Let $\hat{y}$, $\hat{\pi}$, $\widehat{psbr}$, $\widehat{bal}$ be the policymaker's desired values for the target variables and $\hat{g}, \hat{r}, \hat{t}$ be the corresponding desired values for instruments. Then we may write down a general quadratic welfare loss function for the policymaker at time $t = 0$ as:

$$W_0 = \Sigma_{t=0}^{t=T} \lambda^t \{a(y_t - \hat{y}_t)^2 + b(\pi_t - \hat{\pi}_t)^2 + c(psbr_t - \hat{psbr}_t)^2 + d(bal_t - \hat{bal}_t)^2 + e(g_t - \hat{g}_t)^2 + f(r_t - \hat{r}_t)^2 + h(\tau_t - \hat{\tau}_t)^2\} \quad (1)$$

where $\lambda \epsilon (0,1)$ is a discount factor, T is the time horizon and $a,b,c,$ are weights reflecting the policymaker's priorities for the achievement of 'bliss' values $y_t = \hat{y}_t$ and so on.

The control problem to minimise (1) subject to the dynamic constraints of a rational expectations model has been addressed by Driffill (1982), Buiter (1985), Levine and Holly (1988) for linear models and by Holly and Zarrop (1979), Holly and Zarrop (1983), Hall (1985) and Holly and Hughes-Hallett (1988) for non-linear models. Optimisation on non-linear models is computationally very expensive. When one considers the need to search intensively over different combinations of coefficients in (1) to reveal the preferences of the policymaker, this can become a major drawback even if one has access to a high-speed computer. This is one reason why we have chosen the route of model linearisation to carry out this exercise.

There are other good reasons for working a linearised model. Most work on reputational issues, including time-consistent solutions to the optimisation problem, assume linearity (see Levine and Holly, 1988, for a survey of this literature and Levine, 1987). In addition the linear framework allows one to use frequency domain techniques to design simple and robust controllers (Christodoulakis, 1984).

The case for designing policy on a linearised model is strengthened if an accurate linear representation can be found. The linearisation procedure described in Appendix 3.2 proved to be very satisfactory in this respect. Our assessment of the accuracy of this procedure is that any modelling errors introduced are likely to be small in comparison with errors due to imprecise estimates, specification errors and so on. If W_0, given by (1), is minimised, subject to a linear rational expectations model, we obtain an optimal open-loop policy (that is, trajectories) for instruments g_t, r_t and τ_t for $t = 0,1,\ldots T$. If we put $T = \infty$ then in addition the optimal policy may be represented as a constant coefficient feedback rule which, in the face of unexpected exogenous disturbances or modelling errors, will stabilise the economy about the open-loop trajectories. Feedback rules are in effect correction mechanisms which prescribe how instruments are to be revised when the actual outturns of the economy depart from its deterministic, forecasted course.

So far we have presented a fairly conventional approach to policy design by control methods which result in open-loop plus feedback components of policy. We now look at some problems with this design strategy which we consider in turn.

The complexity of the optimal feedback rule

The optimal rule is exceedingly complex involving a feedback on the entire state vector of the linear model. Moreover, for the linearised model, the state vector turns out to be a composite vector of variables with no economic interpretation. It has been argued that rules which can be practically implemented, intuitively convincing to policymakers and easily monitored by the private sector (the latter being particularly important in a rational expectations setting) must be simple (see Kydland and Prescott, 1977, Currie and Levine, 1985a, Taylor, 1985, Vines, Maciejowski and Meade, 1983 and Edison, Miller and Williamson, 1987). Simplicity means, among other things, that feedback must be on a limited number of economic variables or indicators. Perhaps the most straightforward form of simple rule is for instruments to feed back on a subset of the target variables in W_0, namely y_t, π_t, $psbr_t$ and bal_t.

Another consideration in designing rules is that some instruments can be changed more frequently than others and for some, changes must be announced in advance. In particular, for the United Kingdom, the practice is that two instruments, interest rates, r_t, and government spending, g_t, can change each quarter (at least) whereas it has generally been the practice, until very recently, to change tax rates, τ_t, every few years. In the stylised exercise of the chapter we shall allow the tax rate to be changed only once at the beginning of the exercise.

Of the two remaining instruments, plans for government spending in Britain are usually revised annually. The form of the feedback rule we adopt allows for annual white papers prescribing government spending plans for the future. For the interest rate, quarterly revisions are allowed by our rule. These institutional features of the use of instruments are summarised in table 3.4. The precise form of the simple rule chosen is a proportional–integral (PI) controller on the primary targets in (1), output and inflation. Assuming these economic variables can be observed (or estimated) with a lag of one quarter, a PI controller with the frequency characteristics of table 3.4 takes the form:

$$\Delta(r_t - \bar{r}_t) = \theta_{11}\Delta(y_{t-1} - \bar{y}_{t-1}) + \theta_{12}(y_{t-1} - \bar{y}_{t-1}) + \theta_{21}\Delta(\pi_{t-1} - \bar{\pi}_{t-1}) + \theta_{22}(\pi_{t-1} - \bar{\pi}_{t-1}) \quad (2)$$

Table 3.4 The instruments: frequency of change and policy revisions

Instrument	Frequency of change	Frequency of policy revisions (in relation to open loop policies)
short-term interest rates r_t	quarterly	quarterly
government spending g_t	quarterly	annual
tax rate τ_t	once at $t=0$	no revision

$$\Delta(g_t - \bar{g}_t) = \theta_{31}\Delta(y_{t-4} - \bar{y}_{t-4}) + \theta_{32}(y_{t-4} - \bar{y}_{t-4}) + \theta_{41}\Delta(\pi_{t-4} - \bar{\pi}_{t-4}) + \theta_{42}(\pi_{t-4} - \bar{\pi}_{t-4}) \quad (3)$$

where Δ denotes a first difference and $\bar{r}_t$, $\bar{y}_t$, $\bar{g}_t$ and $\bar{\pi}_t$ denote open-loop trajectories. By introducing a lag of four quarters in (3) at time t the policymaker can plan and announce revisions in g_t over the next four quarters based on observations of y_t and π_t over the previous four quarters.

The rule (2) and (3) is fairly general and includes a number of simple rules which appear in the literature as special cases. For instance with $\theta_{12} = \theta_{21} = \theta_{32} = \theta_{41} = 0$, and $\theta_{11} = \theta_{22} = \theta_{31} = \theta_{42}$ the rule becomes:

$$r_t - \bar{r}_t = \theta_{11}(y_{t-1} + pc_{t-1} - \bar{y}_{t-1} - \overline{pc}_{t-1}) \quad (4)$$

$$g_t - \bar{g}_t = \theta_{31}(y_{t-4} + pc_{t-4} - \bar{y}_{t-4} - \overline{pc}_{t-4}) \quad (5)$$

which is a proportional nominal income rule. With $\theta_{11} = \theta_{12} = \theta_{21} = \theta_{32} = \theta_{41} = \theta_{42} = 0$, the rule is:

$$r_t - \bar{r}_t = \theta_{22}(pc_{t-1} - \overline{pc}_{t-1}) \quad (6)$$

$$g_t - \bar{g}_t = \theta_{31}(y_{t-4} - \bar{y}_{t-4}) \quad (7)$$

which is the decoupled proportional price and output rule found by Currie and Levine (1985a) to perform well in a small semi-empirical model of the United Kingdom economy.

The optimal open-loop trajectory can be used to find approximate values for θ_{ij} in (2) and (3) which make the simple *PI* rule approximately replicate the full optimal rule. Then either time or frequency domain methods can be employed to fine-tune the coefficients to give the rule good robustness characteristics with respect to modelling errors.

The time inconsistency problem

Another major problem with the optimal policy, whether in open-loop or closed-loop form, is that it is time inconsistent, that is, the policy announced at time $t = 0$ becomes through the mere passage of time, sub-optimal. As Kydland and Prescott (1977) point out, this raises serious problems regarding the credibility of the optimal policy in the eyes of the private sector because of the existence of an incentive to renege.

Kydland and Prescott regard the time inconsistency property as a fundamental problem in the use of optimal control methods for macroeconomic policy design. In the concluding paragraphs of their seminal paper they argue that instead of attempting to select policy optimally, "economic theory be used to evaluate policy rules and that one with good operating characteristics be selected . . . it is preferable that selected rules be simple and easily understood, so that it is obvious when a policymaker deviates from the policy. There should be institutional arrangements which make it a difficult and time-consuming process to change the policy rules in all but emergency situations".

In Barro and Gordon (1983), a different approach to the time inconsistency problem is offered. They examine whether reputational considerations can restore credibility for policymakers and hence avoid the inferior outcome of the time consistency constraint. They assume that policymakers suffer a loss of reputation if they renege on earlier commitments. With this 'punishment' mechanism in place, Barro and Gordon show that policies superior to the time consistent policy exist which can be credible and sustainable.

The model of the Barro–Gordon paper has a natural rate of output and is static. In Levine (1987) a generalisation of the analysis to any structurally dynamic linear rational expectations model is provided. The particular form a 'loss of reputation' takes in this dynamic setting is that the policymaker must pursue a time consistent (or 'non-reputational') policy for the duration of the punishment period. The policymaker's decision to renege can be schematically presented as:

Optimal but time inconsistent policy (OPT). Forward looking variables determined by OPT	→	Cheat (renege) for one period taking forward looking variables as given	→	Pursue time consistent policy (TCT) for P periods	→	Return to OPT
	→	continue with OPT				

The gains from reneging ('temptation') must now be weighed against the costs arising from a loss of reputation for P periods ('enforcement'). Let the welfare loss at time t given a decision to renege be W_t^R (the upper branch in the table) and the corresponding welfare loss along the trajectory of the optimal, time inconsistent policy be W_t^{OPT}. Then no incentive to renege exists if

$$W_t^{OPT} < W_t^R \text{ for all } t \tag{8}$$

This is a necessary and sufficient condition for the optimal policy to be sustainable. Condition (8) is henceforth referred to as the sustainability condition.

Now recall that the optimal policy can be decomposed into an open-loop path plus a feedback rule which will stabilise the system about the open loop in the face of unexpected disturbances. We have argued that there are strong reasons why the feedback rule should be confined to simple PI controllers of the form (3). These rules can never be time consistent in the sense that coefficients θ_{ij} chosen at time $t=0$ are those chosen optimally at $t>0$ (this incidentally is true even in models without rational expectations). There is therefore a problem with the choice of simple, non-reputational rules. However the sustainability condition can be examined for the open-loop component of policy alone without unanticipated shocks. For the case of unanticipated shocks, the optimal (OPT) and time consistent policies (TCT) can both be expressed as rather complex feedback rules. Sustainability can then be examined on the assumption that these rules can be implemented. The question of sustainability under simple rules is pursued further in the next section.

To summarise this section, a general welfare loss function is specified with targets for GDP, inflation, the public sector borrowing requirement and the current account surplus. Instruments are the short-term interest rate, government spending on goods and services and the standard rate of income tax. Using a linearised LBS model, an optimal policy is computed which consists of open-loop trajectories for instruments plus a feedback rule which stabilises the economy about its open-loop path in the face of exogenous or modelling uncertainties.

Simplicity constraints on policy design are introduced as follows: the tax rate is changed only once at the outset of the new policy. The interest rate can be revised quarterly about its open-loop path but government spending can only be revised annually. In addition the feedback rule for those two instruments is restricted to a proportional–integral controller.

The policy thus obtained is time inconsistent. Its credibility requires that there is no incentive to renege at any time during its implementation. This feature may be achieved if it is assumed that reneging leads to 'loss of reputation' and an inability to pursue a time inconsistent policy for some interval of time. This leads to a sustainability condition which must be examined empirically.

Results

The optimal open-loop policies

The control exercise is carried out assuming two policymakers with contrasting welfare loss functions. Both policymakers have the same targets $\hat{y}$ and $\hat{\pi}$ for higher output and lower inflation. These, in deviation form, are taken to be $\hat{y} = 5$ per cent (achieved by higher capacity utilisation or a higher level of capital stock) and $\hat{\pi} = -3$ per cent which would reduce inflation to almost zero in the long run.

The priority of policymaker 1 is to raise output towards its 'bliss' value whilst policymaker 2 aims to reduce inflation. Thus the weights *a* and *b* in the welfare loss function attached to output and inflation respectively are set such that *a* is much greater than *b* for policymaker 1 and *b* is much greater than *a* for policymaker 2.

Regarding taxation, policymaker 1 is satisfied with the present standard rate of income tax of 27p in the pound. The baseline forecast assumes this will be reduced to 25p in 1988(2). Thus we may set $\hat{\tau} = -2$ for policymaker 1 from that date. For policymaker 2, $\hat{\tau} = 0$ and the remaining targets $\hat{bal}$, $\hat{psbr}$, $\hat{r}$ and $\hat{g}$ are set at zero indicating that the baseline forecasts are satisfactory. The assumptions regarding the two policymakers are summarised in table 3.5.

Table 3.5 The policymaker's preferences

	Policymaker 1	Policymaker 2
Output, inflation and taxation targets	$\hat{y} = 5$ $\hat{\pi} = -3$ $\hat{\tau} = 2$	$\hat{y} = 5$ $\hat{\pi} = -3$ $\hat{\tau} = 0$
Weights in welfare loss function	*a* much greater than *b*	*b* much greater than *a*

The next step is to imagine an interactive process between ourselves and the policymaker to reveal the appropriate values of the weights *a*, *b*, *c*, . . ., in the welfare loss function (1). The achievement of bliss points $y = \hat{y}$ and $\pi = \hat{\pi}$ is not possible (on the LBS model) and both policymakers know this. Policymaker 1 will be satisfied with an outcome that has output rising by as much as possible, subject to an upper limit on inflation, the PSBR and the current account deficit. From past experience of simulations on the LBS model we know that the inflation and current account constraints are the crucial ones. For inflation an upper limit of 1.5 per cent (relative to the baseline forecast), averaged over the eight years of the simulation, is set. For the current account deficit an upper limit of 1 (as per cent of nominal GDP) relative to the base is chosen. Experimentation with numerous combinations of weights on the linear model led to the following choice: $a = 10$, $b = 1$, $c = 0$, $d = 10$, $e = f = 1$ with the tax rate τ fixed once for all in 1987(4) at $\tau = \hat{\tau} = 2$. For both policymakers the discount factor is set at $\lambda = 0.988$ implying a 5 per cent discount rate a year.

Similarly for policymaker 2 the objective to squeeze inflation out of the economy is constrained by a concern that output does not fall too much. A maximum fall of 1 per cent in output is permitted. Policymaker 2 is also concerned that nominal and real interest rates do not rise excessively. Thus the weight (f) on the instrument r_t is set greater than the weight (e) on g_t. By experimentation the following choice of weights for policymaker 2 was made: $a = 2$, $b = 10$, $c = d = 0$, $e = 1$, $f = 2$.

The open-loop trajectories for the optimal policies obtained from the linear model are shown on table 3.6 along with the outcomes for important endogenous variables obtained by simulation on the full LBS model. For policymaker 1 government spending is raised by around 7 per cent in real terms and the interest rate lowered by between 1 and 2 per cent over the eight years. The exchange rate falls immediately (in quarter 1) by 14 per cent and falls slowly thereafter. Output rises as a result of the direct contribution of government spending to GDP, a fall in the real exchange rate and a fall in real interest rates. The improvement in output peaks at almost 3 per cent above the baseline after two years and falls back to the initial increase which is approximately the contribution to GDP from the increase in government spending. Thus the increase in private sector output fades out mainly as a consequence of the rise in inflation of about 1.3 per cent a year on average over the eight years. This has the effect of reducing demand through wealth and direct inflation effects on consumption. Raising tax by 2p compared with the forecast helps both to contain inflation and the current account deficit which after an initial surge remains within an extra 1 per cent of nominal GDP, falling slowly towards the end of the simulation period. the PSBR presents no problem; in fact

Table 3.6 Open-loop optimal trajectories: LBS model

	Policymaker 1				Policymaker 2			
Economic variable	1 quarter	2 years	5 years	8 years	1 quarter	2 years	5 years	8 years
GDP (y)	1.8	2.8	2.2	1.6	−0.3	−1.1	−1.0	−0.80
Consumer price index (pc)	0	3.6	7.7	11.0	0	−1.5	−3.6	−5.6
Unemployment rate (u)	−1.1	−1.6	−1.7	−1.5	0.2	0.6	0.7	0.7
PSBR ($psbr$)	0.2	−0.8	−1.2	−1.5	0.0	0.0	0.1	10.2
Current account BOP (bal)	−1.3	−0.4	−0.9	0.9	0.3	0.2	0.3	0.3
Exchange rate (er)	−13.81	−14.1	−16.4	−17.6	4.4	6.2	8.2	9.5
Government spending (g)	7.0	6.3	7.1	7.6	−1.3	−2.2	−2.3	−2.4
Interest rate (r)	−1.3	−1.1	−1.4	−1.7	−0.2	0.1	0.1	0.2
Tax rate (τ)	2.0	2.0	2.0	2.0	0	0	0	0

after two years the PSBR as a percentage of nominal GDP actually falls.

For policymaker 2, subject to the constraint that output must not fall by more than 1 per cent, inflation is reduced by around 0.7 per cent a year. This is achieved by a real reduction in government spending initially by 1.3 per cent rising to 2.4 per cent after eight years. Interest rates rise initially but fall slightly thereafter. The main asymmetry between the two policymakers is that policymaker 2 is inhibited from raising interest rates and taxation. Without these available changes the scope for reducing inflation is greatly reduced.

Table 3.7 summarises the gains from optimal control for the two policymakers. The control exercise considered up to now has been the pursuit of output and inflation targets ($\hat{y}$ and $\hat{\pi}$ respectively). The first row of the table compares the welfare loss under control under optimal, time-inconsistent and time-consistent policies (W_O^{OPT} and W_O^{TCT} respectively) with the welfare loss under 'no control' which is the baseline forecast (W_O^{NC}). Under control the welfare loss is reduced to 64 per cent of that under no control for policymaker 1 and to 86–8 per cent for policymaker 2. A striking

Table 3.7 Gains from optimal control: linear model

	Policymaker 1		Policymaker 2	
Policymaker's objective	W_0^{OPT}/W_0^{NC}	W_0^{TCT}/W_0^{NC}	W_0^{OPT}/W_0^{NC}	W_0^{TCT}/W_0^{NC}
Pursue targets $\hat{y}$, $\hat{\pi}$	0.64	0.64	0.86	0.88
Stabilise in response to				
shock: *AEM*	0.40	0.41	0.41	0.41
IPW	0.61	0.61	0.58	0.66
POIL$	0.68	0.68	0.82	0.84
RSW	0.73	0.75	0.67	0.88

Note: W_0^{OPT}, W_0^{TCT}, W_0^{NC} = welfare loss at time $t=0$ for optimal policy, time consistent policy and 'no control' (baseline forecast) respectively. *AEM* = manufacturing earnings; *IPW* = OECD industrial production; *POIL$* = dollar price of oil; *RSW* = world interest rate.

result is that there is almost no time inconsistency involved for either policymaker in policies aimed at targets for output and inflation.[6]

Suppose now that the policymaker is implementing an open-loop policy and the economy is subjected to exogenous shocks. The four shocks considered are permanent changes to: earnings in manufacturing (LBS notation, *AEM*); OECD industrial production (*IPW*); dollar price of oil (*POIL$*); world short-term interest rate (*RSW*). If these shocks are unanticipated, the policymaker must implement the optimal or time-consistent policy in feedback form. As mentioned in the previous section, this involves a very complex form of rule. But putting this problem to one side for the moment, let us consider the welfare loss measured about the open-loop trajectories of the controlled economy with and without this added feedback rule. The ratios given in the bottom part of the table show the gains from feedback control in the face of the four permanent shocks. These gains are considerable especially for an *AEM* shock. For policymaker 1 there is again practically no time inconsistency in the feedback rule for any of the shocks. For policymaker 2 there is significant time inconsistency for two of the shocks, *IPW* and *RSW*.

It would appear then that the extent to which time inconsistency is a problem depends on the priorities of the policymaker. To develop this point table 3.8 displays values for the ratio W_0^{TCT}/W_0^{OPT} as the weight on inflation, b, increases from 1 (policymaker 1) to 12.5 (which exceeds $b = 10$ chosen for policymaker 2).[7] For shocks *IPW* and *RSW* this ratio increases from 1 for $b = 1$ to 1.16 and 1.37 respectively for the two shocks for $b = 12.5$.

Table 3.8 Time inconsistency and the welfare function: linear model

Target or shock	W_o^{TCT}/W_o^{OPT}			
Objective function	$a=2{:}h=1$	$a=2;h=2.5$	$a=2;h=10$	$a=2;h=12.5$
$\hat{y}$, $\hat{\pi}$	1.00	1.00	1.00	1.00
AEM	1.00	1.00	1.01	1.01
IPW	1.01	1.04	1.14	1.16
POIL	1.00	1.01	1.02	1.03
RSW	1.03	1.12	1.31	1.37

This is an interesting result which contrasts with that in Barro and Gordon (1983) where a high weight on inflation reduced the degree of time inconsistency. The reason for this difference is that the source of time inconsistency is different for the two models involved. Barro and Gordon use a static natural rate model in which time inconsistency arises from the benefits of surprise inflation only. In the LBS model surprise inflation effects in the labour market are not significant and time inconsistency arises mainly from the ability to manipulate the forward-looking exchange rate. This feature is more pronounced for the second policymaker for whom exchange rate appreciation is the main mechanism for reducing inflation. For the first policymaker, raising demand is the principle mechanism for increasing output and exchange rate depreciation is a consequence.

Stabilisation using a simple rule

We now turn to the design of a simple feedback rule for fiscal and monetary policy which can get as close as possible to emulating the performance of the optimal feedback rule. In principle each policymaker could adopt a different feedback rule reflecting the contrasting priorities for stabilisation of output and inflation. We shall consider, however, a 'neutral' policymaker who places equal weights on output and inflation. The weights chosen are: $a = b = 5$; $d = 10$; $e = f = 1$. The rule that emerges from this neutral policymaker could be thought of as a 'technocrat's rule', which is a constitutionally binding form of precommitment as recommended by Kydland and Prescott in their seminal paper on time inconsistency. Following the procedure described in Appendix 3.3, the following price and output rules were obtained:

$$\Delta r_t = 0.21\ \Delta y_{t-1} + 0.06 y_{t-1} + 0.2\ \pi_{t-1} \qquad (9)$$

$$\Delta g_t = 1.3\ \Delta y_{t-4} - 0.1\ y_{t-4} - 0.3\ \pi_{t-4} \qquad (10)$$

where all variables are now measured in deviation from about open loop trajectories. These rules are particularly simple, consisting of proportional integral control on output and proportional control only on the price level. Table 3.9 shows the gains from using the rules to stabilise the economy about some desired path in the face of the four unanticipated permanent shocks considered previously. The ratios shown are the welfare loss under feedback control relative to that under no control for three different time horizons. Although these ratios are not strictly comparable to those in table 3.7 (which refer to different welfare loss functions and an infinite time horizon on the linearised model), a rough 'orders of magnitude' comparison is permissible.

Table 3.9 Gains from stabilisation using simple rule: LBS model

	8 quarters	20 quarters	32 quarters
AEM	0.88	0.94	0.94
IPW	1.01	1.00	0.97
POIL$	0.86	0.65	0.60
RSW	0.58	0.69	0.71

Clearly the simple rule performs extremely well for shocks *POIL$* and *RSW* but is only slightly better than no control (over eight years) for the remaining shocks. This demonstrates the main problem with simple rules (highlighted by Levine and Currie, 1987a). The problem is that whereas the fully optimal (and time-consistent) rules are certainty equivalent, that is, they are optimal for any shock, this property breaks down if simplicity constraints are imposed on the rule. It is quite possible that rules which perform exceedingly well for some shocks are worse than no feedback control at all for others. Nevertheless, we have managed to produce a rule which is welfare-improving for all four shocks.

Charts 3.1–3.4 provide trajectories for *GDP*, *PC*, *GOV* and *R* (relative to the base) with and without control (*C* and *NC* respectively) under four shocks of magnitudes stated on the graphs. For example, taking the *POIL$* shock (chart 3.3) in the absence of control a 10 per cent increase in *POIL$* leads to an appreciation of the exchange rate which causes *PC* to fall but, due to the loss of competitiveness, *GDP* also falls. The feedback rule responds by

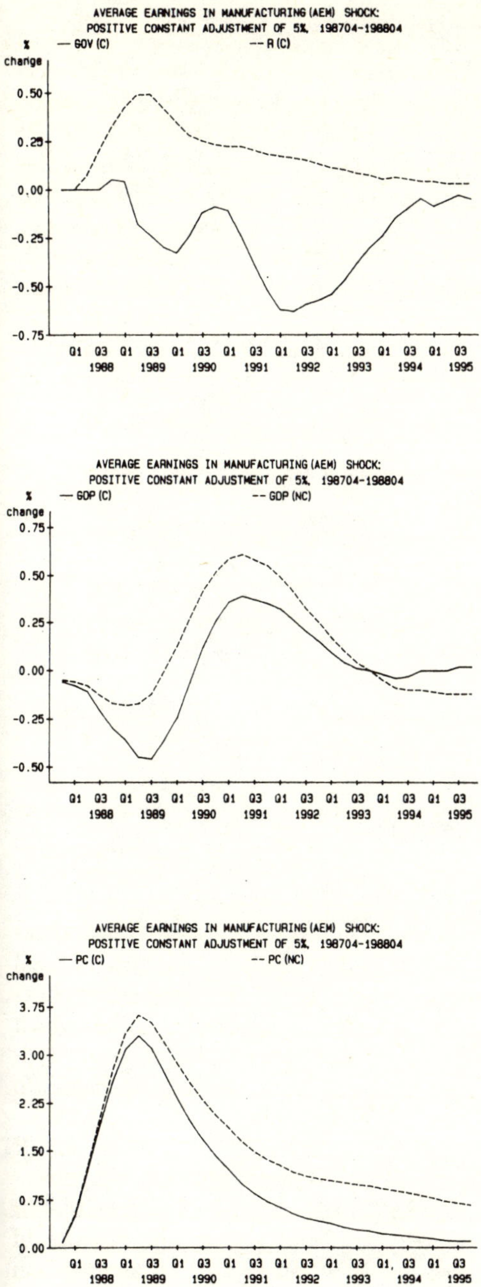

Chart 3.1 Stabilisation under AEM shock

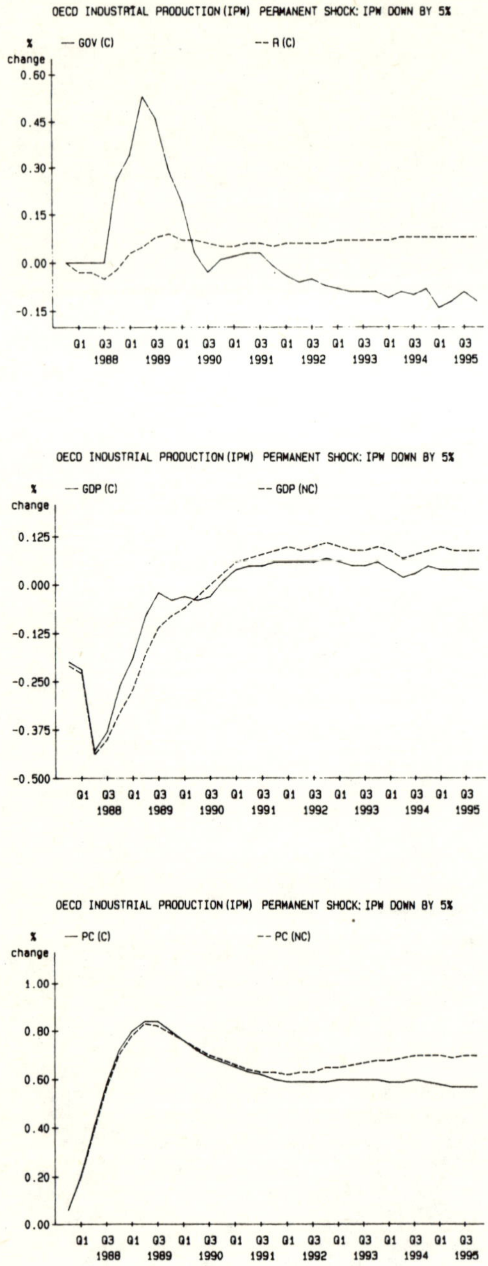

Chart 3.2 Stabilisation under IPW shock

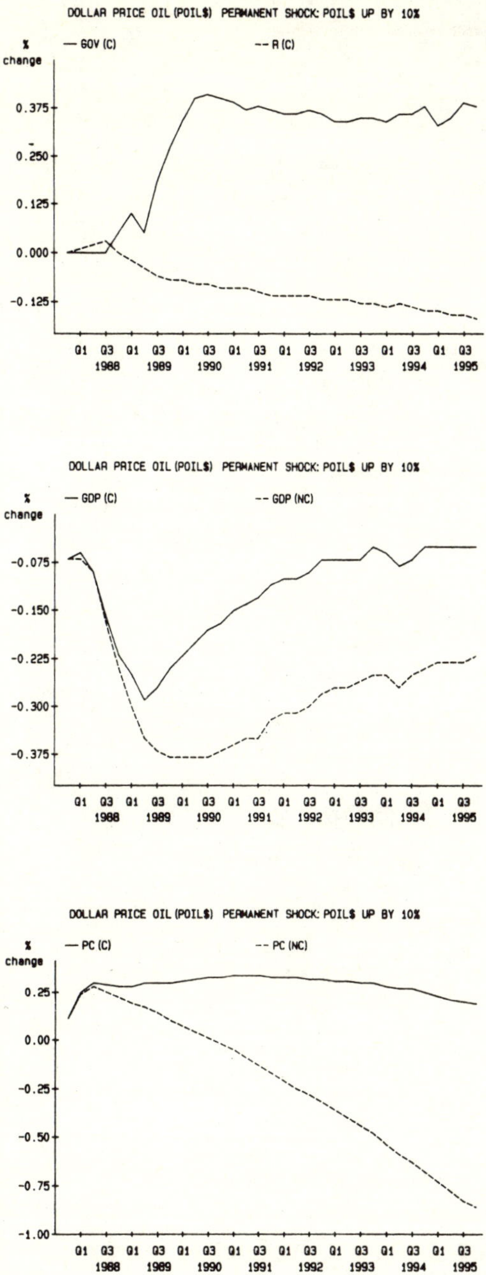

Chart 3.3 Stabilisation under POIL$ shock

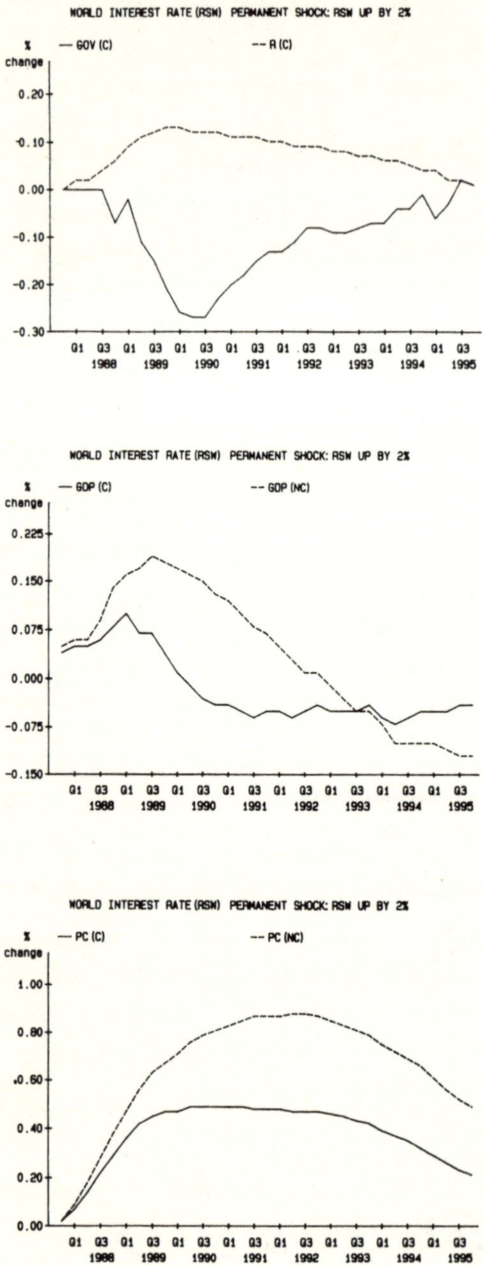

Chart 3.4 Stabilisation under RSW shock

relaxing both fiscal and monetary policy. *GOV* rises and *R* falls which has the effect of curtailing the fall in both *GDP* and *PC*.

Research is currently being carried out to find simple rules which improve upon the performance of (1) and (2). There are a number of ways of proceeding. Firstly, more complicated rules involving feedback on y_t and π_t are being investigated, including *PID* (proportional–integral–derivative) controllers. The drawback with this route is that the improvement in stabilisation performance is being obtained at the expense of complexity. This trade-off is inevitable in the design of simple rules (see Christodoulakis and Levine, 1987).

A second possibility is to examine feedback involving different targets or indicators. For example monetary policy could be used to stabilise the real exchange rate (Edison, Miller and Williamson, 1987). Fiscal policy could be based on a *PSBR/£GDP* target as in the medium term financial strategy. The current account BOP surplus is another possible candidate for a target.

Finally we are investigating the effects of including feedforward control action on selected exogenous shocks in the rule. Again this adds complexity to the rule which must be weighed against any welfare improvement.

Time inconsistency and sustainability

We now turn to the problem of sustaining the optimal policy, given that it is time inconsistent and there may therefore be an incentive to renege. As we have seen, time inconsistency is only a problem for policymaker 2 and so we focus on this case. Furthermore, even for the second policymaker there is only a significant degree of time inconsistency in the face of exogenous shocks *IPW* and *RSW*.

Consider then the stabilisation problem of responding to permanent shocks to *IPW* and *RSW*. Suppose that these shocks are anticipated and occur at the beginning of the new regime. The control problem is then purely deterministic and we can examine sustainability by comparing the welfare loss along the open-loop optimal trajectory with that if reneging occurs according to the schema on page 59. In this chapter we only examine the case where reputation is lost for ever if the policymaker reneges and the case where there is one period of 'cheating' is ignored. The results are displayed in tables 3.10 and 3.11.

Column 1 of the tables shows the welfare loss, W_t, from time t onwards ('cost-to-go'). Column 2 is the welfare loss following reoptimisation if the newly reoptimised policy is believed. This is usually referred to as the 'perfect cheating' policy. It is highly implausible that the private sector would believe each new policy

Table 3.10 The sustainability of the optimal policy: permanent shock: IPW = −1: linear model

Time (quarter)	Welfare loss along *OPT* policy	Welfare loss along perfect cheating policy	Welfare loss after reneging to *TCT*
0	0.52	0.52	0.59
4	0.32	0.31	0.33
8	0.21	0.20	0.20
12	0.20	0.19	0.20
16	0.19	0.19	0.19
20	0.20	0.20	0.20
24	0.20	0.20	0.20
28	0.20	0.20	0.20
32	0.20	0.20	0.20

Table 3.11 The sustainability of the optimal policy permanent shock: RSW = 2: linear model

Time (quarter)	Welfare loss along *OPT* policy	Welfare loss along perfect cheating policy	Welfare loss after reneging to *TCT*
0	7.11	7.11	9.32
4	5.89	5.71	7.21
8	4.44	4.07	4.85
12	3.57	3.21	3.54
16	2.99	2.74	2.86
20	2.61	2.48	2.51
24	2.32	2.27	2.28
28	2.11	2.09	2.10
32	1.94	1.94	1.96

announcement if previous ones had been reneged upon, but we include this case to indicate the degree of time inconsistency along the optimal policy. The third column gives the welfare loss if reneging is accompanied by an instant loss of reputation which lasts forever and forces the policymaker to pursue the time consistent 'non-reputational' policy. If this value dips below the cost-to-go in

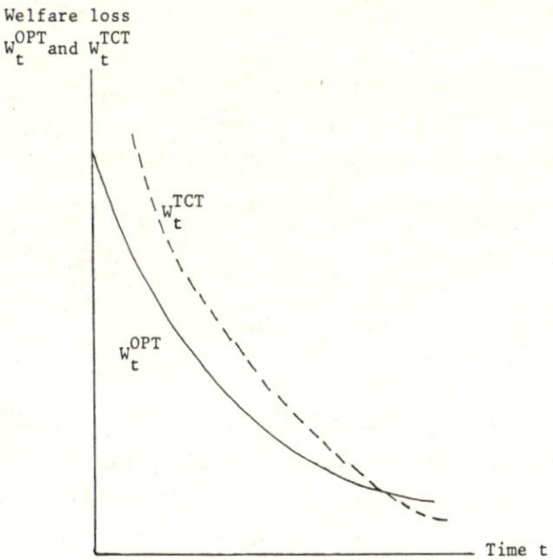

Chart 3.5a Sustainability: deterministic case

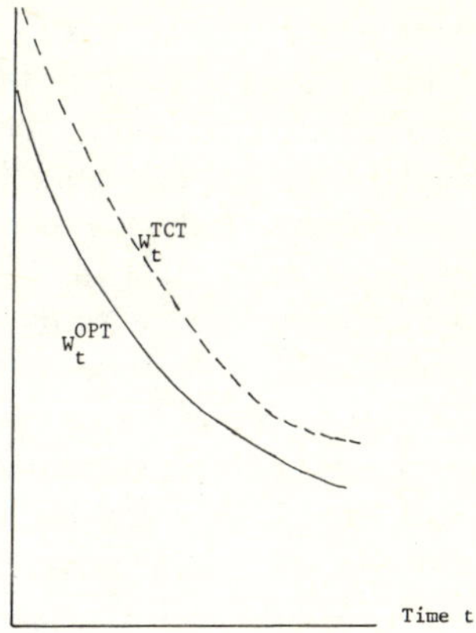

Chart 3.5b Sustainability: stochastic case

column 1 then the sustainability condition (8) is not satisfied.

Table 3.10 shows that the sustainability condition is satisfied for anticipated shock *IPW* (although it must be said that there is no time inconsistency at all after one year). By contrast table 3.11 shows that there is an incentive to switch to a non-reputational policy in response to an anticipated permanent shock to *RSW*. The numbers in italics indicate where the welfare loss, after reneging, falls below that under the optimal policy.

We have not succeeded, then, in establishing sustainability for open-loop policies in response to an anticipated permanent change to *RSW*. This is not the end of the matter however, because, as Currie and Levine (1987) and Levine (1987) have shown, the addition of stochastic disturbances can completely alter the picture.

In chart 3.5a the deterministic case is shown for a hypothetical example in which W_t^{TCT} falls below W_t^{OPT} between three and six years, signifying that sustainability is not achieved. The effect of adding a stochastic element is to introduce a permanent wedge between W_t^{TCT} and W_t^{OPT} as in chart 3.5b. This arises from the feedback component of policy which is able to provide better protection against continuous shocks under the optimal than under the time consistent policy. All this assumes that both these policies may be implemented in their full feedback form. But suppose this is not possible and the policymaker is constrained to use simple feedback rules of the type (9) and (10). Then we must reconsider the appropriate private sector punishment mechanism in the event of reneging.

For the case of full feedback rules the punishment strategy, generalised from Barro and Gordon, is that the private sector only believes in a time consistent rule for some punishment period. Since simple rules cannot be time consistent, a logical (and, we would argue, plausible) extension of this is that under the constraint of simplicity the analogous punishment is that the private sector ceases to believe in any feedback rule and assumes open-loop policies for some period of time. The wedge in chart 3.5b will then exist and ensure sustainability for all shocks if the simple rule improves welfare for all shocks. As we have seen this has been achieved for our simple rule, at least for the four shocks selected. We conclude that the time inconsistency of the simple rule need not undermine credibility.

Conclusions

Ball and Burns (1978) identified two limitations of their study of stabilisation policy. In the absence of a fully specified model of capital flows they could not model the case of a freely floating exchange rate. They also said that the discussion of policy recommendations might have been carried out in the context of an optimal control application but they had not attempted it. Since 1977 the LBS model has been developed to incorporate a financial sector in which the exchange rate is determined *inter alia* by international capital flows. We have also developed the techniques for conducting optimal control exercises using a linearised version of the model. Unlike the 1977 exercise we have not attempted to reconstruct history to show how a 'better' outcome might have been achieved since 1977. We have, however, suggested policy paths for the years to 1995 and have designed policies to respond to shocks.

The policy paths to 1995 were of two kinds. The first path was for a policymaker who was primarily concerned with reducing inflation and the second path was for one who was primarily concerned with increasing output, though of course both policymakers were interested in both output and inflation. The two paths are open-loop in the sense that they do not respond to shocks in the future.

The problem with an open-loop policy is that it is ill-equipped to deal with unanticipated shocks to the economy. We have shown that a flexible response, in the form of a simple feedback rule, is capable of holding the economy more closely to the open-loop path than if an inflexible approach, of sticking to the previously announced policy, is adopted. Given the experiences of the past ten years we would particularly draw attention to the response to an oil price shock and to an unexpected rise in earnings in manufacturing.

To assess what might have been if feedback control in the form of our simple rule had been in operation in the recent past, consider the oil price shock. Assuming approximate linearity we can deduce the following from the 10 per cent permanent shock to the dollar price of oil (chart 3.3). Without feedback control the effect of a doubling of the oil prices experienced in 1979–80 is that real output falls by almost 4 per cent and recovers slowly over the eight year simulation period to around 2.5 per cent below the baseline at the end. The price level falls by about 8 per cent representing about 1 per cent off inflation a year. With the feedback rule output falls by 3 per cent but quickly recovers to 0.75 per cent below its baseline after five years. The cost of considerable output gains over the period is that the price level remains close to the baseline and there are no gains for inflation control.

For the earnings shock it is more difficult to determine how much of the rise in earnings in 1979 and 1980 could be considered as unexpected. But we can observe in chart 3.1 that fiscal and monetary policy is tightened in response to a 5 per cent rise in earnings. This helps to ameliorate the effects on inflation though output is lower, initially, than if there was no response.

The question is, what lessons can be learned for economic policy between 1979 and 1982? At that time, as we describe in the first part of this chapter, the economy was subjected to both a large rise in oil prices and a large rise in earnings. In 1980 the medium term financial strategy was announced. This involved a major change to the conduct of macroeconomic policy and a commitment to reduce inflation by fiscal and monetary means. At that time the government was under pressure to relax policy and to expand the PSBR. In fact in 1981 fiscal policy was tightened by between £4 billion and £5 billion compared with a neutral budget. Do the results of the optimal control exercise above suggest an alternative policy? For the neutral policymaker the results of feedback control suggest that fiscal and monetary policy should be relaxed in response to an oil price shock. Of course this result depends upon what kind of policymaker we have.

There is also the problem that the Conservative government needed to establish the credibility of its anti-inflation policy. If at the time it had been 'flexible', the question arises whether the underlying medium term strategy would have carried any conviction, and an opportunity to reduce inflationary expectations may have been lost. The distinctions we have drawn between an open-loop policy and a feedback policy are important but there is also a useful distinction which can be drawn between that part of the policy which is directed at correcting major imbalances in the economy – and this is likely to be concentrated in the early part of any strategy, and will coincide with the time when credibility needs to be established – and that part of the policy associated with the period once the corrections have been made, and the government has established its credibility.

During the period of transition, flexibility may provide the wrong signal and may be interpreted as an abandonment of the anti-inflationary policy. This is one reason why we have emphasised the value of feedback rules which can be understood readily and monitored by the private sector. However, once the inflation rate has been stabilised, there may be more opportunity to be flexible, not in the sense of a weakening of commitment to lower inflation, but by having a feedback response to disturbances which make it more likely that the economy can be kept along its low inflation path. These sorts of problems of reputation under feedback rules rather than open-loop policies are clearly important and an as yet relatively unexplored area for future research.

The final issue addressed here is the question of time inconsistency. Our principle results are as follows. There is no significant time inconsistency associated with the open-loop policies aimed at increasing output or reducing inflation. Time inconsistency only arises when the optimal rule has to respond to shocks to oil prices or world short-term interest rates. Moreover, time inconsistency is still only a problem for the second policymaker who is particularly concerned with inflation. For this case we investigate whether a permanent loss of reputation is sufficient to deter the policymaker from reneging. We conclude this will be the case, but only if disturbances to the economy are repeated and unanticipated.

Appendix 3.1

LBS model variables

The variables and notation used here follow the usage in the July 1987 model manual except for the following

Here		*LSB Model*
INF	Annual inflation (consumer prices)	*D4PC*
GDP£	Nominal *GDP*	*GDP£0*

GOV	Real government spending	Composite variable consisting of *EEGG* (government employment), *PROC* (procurement), *IHG* (residential *GDFCF*), *INGG* (non-housing *GDFCF*) and *IPCOR* (public corporations *GDFCF*)
R	Short-term interest rate	*RLB* (Clearing bank base rate) with which other short-term rates change.
TAX	standard rate of income tax	*TRY*
ER	Exchange rate ($ per £)	PO^{-1}

Table 3.A1 The October 1987 forecast

Economic variable	8704	8904	9204	9504
GDP[a] £bn	59.641	63.180	69.000	73.215
Consumer price index (*PC*)	152.0	165.7	180.9	204.9
Unemployment rate (*U*) %	9.9	9.5	8.2	9.5
PSBR[a]	0.8	0.6	0.2	−0.04
Current account *OP*[b] (as % of *GDP£*)	−0.4	−0.5	−0.1	−0.4
Exchange rate (*ER*)	73.0	71.7	72.1	82.4
Government spending[a] (*GOV*) £bn	15,142	15,187	15,231	15,505
Interest rate (*RLB*) %	10.0	9.6	8.0	8.0
Tax rate (*TAX*) p/£	27	25	25	25

[a] 1980 prices.

[b] These values are averages over the previous four quarters.

Appendix 3.2

Linearisation of the LBS model

The following is a brief summary of the generalisation by Christodoulakis (1987) of the Vines and Maciejowski (1983) linearisation procedure to rational expectations models. Let

$$P_t = \begin{bmatrix} PO_t \\ PE_t \\ PGILT_t \end{bmatrix} \tag{A1}$$

be a vector of the three forward-looking variables in the LBS model, PO_t (price of overseas assets), PE_t (price of equity) and $PGILT$ (price of gilts). Let

$$W = \begin{bmatrix} GOV_t \\ R_t \\ TAX_t \end{bmatrix} \tag{A2}$$

be a vector of instruments.

$$Y = \begin{bmatrix} GDP_t \\ PC_t \\ PSBR_t/\pounds GDP_t \\ BAL_t/\pounds GDP_t \end{bmatrix} \tag{A3}$$

be a vector of outputs and

$$V_t = \begin{bmatrix} AEM_t \\ IPW_t \\ POIL\$_t \\ RSW_t \end{bmatrix} \tag{A4}$$

be a vector of exogenous shocks. Consider the vector of expectational variables.

$$P^e_{t+1,t} = \begin{bmatrix} PO^e_{t+1,t} \\ PE^e_{t+1,t} \\ PGILT^e_{t+1,t} \end{bmatrix} \tag{A5}$$

where $P^e_{t+1,t}$ is the rational expectations of P_{t+1} formed at time t. Denote deviations from the baseline forecast by lower case symbols as in the third section of this chapter. Then the first stage of the method is to apply the Maciejowski-Vines linearisation procedure, regarding $p^e_{t+1,t}$ as exogenous, to obtain a state-space system of the form

$$x_{t+1} = \tilde{A}x_t + \tilde{B}\begin{bmatrix} w_t \\ v_t \\ p^e_{t+1,t} \end{bmatrix} \tag{A6a}$$

$$\begin{bmatrix} y_t \\ p_t \end{bmatrix} = \tilde{C}x_t + \tilde{D}\begin{bmatrix} w_t \\ v_t \\ p^e_{t+1,t} \end{bmatrix} \tag{A6b}$$

where x_t is a composite variable with no economic interpretation, considered as predetermined with initial conditions $x_o = 0$.

After some straightforward matrix algebra (A6a) and (A6b) may be written in the familiar representation of rational expectations models:

$$\begin{bmatrix} x_{t+1} \\ p^e_{t+1,t} \end{bmatrix} = A\begin{bmatrix} x_t \\ p_t \end{bmatrix} + B\begin{bmatrix} w_t \\ v_t \end{bmatrix} \tag{A7a}$$

$$y_t = Cx_t + D\begin{bmatrix} w_t \\ v_t \end{bmatrix} \tag{A7b}$$

where x_t are predetermined and p_t are non-determined. Equations (A7a and A7b) are in the form for which both the Blanchard-Kahn solution procedure and the optimal control solutions given in Levine and Holly (1988) can be applied.

Notes

1 There had been earlier informal cooperation. The LBS model was used by the PREM group in some of its earlier work on applying linear controllers to large models (Zarrop *et al.*, 1978). After 1979 the PREM group obtained a copy of the NIESR model, and ultimately the Treasury model.

2 See Chow (1975), Wall and Westcott (1976), Bray (1975), Holly *et al.* (1979).

3 The first work of this kind in economics is that of Theil (1964) with linear models. See also Livesey (1979), Zarrop, Holly, Rustem and Westcott (1979a and b) and Rustem and Zarrop (1979) who used non-linear models.

4 Baker (1979) linearised the Cambridge Growth Project model and used a targets–instruments approach. However, there was no explicit optimisation criterion employed. In Holly, Zarrop and Westcott (1978) the LBS model was linearised by stochastic perturbation and the LQG framework applied to the linearisation. The optimal feedback rule was then applied back to the non-linear model. The

Cambridge Group has applied classical control techniques to linearised versions of large models using the reduced-order techniques of Maciejowski (Maciejowski and Vines, 1982). Even more recently, Christodoulakis (1987) has extended Maciejowski's technique to handle rational expectations models. This linearisation technique has been combined with the LQG rational expectations framework of Levine and Currie (1987a) and Christodoulakis and Levine (1987) and used here.

5 For an extensive review of these various approaches see Holly and Hughes Hallett (1988).

6 The reason for this result may be the nature of the terminal condition. The linearised model solved under rational expectations imposed the same long-run inflation rate as the baseline forecast for both optimal and time consistent policies. Future work will relax this assumption, allowing for the possibility of an inflationary bias in the long run for the time consistent case (as in the Barro-Gordon (1983) model). Then a greater divergence between the time consistent and optimal policies may emerge.

7 The remaining weights are as for policymaker 1 ($a = 10$, $c = 0$, $d = 10$, $e = f = 1$) so that we are measuring the effect, on time inconsistency, of increasing the priority attached to inflation control.

Comment on Chapter 3

Michael J. Artis

This chapter is quite a lengthy one and whilst this comment is directed at the innovative last section, it bears mention that there is a great deal of valuable and interesting material in the earlier sections.

The rational expectations revolution posed critical problems for model simulation activity – the Lucas Critique and the problem of time inconsistency. Modellers have long since ceased to be paralysed by the Lucas Critique, though the steps that have been taken to meet it – isolating expectational variables and solving models under explicit consistent expectations assumptions – do not in truth guarantee immunity from it. This chapter, typical of its genre, assumes away the Lucas Critique and concentrates on meeting the time inconsistency problem.

The reason why time inconsistency is a problem is that, in a model with forward looking expectational variables like the present one, a policy computed as optimal will become sub-optimal with the sheer passage of time. Since this can be recognised *ex ante*, agents will believe that the authorities will abandon the policy first computed and will therefore place no credence in it. To meet this problem, the authors seek to show that a combination of an optimal open-loop strategy and a simple feedback rule welfare-dominates an alternative time consistency policy with no feedback and would therefore be a sustainable and credible combination.

The solution suggested exploits the fact that in the presence of innovations, a feedback rule will generally be welfare-improving (but whether, and how much, depends on the shock, the precise form of the rule, the model and the objective function of course), so that adding the rule to the optimal policy open-loop baseline trajectory offers quite a good deal. Yet it would be inappropriate to complement the time consistent strategy in the comparison with a comparable simple feedback rule, because a simple feedback rule is certain to be time inconsistent, and cannot therefore be part of a time consistent package.

For the particular set-up entertained here, the combination of the feedback rule and the open-loop optimal policy trajectory does in fact outperform the time consistent strategy, so that although the example is specific to the set-up (not just the model, but the objective function, shock and precise rule too), the general point is nonetheless established that it is possible to do better than the time-consistent strategy. The time inconsistency problem need not, therefore, enforce the complete abandonment of optimising methods in favour of poor, but time consistent, policies. And whilst the emphasis is on the use of rules, the dividing line between discretion and innovation-contingent rules is a thin one. So this chapter suggests something of a change in typical LBS policy advice.

A question which remains is whether it is possible to do even better. The restriction of the set of feedback rules considered to the class of 'simple' ones follows from an informal optimisation of the degree of complexity with respect to the constraint of transparency in a rule. (Moreover, the choice of rule is conditioned on a very small number of shocks.) A more complex rule would perform better against a range of shocks, but would be more difficult to monitor and could lead to the suspicion of chicanery on the authorities' behalf. Yet a simple feedback rule may be thoroughly, and obviously, inappropriate in some situations and in such circumstances the private sector will expect that it may be abandoned at some point. Then, an intermediate approach that recommends itself is that of the regime-switching rule, where the authorities in predefined circumstances switch from one simple rule to another. (Many countries, including the United Kingdom, have in effect done something like this in switching from monetary to exchange rate targets and a good deal of pain could have been avoided if this could have been more precisely anticipated.)

In the denouement, the authors apply their analysis to the circumstances of post-1979 policy. One remark that this provokes is simply that there is a contrast between the policy procedure recommended which focuses on ultimate goal variables and policy instruments and the policy actually pursued which put the monetary aggregates at the centre of the picture, but could have put alternative intermediate variables there. It would be interesting to see whether there are any advantages in using intermediate variables in this way and, if so, what they are. A second remark is that at one level, the medium term financial strategy has been completely discredited: monetary targets for £M3, centrepiece of the original policy, have been explicitly abandoned. The exchange rate, once the explicit subject of benign neglect, is now a principal declared target of policy. Asserting that the authorities maintained their policy credibility through this 180° about-turn is to credit the public with the ability to 'see through' all the discussion (mumbo-jumbo?) of monetary targets to a test of the government's counter-inflationary stance. This suggests that a more direct statement of policy aims (in terms of the ultimate variable of concern – inflation) would have been better, in removing confusion and uncertainty.

4 A New Classical Policy Programme

*Patrick Minford and Anupam Rastogi**

Mrs Thatcher's government came into office in 1979 committed to gradualism in policy towards inflation. However, there were a number of economists who urged a 'sudden death' or 'cold turkey' approach. These included Professor Hayek and others of the Austrian school, but perhaps the most vociferous were the new classical economists. Sargent (1986) compared Thatcher's method unfavourably with Poincaré; in fact he, like many others, failed to realise that in practice the policies were far from gradualist. Nevertheless, the combination of gradualist rhetoric with the reality of sharp change was suboptimal from a new classical viewpoint (Minford and Peel, 1981). This chapter discusses what difference would have been made had policy been explicitly new classical.

A complete programme of policy must embrace unemployment and the supply side; as is well known, this is, in the new classical view, the province of micro policy on such matters as tax/transfer structure, union laws and regulation. We will comment on this issue later in the context of an extended workfare programme, but the primary focus here is on inflation policy.

We begin with an account of what did happen as seen through the eyes of the Liverpool new classical model; this recaps the material in Matthews and Minford (1987). Using this as the base case, we go on to describe how policy on inflation might have been reconstructed on new classical lines. Then this policy programme is simulated on certain crucial assumptions about credibility. The next section discusses what the effect of a general workfare programme might be and, finally, we conclude with some general comments.

The past as it actually turned out

Matthews and Minford reconstruct the period from 1979 to 1985. The method used is standard. The model is simulated for each year on the basis of previously available information about exogenous

* We are grateful to Kent Matthews for numerous discussions of the issues treated here. The Liverpool model of the United Kingdom has been developed with the financial support of the ESRC and more recently the ESRC Consortium for Macroeconomic Modelling and Forecasting. This support is gratefully acknowledged.

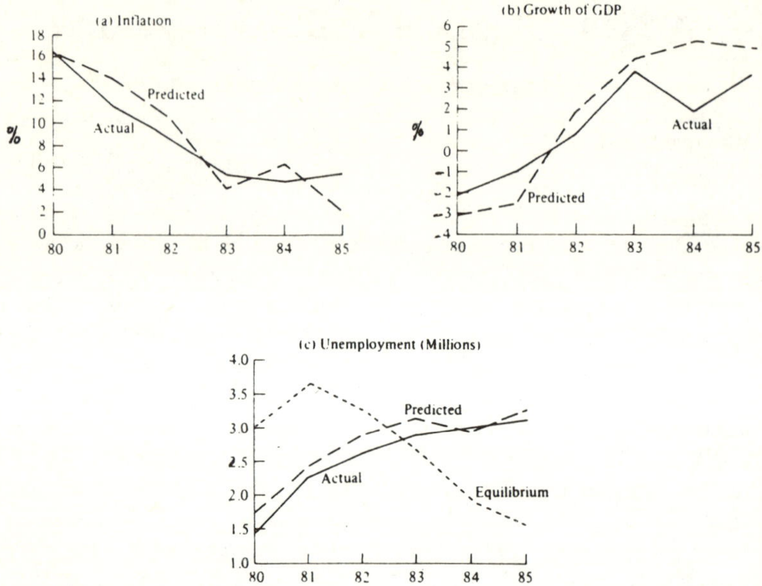

Chart 4.1 Predicted and actual values of inflation, GDP growth, and unemployment

variables to obtain the expected outcome; the actual exogenous variable values for the year (and their correspondingly revised values for future years) are then input to obtain the actual outcome. (The dating of expectations differs between labour and financial markets; wages rely on the previous year's data because of a contract lag, but interest and exchange rates react to current information.)

The summary results of this process are shown in chart 4.1 and tables 4.1 and 4.2, reproduced from Matthews and Minford (1987). From our viewpoint here the key assumptions concern the way in which expectations about future fiscal and monetary policy were formed.

From our experience of forecasting over this period as confirmed by simulations for this exercise, the medium term financial strategy (MTFS), much as we supported it and would have liked it to be believed, decidedly did not determine these expectations in the important early 1979–82 inflation battle. That this is so, is obvious from the behaviour of long-term interest rates, which would have fallen dramatically had the MTFS been believed, but in fact stayed

Table 4.1 Shocks during 1980–85

		1980	1981	1982	1983	1984	1985
Domestic							
M0 growth (%)	Actual	8.0	4.6	3.3	5.7	5.7	4.6
	Expected	12.8	10.6	8.4	6.4	5.1	6.3
	Shock	−4.8	−6.0	−5.1	−0.7	0.6	−1.7
Long-term growth of money (%)	Actual	10.6	8.4	6.4	5.1	6.3	4.2
	Expected	12.8	10.6	8.4	6.4	5.1	6.3
	Shock	−2.2	−2.2	−2.0	−1.3	1.2	−2.1
Govt. receipts as percentage of GDP	Actual	28.0	29.0	33.6	31.0	31.7	31.2
	Expected	28.0	28.0	30.9	33.6	31.0	31.7
	Shock	0.0	1.0	2.7	−2.6	0.7	−0.5
External							
World trade growth (%)	Actual	1.0	−1.0	−1.0	2.0	8.0	3.7
	Expected	6.2	6.2	6.2	6.2	6.2	6.2
	Shock	−5.2	−7.2	−7.2	−4.2	1.8	−2.5
Foreign real short interest rates	Actual	3.4	6.0	5.0	5.0	8.0	4.5
	Expected	1.7	0.8	3.5	5.4	5.0	6.6
	Shock	1.7	5.2	1.5	−0.4	3.0	−2.1
Foreign real long interest rates	Actual	3.1	4.0	5.0	3.7	6.3	5.0
	Expected	2.2	0.6	4.1	5.3	5.0	6.6
	Shock	0.9	3.4	0.9	−1.6	1.3	−1.6
Supply							
Employers' NI contributions	Actual	13.7	13.7	13.2	11.9	11.2	10.4
	Expected	13.1	13.7	13.7	13.2	11.9	11.2
	Shock	0.6	0.0	−0.5	−1.3	−0.7	−0.8
Real unemployment benefits 1980 = 100	Actual	100.0	106.7	104.2	104.2	103.9	103.2
	Expected	98.1	100.0	106.7	104.2	104.2	103.9
	Shock	1.9	6.7	−2.4	0.0	−0.3	−0.7
Average amount lost in taxes and NI (%)	Actual	23.8	25.5	26.1	25.4	25.4	24.1
	Expected	22.8	23.8	25.5	26.1	25.4	25.4
	Shock	1.0	1.7	0.6	−0.7	0.0	−1.3
Unionisation rate (%)	Actual	58.2	56.9	55.8	54.2	52.4	50.9
	Expected	56.4	58.3	57.1	56.1	54.6	53.0
	Shock	1.8	−1.4	−1.3	−1.9	−2.2	−2.1
Indirect tax rate (%)	Actual	13.6	14.5	15.2	15.2	15.2	15.6
	Expected	13.0	13.6	14.5	15.2	15.2	15.2
	Shock	0.6	0.9	0.7	0.0	0.0	0.4

high throughout, only moving down to a plateau of about 10 per cent in late 1981, after the tough budget of that March began to show up in a falling PSBR. (Walters, 1985, put a lot of stress on that budget as building financial confidence, very much in line with our simulated reconstruction of events.)

Our assumptions, which we justify by reference empirically to the

Table 4.2 Decomposing the effects of shocks: a summary

		Effects of shocks from					
		Domestic	External	Supply	Total	Fitted value	Actual value
Inflation (%)	80	−6.6	2.1	1.5	−1.6	16.4	16.4
	81	−6.4	4.9	1.3	1.0	14.0	11.5
	82	−4.2	2.3	−0.6	−0.4	10.3	8.5
	83	−4.7	1.6	−0.4	−5.1	4.0	5.2
	84	2.7	0.8	−0.9	2.6	6.2	4.6
	85	−4.6	−0.9	−0.7	−4.4	1.9	5.3
GDP growth (%)	80	−0.6	−2.0	−1.8	−4.0	−3.1	−2.1
	81	−0.3	−3.8	−0.9	−5.1	−2.5	−1.0
	82	0.0	−2.5	0.7	−1.7	1.9	0.8
	83	−0.6	−2.0	1.9	1.4	4.4	3.8
	84	0.1	−0.4	1.4	1.0	5.3	1.8
	85	−0.2	0.4	1.2	1.1	4.9	3.7
Unemployment (000)	80	145	80	120	323	1,750	1,450
	81	185	195	180	475	2,420	2,270
	82	140	190	−50	200	2,890	2,625
	83	265	190	90	20	3,135	2,885
	84	−130	10	−200	−270	2,940	3,000
	85	190	200	−185	15	3,255	3,115
Real exchange rate (1980 = 100)	80	7.6	−2.7	1.2	4.2	92.1	100.0
	81	7.6	−6.1	2.2	1.8	103.3	100.2
	82	5.1	−3.0	1.4	0.9	102.8	96.4
	83	5.6	−1.7	0.1	−4.1	91.8	88.4
	84	−3.4	−1.5	−0.6	−3.9	85.8	82.8
	85	4.8	0.5	−0.3	5.3	87.8	83.3

Notes: Effects of domestic, external, and supply shocks do not sum to total shock because of nonlinearities in the model. The base run is not shown but may be calculated by subtracting total shocks from fitted values.

relatively good fit the model achieves with it and theoretically to the intertemporal budget constraint on government in a world of political constraints on tax and public spending, is that expected money growth is fixed by 'balanced financing' of the expected PSBR; and that the PSBR is expected to be constant as a fraction of GDP at its latest value.[1]

A political economy interpretation of this would be that with debt, both public domestic and overall foreign, high relative to GDP, at least in the eyes of overseas markets, it would require high and rising interest rates to keep money growth down and 'bond-finance' a continued PSBR of 5–6 per cent of GDP. Such interest rates would be too unpopular to be sustained, leading to higher money growth. As for the prospects of cutting the PSBR in line with the MTFS, this would be prevented by vested spending interests on the one hand and the unpopularity of higher taxes on the other. Hence the markets believed only the 'cuts' that were already delivered and no promised ones; given that static forecast for the PSBR, money growth was forecast on the assumption of constant interest rates, the implication of balanced financing.

In a recent paper (Minford, 1987), one of us argued that 'credibility' is set by observed objective constraints on government's discretionary action. In the absence of constraints government would be expected to pursue the policy that is most in its interests at the time of decision – namely discretion. The MTFS failed to have total credibility because there was nothing to force the government to carry it out. Indeed, it seemed that if Mrs Thatcher and Sir Geoffrey Howe had done so they would lose power to the powerful 'wets' in the party; these would of course preside over a 'U-turn'. The MTFS did, however, make it extremely embarrassing for Mrs Thatcher to move to more inflationary outcomes than she inherited. Faced with these uncertainties, the markets concluded that she would probably survive but at the cost of watering her policies down to the mere containment of the status quo in PSBR and money growth. This indicates that the MTFS did do something; it did at least make it highly unlikely that money growth would *exceed* balanced financing or that the PSBR would *rise*, both active possibilities in the oncoming recession.

What actually happened is well known; policy turned out to be substantially tighter than even the gradual path of the MTFS. In the struggle to bring down inflationary expectations, the PSBR was cut sharply in 1981 in the trough of recession, ensuring an even sharper cut in cyclically adjusted terms, while M0 growth was cut by more than 70 per cent in two years, unintentionally, in pursuit of a target for distorted £M3. These shocks together with their sequels (squeezing inflation down proved to require sustained policy tightness in excess of expectations till 1986) produced, in our account, a cumulative rise in unemployment of about one million by 1986.

The hindsight provided by this experience should make it possible to design an 'immediate' policy which would have brought down inflationary expectations at once and so made the process of getting inflation down less costly in unemployment. However, as is obvious, no claim is made that with the information of the time this could have been designed in 1979; H. Indsight is the true author of this chapter!

Any design should make no unrealistic assumptions about possible constraints on future policy that could have created credibility. For example, no IMF conditionality was possible because there was no external crisis making such a surrender of sovereignty politically saleable; indeed, North Sea oil revenue provided large external surpluses. A different problem attached to the EMS as a discipline; had we joined it, it would have been assumed we would make maximum use of the wide exchange rate limits that Italy used at that time.

As for internally policed mechanisms to stop discretionary backsliding, these require a government able to guarantee its own continuity, otherwise no other commitments are binding. This, as we have seen, was Mrs Thatcher's problem in 1979–80. Any too tough future promissory notes could not merely have been repudiated by the Tory old guard but also could have precipitated effective rebellion against the leadership.

What is left? Only immediate pre-emptive action, which removes future discretion from the agenda. This would take the form of large cuts in the PSBR, bringing it at once to its long-run target level, consistent with stable prices; this target is roughly a PSBR of 0.5 per cent of GDP, since stable prices require roughly 1 per cent M0 growth per annum. Politically, such cuts are made possible by the honeymoon effect of election victory; in this first '100 days' governments have brief freedom of action to set a new direction and even to renege on past promises in the light of new information denied to them in opposition. Such reneging would have been desirable in the case of the large Clegg commission awards to public sector workers.

In what follows we assume this strategy is followed. But while this conditions, according to our previous argument, expected future long-term money supply growth, it requires to be accompanied by accommodative movements in money, as real balances react sharply to the drop in inflation expectations and the swing in real activity. This problem is familiar to students of the ends of hyperinflations. So we allow for this by assuming that money growth is temporarily accommodative. We now turn to our simulation of these policies.

The simulated results of immediacy

The simulations that follow assume that from the beginning of 1980 public expenditure was held down and taxes raised sharply in order to bring the PSBR down at once to approximately 0.5 per cent of GDP on a cyclically adjusted basis. (Since inflation is planned to fall to zero also in short order, inflation adjustment is irrelevant.)

Money growth (M0) is cut in parallel – implying a steady growth of around 1 per cent per annum for stable prices – apart from the temporary accommodation above. So, for example, in 1980 instead of dropping to 1 per cent growth as the rule implies, M0 rises 8 per cent to accommodate higher real balances (so dampening the very sharp rise in the real exchange rate); and in 1981 M0 falls somewhat as real balance demand and real activity fall. From 1982 money growth settles down in the more stable conditions.

From 1981 onwards fiscal and monetary policy is sustained in this mode; whereas in 1980, of course, the policy is a shock, on a major scale, from 1981 it is fully anticipated for reasons discussed above. Thus, in terms of the fiscal and monetary policy rules in operation, these policy changes are treated as pure one-off shocks in 1980, and only 1980.

The actual PSBR does of course rise in 1981–4 as the economy falls below its normal rate of capacity utilisation. But it is assumed that the markets appreciate, after the harsh medicine of 1980, the cyclically adjusted balance of the public accounts; after 1985 the projected PSBR is for comfortable balance.

Public spending on goods and services follows a path similar to that actually followed except that it is cut less in 1981, the year of worst recession, and more in 1982 as recovery occurs; thereafter it recovers to the actual path, overtaking it as real GDP exceeds the actual 1985 level by 4.4 per cent, producing more tax revenue. Of course, this would also make possible supply-side cuts in tax rates; these would improve output and employment more quickly. But we have deliberately excluded these here to focus solely on cyclical responses to counter-inflation policy.

All other exogenous shocks from 1980 onwards are assumed to be exactly as in Matthews and Minford (1987); we also include the single equation errors (that would, if included in Matthews and Minford, have replicated actual events). The path from 1981 onward takes as lagged information the *predicted* values of the previous year, not the actuals which are assumed to be the result of the different actual policies carried out. Thus our comparison is between what actually happened and what would have happened under the immediacy policies, had everything else remained exactly the same.

The basic picture is clear (see chart 4.2 and table 4.3). There would have been a much deeper recession in 1980–81 and a quicker rise in unemployment, reaching three million by 1981. However, because there are no further negative fiscal/monetary shocks after 1980, unemployment starts to fall sooner and by 1985 it is below three million.

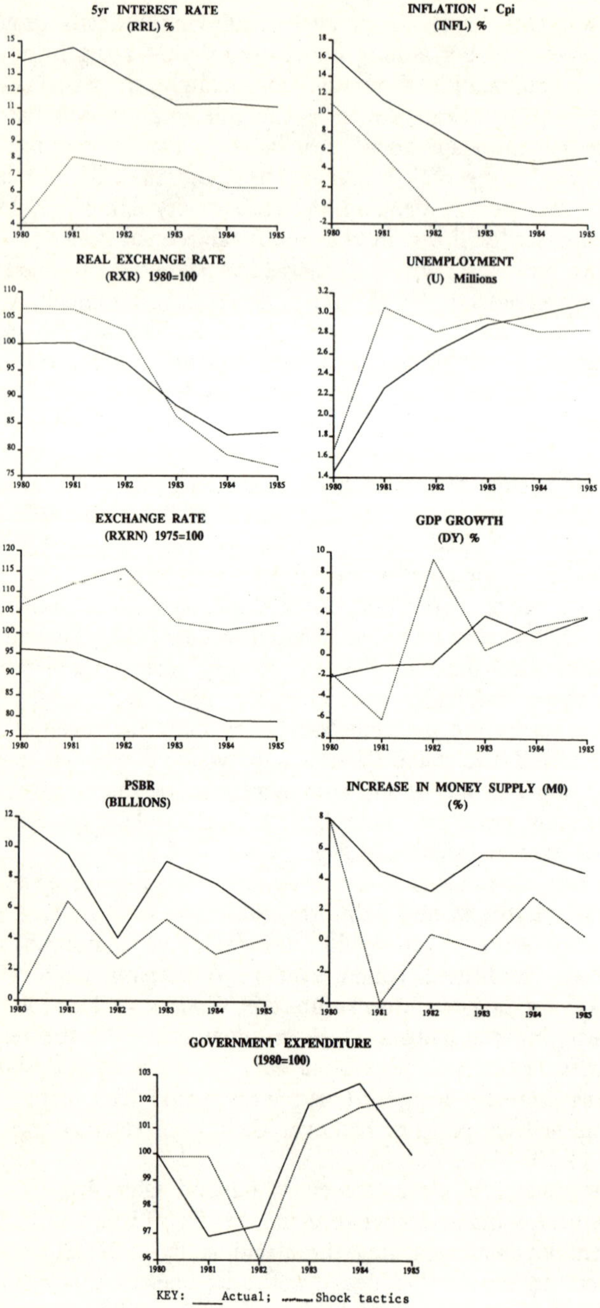

Chart 4.2 Shock-tactics simulations

Table 4.3 Simulation results

		Actual	Shock tactics
5-year interest rate (*RRL*) %	1980	13.8	4.2
	1981	14.6	8.1
	1982	12.8	7.6
	1983	11.2	7.5
	1984	11.3	6.3
	1985	11.1	6.3
Inflation - CPI (*INFL*) %	1980	16.4	11.0
	1981	11.5	5.6
	1982	8.5	−0.5
	1983	5.2	0.5
	1984	4.6	−0.7
	1985	5.3	−0.3
Real exchange rate (*RXR*) 1980 = 100	1980	100.0	106.8
	1981	100.2	106.6
	1982	96.4	102.5
	1983	88.3	86.3
	1984	82.8	79.0
	1985	83.3	76.7
Unemployment (*U*) '000	1980	1452.0	1656.0
	1981	2269.8	3059.6
	1982	2626.1	2816.7
	1983	2886.0	2958.0
	1984	2998.3	2820.8
	1985	3113.1	2840.0
GDP growth (*DY*) %	1980	−2.1	−1.7
	1981	−1.0	−6.2
	1982	0.8	9.3
	1983	3.8	0.5
	1984	1.8	2.8
	1985	3.7	3.8
Exchange rate (*RXRN*) 1975 = 100	1980	96.1	106.8
	1981	95.3	111.8
	1982	90.7	115.6
	1983	83.3	102.5
	1984	78.8	100.7
	1985	78.7	102.5
PSBR (£ millions)	1980	11816.0	342.9
	1981	9495.0	6474.6
	1982	4094.0	2744.5
	1983	9148.0	5311.6
	1984	7667.0	3079.3
	1985	5399.0	4038.9

Table 4.3 contd.

		Actual	Shock tactics
Govt. expenditure (1980 = 100)	1980	100.0	99.9
	1981	96.9	99.9
	1982	97.3	96.0
	1983	101.9	100.8
	1984	102.7	101.8
	1985	100.0	102.2
Increase in money supply (*M*0) %	1980	8.0	8.0
	1981	4.6	−4.0
	1982	3.3	0.5
	1983	5.7	−0.5
	1984	5.7	3.0
	1985	4.6	0.5

The inflation rate falls more rapidly and settles at zero from 1982. It does not drop at once to zero in 1980 in spite of the immediacy because the world recession and other negative shocks on the supply side reduce money demand in 1980–81 and cause 'defensive' price rises.

The real exchange rate similarly rises more sharply in 1980 but thereafter drops back more quickly as there are no more negative fiscal/monetary shocks.

So far we have found rather what we might have expected from a model such as this. It does suggest in line with new classical advice that the short sharp shock that cannot be reversed, and so bypasses issues of credibility, gives better longer-term results than gradualism. The question that remains is whether the treatment was too brutal to be a practical possibility even in the honeymoon period of the first six to twelve months.

The scale of the cuts or tax rises needed would have been of the order of 10 per cent of total government expenditure and 4 per cent of GDP. By contrast, even with the Clegg awards, actual government spending in 1980 remained roughly constant in real terms (that is, deflated by the GDP deflator). It is not that difficult to imagine a crisis package that could have been politically viable: withdrawal of Clegg awards, freezing of all benefits in money terms, general 10 per cent programme cuts, raising of the discount factor on capital projects, or bringing forward the tax rises of the 1981 budget (worth about 4 per cent of GDP). In our programme here we assume, as noted earlier, that government spending on goods and services moves much as it in fact did, but that tax rates rise by 4 per cent of GDP in 1980, remaining at this level throughout the period. So in effect we bring forward the tough 1981 budget by eighteen months.

Judgement of political viability would require an extended discussion which we are not competent to undertake and would take us too far from the focus here: that is, assuming viability, what would have resulted. But when the opposition has itself been practising or advocating cuts, experience shows it can be done; witness the recent policies of Haughey in Eire and Lange in New Zealand in just such circumstances.

In summary, the policies here would have caused substantial dislocation during 1980–81, with the real exchange rate appreciating about twice as much as it actually did and GDP falling 7 per cent, also about twice as much. But the recovery would have been faster with inflation eliminated; by 1985, GDP would have been nearly 5 per cent higher. Would such a cure have been so much more painful than what actually happened, that its speed and long-term gain would still not have seemed attractive?

A programme of workfare to eliminate long-term unemployment

The remaining simulation extends new classical thinking to the supply side. In their simulations, Matthews and Minford found the equilibrium unemployment rate to have fallen steadily since 1982 to around one million or less by 1986; but for reasons of credibility that should be obvious from the preceding pages, we opposed reflationary policy as a way of closing the gap between actual and equilibrium unemployment. That leaves further cuts in the equilibrium as a way of reducing unemployment faster.

We identified various policies that could do this, including further reduction in union powers, housing deregulation, a crackdown on benefit fraud and benefit cuts to the unemployed. The first three are being pursued to varying degrees but the fourth has proved to be politically unpopular because people feel, whether rightly or wrongly, that the genuinely needy would be hurt along with those who could get a job. An alternative, which has a similar effect but is subject to administrative screening of need, so potentially avoiding harm to the needy, is workfare.

Lowering equilibrium unemployment can be done either by raising the marginal product of the unemployed or by lowering the wage at which they will work (and so the general level of wages). Workfare must, to be effective, do one of these; it may train or it may provide cheap labour. But in either case it must be sustainable permanent change in the institutions and not a temporary measure which, once reflationary finance for it disappears, must be

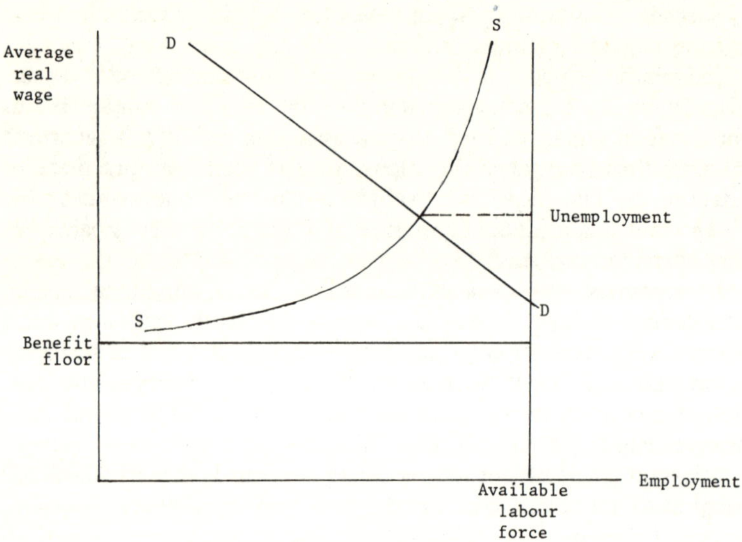

Key: SS = labour supply (supply withdrawn as average real wage declines to benefit floor, drawing increasing numbers into 'unemployment trap')

DD = labour demand (marginal product in terms of affordable real wage; influenced by real exchange rate; position of DD set by international conditions, on assumption of current account balance, and profit-maximisation by firms subject to production function).

Source: Minford *et al* (1985).

Chart 4.3 Labour supply and demand in general equilibrium in the open economy

abandoned for lack of finance. Therefore, any proposal must be costed on the assumption that it is fully tax financed to test its durability. Many costings of special measures do not meet this rigorous requirement.

The general equilibrium long-run supply and demand curves for labour shown in chart 4.3 can be used to clarify this point. The scheme when paid for in higher taxes must shift their intersection to the right; thus the change in implicit tax/benefit structure must increase incentives to work for a given pre-tax wage or must increase the marginal product at that wage.

Proposals to increase allowances under existing job and training schemes to make them more attractive to the unemployed, such as are currently reported to be under consideration, will not satisfy this test, because the extra cost has to be borne by employers or employees in higher tax; the supply curve may well shift rightward but the demand curve shifts leftward, and there is no basis for believing the net effect will be positive.

The scheme considered here assumes that after a year it becomes compulsory to take workfare, as in Sweden. This limits the extra cost for obtaining the rightward move of the supply curve. As is recognised currently by the Department of Employment, existing schemes are unattractive to many or perhaps most of the long-term unemployed. Politically, however, the idea of making work compulsory for those on benefits is acceptable because it is felt that society should not support those who can support themselves but only give supplementary support to agreed minimum standards of living, once people are doing the best they can for themselves. Workfare achieves this while ensuring an administrative screening so that no-one is victimised.

Our costings are crude. There are 1.2 million long-term unemployed, whom workfare would compel to work for existing benefits; for these people the replacement ratio falls to zero since if they do continue as unemployed they lose benefits, or more relevantly perhaps there may be other sanctions so that they do not refuse. We simulate this by cutting our average benefit variable by one third, roughly the proportion of those unemployed in the total. At the same time there will be some costs in expenses of workfarees, supervision, and machinery/premises; we assume a figure of £2,500 gross per workfaree for these, making a total cost of some £3 billion per year for the programme in current prices. This is added permanently to public spending with the constraint that the PSBR be unchanged on average long-term. The whole programme is phased in over three years in recognition of the problems in involving all the long-term unemployed.

The results can be seen in chart 4.4. They can only be indicative because our calculation of equivalent benefit and of cost are so rough.

But the general effect is clear. Compulsion, Swedish-style, reduces unemployment rapidly, cutting public expenditure costs as tax revenues increase from the marginal product of the newly employed, and raising output significantly. Because the direct cost of the programme is kept down by paying only existing benefits plus expenses and relying on compulsion to induce participation, the net PSBR cost is negative to the tune of £4 billion per annum.

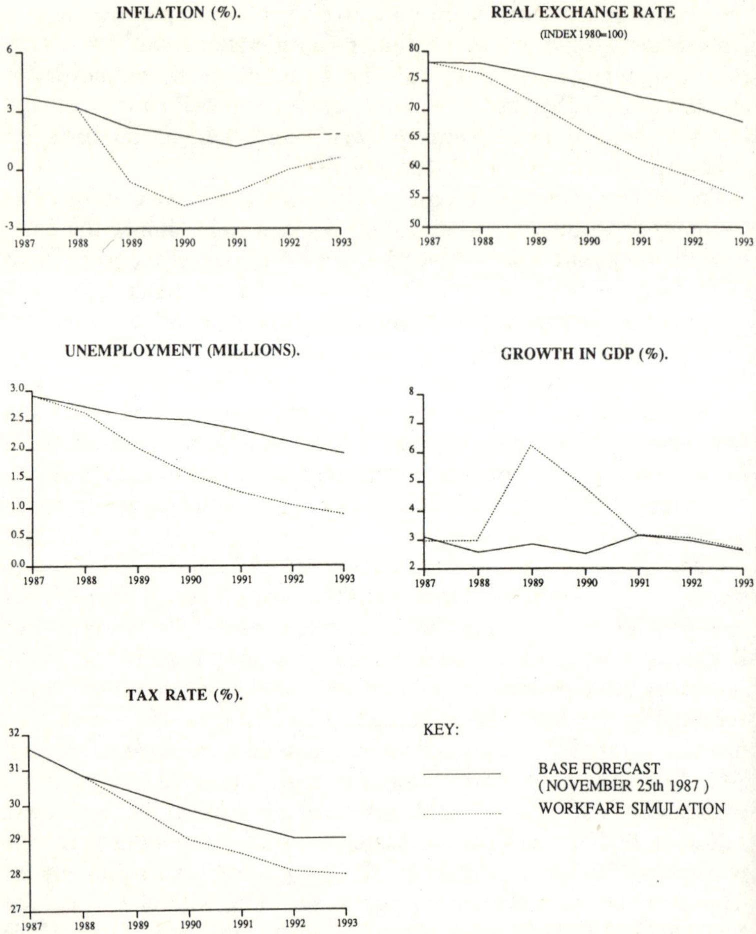

Chart 4.4 Workfare simulations

This is assumed to enable tax cuts but no allowance has been made for any further supply-side effect of this because the effect in the model is mainly connected with the unemployment trap and this is reduced to insignificance with the workfare programme assumed here.

Again the question of political viability arises and again we propose to avoid it except to note that if it can be accepted both in socialist Sweden where benefits are similarly high for low-paid workers and in capitalist United States where benefits run out after six to twelve months, it should be saleable here.

Conclusions

This chapter has considered two important issues of macroeconomic policy from a new classical perspective. One conclusion has been that because of the credibility problem the results of 'cold turkey' in fiscal/monetary policy are more attractive as a way of stabilising prices than gradualism. The other is of more immediate relevance: that in designing programmes to reduce unemployment, the workfare principle offers great advantages – without it the cost of inducing the unemployed to participate in JTS[2] is likely to require tax rises that would reduce private sector employment by as much or even more. Not everyone will agree with the model used to generate these conclusions; but it should at least lead the increasing number of economists who take rational expectations and the supply side seriously to reflect carefully on what *they* would expect.

Note

1 This implies that the model under rational expectations is augmented by two rules governing fiscal and monetary policy: $d_t = d_{t-1} + v_t$ and $\Delta m_t = Pd_t + u_t$, where d_t = ratio of PSBR to GDP, m_t = log of M0, P = average ratio of GDP to government financial liabilities, v_t and u_t are random errors.

2 The Job Training Scheme intended to offer training places to all the long-term unemployed who cannot be placed in a job.

Comment on Chapter 4

Paul Levine

Patrick Minford and his co-author, Anupani Rastogi, have written a very clear and succinct chapter. It addresses two quite separate issues: the first is to do with the credibility problem facing the Thatcher government in 1979 and the second is the use of a workfare programme to eliminate long-term unemployment. The first part of the chapter is probably the more novel. Since most people should be familiar with the Liverpool group's supply-side views, the credibility issue will be concentrated on here.

Minford makes the case that a 'cold turkey' rather than gradualist approach would have been more appropriate for the incoming Thatcher administration. The argument may be summarised as follows. The Conservative government faced a serious credibility problem at the outset of the medium term financial stategy (MTFS). A commitment was made to reduce inflation and interest rates by reducing £M3 growth from 7–11 per cent to 4–8 per cent over four years and the PSBR–GDP ratio from 3¾ per cent to 1½ per cent. However, markets did not believe this would be carried out. The continuing existence of powerful 'wets' in the cabinet and the early unpopularity of the government meant that a reputation for dryness was not achieved until 1982. The behaviour of long-run interest rates which only began falling in 1982 is evidence that the expected inflation rate remained high in the early years of the administration.

Instead of believing the announced MTFS, markets only believed policies that were delivered. Thus, in the eyes of the private sector, the PSBR–GDP ratio followed a random walk or, in other words, current values of the ratio were assumed to continue indefinitely. Assuming constant inflation and real interest rates in the long run, this ratio then determines expectations of long-run inflation, a crucial determinant of current, actual inflation.

Given these beliefs by the private sector, a cold turkey policy which rapidly reduced the PSBR to zero would have quickly reduced actual inflation as well. The result according to simulations by the Liverpool model would have been a deeper recession at first, but a more rapid reduction in inflation compared with gradualism. Output would then have recovered quickly so that, after two years of the cold turkey MTFS, unemployment would have begun to fall.

The first point to stress about this argument is that it applies only to policies without reputation. If the Thatcher government had enjoyed a reputation for precommitment to its announced MTFS in 1980, it is not true in general that cold turkey would have been preferable to gradualism. To demonstrate this point two simulations on the LBS model have been carried out assuming policy announcements are believed. Charts 4.5 and 4.6 show optimal policies for 'policymaker 2', in the chapter by Budd *et al.* (chapter 3) who are concerned primarily with stabilising inflation. In the exercise here larger weights for inflation have been chosen than in chapter 3 and monetary policy has been allowed a bigger role by reducing instrument costs on inflation rates. In the resulting optimal policies government spending falls gradually to 2 per cent in the long run and short-term interest rates rise gradually to 1.2 per cent in the long run.

Now compare these policies with cold turkey alternatives: an immediate sustained fall in government spending by 2 per cent and an immediate, sustained rise in interest rates by 1.2 per cent. The GDP loss under cold turkey takes over five years to recover to its optimal, gradualist level. The price level falls faster but the

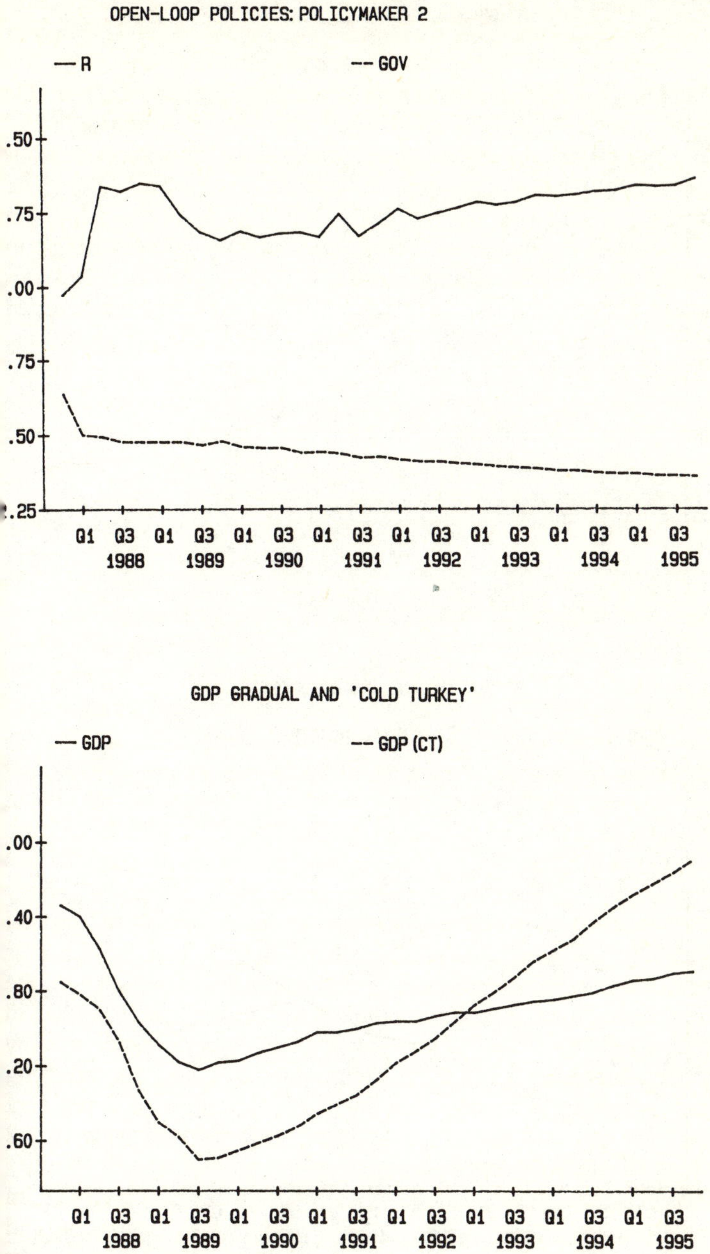

Chart 4.5 Gradualism versus 'cold turkey'

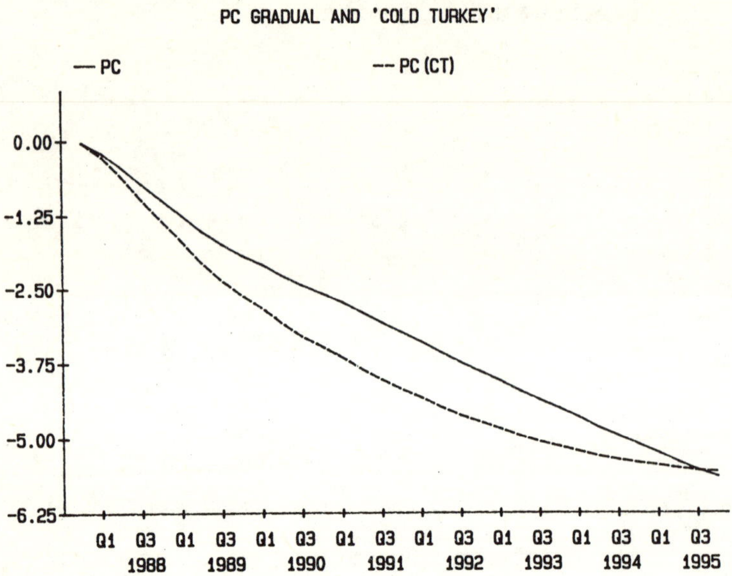

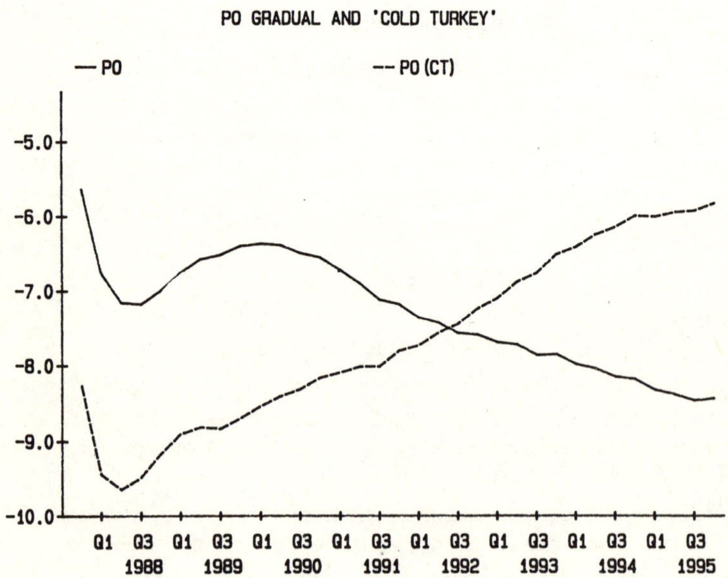

Chart 4.6 Gradualism versus 'cold turkey'

inflationary gains are small. Of course these conclusions are model-specific; but if cold turkey and gradualist policies were compared on the Liverpool model with reputation the results would probably not be too dissimilar.

The case for cold turkey then rests critically on the assumption of no reputation. Furthermore it is clear that it critically depends on the Minford view of how expectations of policy are formed in the absence of reputation. In this chapter reputation is to do with the nature of the government in the eyes of the private sector. In considering policy options, it is assumed that, whatever decision is taken, markets would still believe that a PSBR–GDP ratio follows a random walk. This is certainly a bold empirical assumption which may have accurately reflected the markets' scepticism regarding the new government's counter-inflationary intentions. After all, in this period it did double VAT and introduce large increases in the prices of nationalised industries. But this approach fits uneasily with the Liverpool model which is the most rational of the macroeconomic forecasting models in assuming rational expectations in all markets.

A number of recent papers on uncertainty regarding the policymaker's objective function (or 'type of government') suggest far more plausible models whereby the private sector adjusts its expectations in the light of observed policies in a rational manner. (See, for example, Backus and Driffill, 1985a and 1985b, Barro, 1986, Vickers, 1985, and surveys by Driffill, 1987, and Levine and Holly, 1987.) It seems likely that an application of this type of learning model to the Liverpool model would result in a dry government being drier than its optimal policy implies in order to build up reputation and differentiate itself from wet governments. Whether, however, the policy would be anything approaching cold turkey is an open, empirical question. This is certainly an important area for future research and Minford has provided a very useful start.

Although uncertainty regarding government preferences is an important aspect of credibility, it is not the only aspect. Credibility problems exist whenever *ex post* policies may differ from *ex ante* policies for whatever reason. This can happen even where the type of government is known and thought to be infinitely lived. This is the more familiar time inconsistency problem which is not addressed in this chapter. Even when the private sector has been convinced of the counter-inflationary character of the government, provided that the government has some concern for output there may exist an incentive to undergo a U-turn once inflation expectations and inflation itself have been brought down. Again reputational considerations of the type considered by the literature cited above suggest that this may not be a serious problem; but this needs examining using empirical models.

Turning to the workfare programme, a few brief comments follow. The proposal is essentially to remove benefits for the long-term (over one year) unemployed with exceptions determined through administrative screening. Assuming this latter category is negligible in size, average benefits will fall by one third. The beneficial supply-side effects then follow due to the large impact of benefits on the real wage in the Liverpool model.

A number of references to the Swedish experience are cited in support of the scheme. Of course Minford is very selective in his approval of the Swedish approach to unemployment. In Sweden a tough benefits policy is part of a *quid-pro-quo* which has seen large-scale job creation in the public sector as the principal weapon for keeping its unemployment rate at below 3 per cent.

As for the simulations themselves it is important that they are accompanied by a health warning. This could take the following form (taken from Minford *et al.*, 1984). "It must be stressed that the model is intended to represent what we believe, it has not been our intention to *test* its structure against past data, rather than to use this data to help parameterize the model." In relation to this it is instructive to compare the freely-estimated coefficients of the Liverpool wage equation undertaken by the Macroeconomic Modelling Bureau at Warwick (Wallis *et al.*, 1986) with those reported by the modellers themselves, which imposed some estimates.

In conclusion this chapter provides an interesting view of the credibility problem facing Thatcher in 1979 and a more predictable argument for cutting unemployment benefit. Whilst this author remains unconvinced by either argument, Minford as usual has provided a stimulus which should sharpen future debate regarding expectations and supply-side questions.

5 Using Macroeconometric Models to Evaluate Policy Proposals

*David S. Turner, Kenneth F. Wallis and John D. Whitley**

Introduction

Policymaking with a macroeconomic model often involves the evaluation of new policy proposals, and is seldom limited to standard policy simulations which study the effects of variations in the settings of policy instruments included in the existing specification of the model. Sometimes the new policy proposals are genuine innovations, such as the introduction of new policy instruments or institutional arrangements; sometimes they are new with respect to a given model, in that the policy instruments do not appear in the model's specification, for one reason or another. In using an econometric model to provide a fully elaborated, internally consistent, quantitative assessment of the macroeconomic consequences of a policy proposal, various interventions and adjustments to the model are then necessary, based on prior assumptions and off-model evidence. Such interventions are also required if a relevant policy instrument does appear on the model, but the model's specification neglects important features of the transmission mechanism through which the instrument operates, or other important internal linkages. In this chapter we consider the issues that arise in policy analysis of this kind, and illustrate them by using existing models of the United Kingdom economy, as described by Wallis *et al.* (1987), in three leading examples.

To evaluate a policy proposal, the general procedure is to estimate its effects by comparing two solution paths of the model, one a base run or control solution over some historical or forecast period, and the second a perturbed solution, incorporating the policy changes, over the same period. Clearly there are limitations to the kind of policy that can be simulated in this way. The general assumption is that there are substantial parts of the model that

* The financial support of the Economic and Social Research Council is gratefully acknowledged as are the helpful comments of our colleague Paul Fisher and our discussants Richard Layard and Chris Melliss.

remain invariant to the policy change, and that sufficient information and assumptions are available to allow respecification of those parts of the model that do change. Typically this information covers both the impact of the new policy and its transmission mechanisms, and sensitivity analysis can be undertaken to assess the importance of particular assumptions. However, where the new policy is diffuse, with possibly wide-ranging macroeconomic consequences, being intended to promote broad structural change that cannot be quantified, then model-based analysis is not possible: recent 'industrial policy' proposals fall into this category. Moreover regional and sectoral policies are typically outside the scope of an aggregate model.

Expectations of future values of endogenous variables, such as inflation or exchange rates, are often an important determinant of current behaviour. A traditional way of handling such unobserved expectations is to assume that they are functions of the current and lagged values of a few observed variables and so substitute them out, giving a conventional backward-looking dynamic model. Such a model is unlikely to remain invariant across policy regimes, as noted by Lucas (1976). A practical and increasingly common alternative is to treat expectations variables in an explicit forward-looking manner. Then, in solving the model for the endogenous variable values over a forecast period, an internally consistent solution is calculated, in which each period's future expectations variables coincide with the model's forecasts for that future period. This model-consistent treatment of expectations removes a major source of model instability under policy change, in response to the Lucas critique. It also allows policies to be tested under conditions where their effects are understood, noting Currie's (1985) argument that good performance in these circumstances is a necessary condition for a satisfactory policy. Questions of credibility arise, however, if the new policy represents a situation which is not sustainable in the long run, given the government's intertemporal budget constraint, for example. How existing simulation techniques might be modified to reflect such factors as uncertainty about the eventual reversal of an unsustainable policy is an open research problem.

Estimates of the policy response are typically presented as point estimates, and no formal procedures for assessing the uncertainty of these estimates are available. Sensitivity analysis of various kinds may be undertaken, but the interpretation of the results is essentially subjective. Different models of the economy may give different estimates, and comparing these is a further kind of sensitivity analysis. Understanding the reasons for inter-model divergences through systematic model comparisons is one of the objectives of the research programme of the ESRC Macroeconomic Modelling Bureau (Wallis *et al.*, 1984–7), and inter-model comparisons feature in the examples that follow. Such comparisons may contribute to a clearer subjective assessment of the uncertainty surrounding empirical model-based results.

A further objective of the Bureau is to improve the accessibility and openness of models and model-based work. Considerable progress has been made in respect of the models themselves and their associated forecasts, which the ESRC-supported teams deposit in sufficient detail so that the Bureau can replicate the forecasts and subsequently analyse the contributions of exogenous projections and residual adjustments. An implicit theme of the present chapter is that the same principles should apply to policy analysis. A full account of model adjustments and interventions should accompany each policy exercise, so that the results can be replicated and, more generally, so that the relative importance of the various elements of the calculation can be assessed, especially when different modellers present different estimates of the costs or benefits of new policies. If a complete policy package is under consideration, then this requires a detailed specification of the adjustments and interventions made in modelling each component of the package. Of course, through various interactions and non-linearities the total effect of the package may differ from the sum of the individual effects of its components, but this cannot be assessed without a full specification of each component. The examples presented in later sections of the chapter are of individual policies, rather than policy packages, and we indicate by our own example the presentation in detail that is being advocated.

Model-handling for policy evaluation

In this section we describe the techniques employed in evaluating policy proposals with macroeconometric models. To fix ideas, we first use the framework of the *linear* simultaneous equation model, reserving generalisations until later.

The model describes the relations between the elements of a vector of current endogenous variables y_t and a vector of predetermined (exogenous and lagged endogenous) variables z_t together with random errors u_t, and is written in *structural form* as

$$By_t + Cz_t = u_t. \tag{1}$$

Estimates of the structural parameters B and C provide information about elasticities, marginal propensities, reaction coefficients, and so forth. Identities are distinguished as equations in which the numerical values of the parameters are given *a priori* and there is no error term. As the estimation of the model is not a principal focus of the present chapter, no separate notation is used to distinguish a parameter and its numerical value. The contemporaneous feedbacks among the endogenous variables are solved out in the *reduced form*

$$y_t = \Pi z_t + v_t, \; \Pi = -B^{-1}C, \; v_t = B^{-1}u_t.$$

For those elements of the vector z_t that are policy instruments, the associated reduced-form coefficients give the *policy multipliers* or *ready-reckoners*, describing the response of the endogenous variables (targets) to a unit shock in a policy instrument. In a linear model such ready-reckoners may be combined to describe the effect of a policy package. For presentational purposes, however, the impact of the policy change might be described in terms of the difference between two solutions of the model, which, of necessity, is the procedure followed once the linearity assumption is relaxed. First a control solution or base run $\hat{y}_t$, $t = 1,\ldots,T$, satisfying the equations

$$B\hat{y}_t + Cz_t = 0 \tag{2}$$

is obtained over some historical or simulation period for given values of the exogenous variables. Then the vector z_t is replaced by $z_t + \delta_t$, $t = 1,\ldots,T$, where the vector δ_t has most of its elements equal to zero, with non-zero values corresponding to perturbations in selected policy instruments. The perturbed solution or simulation $\tilde{y}_t$, $t = 1,\ldots,T$, satisfying the equation

$$B\tilde{y}_t + C(z_t + \delta_t) = 0 \tag{3}$$

is obtained, and the differences $\tilde{y}_t - \hat{y}_t$ estimate the effect of the policy change. The differences obey the relation

$$B(\tilde{y}_t - \hat{y}_t) + C\delta_t = 0 \tag{4}$$

and this is the equation that must be solved for δ_t if it is desired to find the policy change that will achieve a given deviation in target variables. Clearly, at least as many instruments as targets are required.

To evaluate new policy possibilities, this framework is augmented in various ways, since the policy change is no longer a simple alteration in the value of an element of z_t. Typically the perturbed solution is obtained from the given model augmented by residual adjustments, namely

$$B\tilde{y}_t + Cz_t = a_t \tag{5}$$

and the problem is to assign appropriate values to the relevant elements of a_t. The standard case of the preceding paragraph corresponds to this equation if $a_t = -C\delta_t$, but in the present case the model does not immediately provide the information required for this calculation. A simple example is that of the introduction of a new tax: if this serves to augment a price variable that appears in the model in an appropriate way, then the relevant adjustment is given as the tax multiplied by the price coefficient, in every equation in which the price variable appears. However, if the price variable does not appear in the model, perhaps because it has exhibited insufficient variation in the historical data to allow its coefficient to be estimated, then evidence from statistical or accounting sources, or from other econometric or survey research, must be drawn on to calculate the relevant adjustment.

In a frequently-occurring case, the appropriate variable(s) appears on the model, but in an aggregate form, and it is desired to perturb a specific component of the aggregate, which at least in some part of the model has a differential impact. Let the aggregate variable be z_{1t}, the first element of the vector z_t, which appears in the equation of interest, taken to be the first equation, with coefficient c_{11}. However the perturbation δ_{1t} applies only to a component of the aggregate, which is assumed to have coefficient $c^\star_{11}$. Then in a single-equation context it might suffice to scale the perturbation, obtaining the solution $\tilde{y}_t$ from a model containing the term $c_{11}(z_{1t} + \delta^\star_{1t})$, where $\delta^\star_{1t} = c^\star_{11}\,\delta_{1t}/c_{11}$. But it is often the case that the variable appears elsewhere in the model with no differential disaggregated effects. Then the perturbation should be retained as δ_{1t}, and allowance made in the first equation through an additional residual adjustment $a_{1t} = (c_{11} - c^\star_{11})\delta_{1t}$.

In some circumstances the impact of the new policy on a particular behavioural equation may be specified sufficiently precisely that the required residual adjustment to that equation can be calculated, for example, as the change in a particular variable which is omitted from the equation multiplied by its coefficient, whose value rests on off-model evidence. More generally, assumptions about the policy relate to its impact on the solution (the reduced-form values) for particular endogenous variables. There are various methods of obtaining a model solution in which certain endogenous variables are constrained to have given values. First, this may be achieved by the choice of appropriate values for the variables' own residual adjustments, and procedures for producing these adjustments automatically are known as *type 1 fixes*. A second procedure, known as *exogenisation*, is to include the endogenous variables with pre-assigned values among the predetermined variables, delete the equations which are normalised on those variables, and solve the slimmed model for the remaining endogenous variables.

To consider these possibilities we partition the vector y_t into subvectors y_{1t} and y_{2t}, and assume that the variables whose values are constrained are collected in the first subvector. Partitioning the structural form conformably, equation (1) may be written

$$\begin{bmatrix} B_{11} & B_{12} \\ B_{21} & B_{22} \end{bmatrix} \begin{bmatrix} y_{1t} \\ y_{2t} \end{bmatrix} + \begin{bmatrix} C_1 \\ C_2 \end{bmatrix} z_t = \begin{bmatrix} u_{1t} \\ u_{2t} \end{bmatrix}. \qquad (6)$$

Denoting the preassigned values of the endogenous variables in the first block by $y^{\star}_{1t}$, the associated solution for the unconstrained variables is then obtained (with $u_{2t} = 0$) as

$$y^{\star}_{2t} = -B_{22}^{-1} (B_{21}y^{\star}_{1t} + C_2 z_t). \qquad (7)$$

In this calculation the variables y_{1t} are treated in the same way as z_t, hence the term exogenisation; one might alternatively say that the first block of equations has been switched out. The type 1 fix that ensures that $y^{\star}_{1t}$ and $y^{\star}_{2t}$ also represent a solution to the first block of equations is

$$a_{1t} = B_{11}y^{\star}_{1t} + B_{12}y^{\star}_{2t} + C_1 z_t.$$

The solution obtained from the general model

$$By^{\star}_t + Cz_t = a_t$$

with this residual adjustment, the subvector a_{2t} being zero, is clearly identical. Thus using a_{1t} to control y_{1t} is numerically equivalent to switching out the first block of equations, that is, treating y_{1t} as predetermined in the second block.

A further method of constraining an endogenous variable to have a given value is to adjust some other variable to which the constrained variable is related. For example, a price variable may be adjusted in order to achieve a desired variation in a quantity variable. The calculation and imposition of the required adjustment is known as a *type 2 fix*. It can be accomplished by adjusting the residuals on other endogenous variables, or by adjusting appropriate exogenous variables (policy instruments) by an amount δ_t, using the notation introduced in equation (3). In the context of the partitioned model (6), the adjustment required to achieve the target value of the first subvector satisfies the equation

$$(B_{11} - B_{12} B_{22}^{-1} B_{21}) y_{1t}^{\star} = -(C_1 - B_{12} B_{22}^{-1} C_2) (z_t + \delta_t).$$

Given $y_{1t}^{\star}$, the existence of a solution for δ_t rests on the existence of appropriate channels of influence, which may be direct, as represented by the matrix C_1, or indirect, as represented by C_2 and B_{12}. In the context of a single equation, the required calculation amounts to an inversion of the equation, obtaining the value of the explanatory variable that is needed to produce the desired value of the dependent variable, for example adjusting interest rates to achieve a monetary target. The classification of variables as endogenous or exogenous is not changed by this calculation, however: in this example it is precisely because interest rates are treated as exogenous that they can be manipulated to produce the desired response of endogenous money.

In a type 2 fix, the associated solution for the variables that are not targeted is

$$y_{2t}^{\star} = -B_{22}^{-1} \{B_{21} y_{1t}^{\star} + C_2(z_t + \delta_t)\} \tag{8}$$

This differs from the case of exogenisation or a type 1 fix, given in equation (7), by including the explicit policy adjustment. If the policy instruments used in targeting y_1 have a direct effect through the second block of equations, that is, the relevant elements of C_2 are non-zero, then the solution for y_2 is different.

Apart from this last possibility, the various procedures – type 1 and type 2 fixes, exogenisation – produce identical results in a single run. In subsequent simulation exercises, however, they may have different implications, since exogenisation eliminates feedbacks through the first block of equations. For example, if it is desired to perturb the pre-assigned values $y_{1t}^{\star}$, in the exogenisation case this may be done directly, whereas in the type 1 fix case the residuals a_{1t} may be perturbed. The latter case admits the distinction between an *ex ante* and an *ex post* adjustment, since a change in a_{1t} produces a change in $y_{1t}^{\star}$ of

$$\Delta y_{1t}^{\star} = (B_{11} - B_{12} B_{22}^{-1} B_{21})^{-1} \Delta a_{1t}.$$

Thus in the scalar case, with $B_{11} = 1$, Δa_{1t} and $\Delta y_{1t}^{\star}$ differ unless B_{12} or B_{21} is identically zero, that is, the model is decomposable, while in the vector case, even if the model is decomposable, feedbacks within the first block in general cause $\Delta a_{1t} \neq \Delta y_{1t}^{\star}$.

As a second example, suppose that it is desired to maintain the target values y^*_{1t} in the face of an exogenous shock, say, a fall in the world price of oil. This may be represented by introducing a further vector of perturbations γ_t, defined in the same way as δ_t, but with non-zero elements corresponding to changes in external variables, not policy instruments. In the exogenisation case, the values of y^*_{1t} are implicitly assumed to be maintained, and the associated change in the remaining endogenous variables is $\Delta y^*_{2t} = -B_{22}^{-1} C_2\gamma_t$. In the case of a type 2 fix, further adjustments $\Delta\delta_t$ to policy instruments are explicitly required to maintain the target values y^*_{1t}, which may give an additional effect on the remaining endogenous variables, as in equation (8) above. Hence the exogenisation procedure is likely to produce biased results.

In all these cases, a statement of the premise on which the intervention rests is essential. This is straightforward in the case of a type 2 fix using exogenous variables that are part of the model's specification, but less so in the case of a type 1 fix or exogenisation. Unless a mechanism whereby a direct reduction in an endogenous variable can be achieved is put forward, however, such exercises make no contribution to the analysis of policy *per se*. Without a statement of the implicit model or side calculation that underpins the assumption of an exogenous shift in an endogenous variable, the result can be described as, at best, not 'what-if' but 'if-only' analysis (Andrews *et al*., 1985).

Nonlinear models

The specific context of the previous discussion, namely that of a linear simultaneous equation model, is unrealistic, since the practical models are nonlinear in variables. The nonlinear system is usually written formally, in its structural form, as

$$f(y_t, z_t, \alpha) = u_t$$

where f is a vector of functions having as many elements as the vector y_t, and α is a vector of parameters. This notation is convenient, although it is more general than is necessary, since the equations of empirical macroeconomic models are usually linear in simple transformations (such as logarithms) or simple functions (such as products or ratios) of variables. Nonlinearity in parameters is relatively rare.

It is assumed that there exists, at least implicitly, a single inverse relationship

$$y_t = g(u_t, z_t, \alpha)$$

valid for relevant z-values, analogous to the reduced form in the linear case. In general an explicit analytic expression for g does not exist, but it can be approximated numerically to any desired degree of accuracy. Forecasting and policy analysis exercises usually ignore the impact of the random error term and utilise the *deterministic solution* of the model, which may be written implicitly as

$$\hat{y}_t = g(0, z_t, \alpha);$$

it is obtained as the numerical solution, to the desired degree of accuracy, of the equations

$$f(\hat{y}_t, z_t, \alpha) = 0.$$

Policy multipliers are calculated as the difference between base and perturbed deterministic solutions: although their definition as the partial derivatives of the conditional expectations of the endogenous variables with respect to the policy instruments suggests that stochastic simulation estimates of the conditional expectations should be used, in practice this results in no appreciable difference from the usual calculation.

Residual adjustments, type 1 and type 2 fixes, and exogenisation exercises likewise proceed through numerical solution methods in the nonlinear case, the underlying concept being unaffected by our inability to express it in convenient linear algebra. Nonlinear models are usually programmed for solution by first inverting any function or transformation applied to the variable on which an equation has been normalised; this then allows the application of an additive residual adjustment specified in the same units as the variable being adjusted. For example, if the endogenous variable y_{it} is consumers' expenditure, and a log-linear consumption function has been specified, of the form

$$\ln y_{it} = b \ln y_{jt} + c \ln z_{kt} + u_{it},$$

then in deterministic solution the transformed equation

$$y_{it} = \exp(b \ln y_{jt} + c \ln z_{kt}) + a_{it}$$

permits the application of the residual adjustment a_{it} to consumers' expenditure in its original units. This example also allows us to illustrate a further possibility, that the adjustment is specified multiplicatively, as a factor m_{it} say taking values on either side of 1.0. In terms of the initial log-linear equation, $\ln m_{it}$ then takes the place of the disturbance u_{it}, with positive or negative values.

Dynamic models

As with nonlinearity, the earlier discussion pays little attention to the dynamic nature of the models. In practice, however, dynamic aspects of the relations among variables are of concern, and the time form of the reaction of a target variable to a policy instrument is often as important as the overall magnitude of the reaction. To consider dynamic models explicitly we distinguish between exogenous and lagged endogenous variables, partitioning z_t into a vector of purely exogenous variables x_t and the lagged variables $y_{t-1}, y_{t-2},\ldots$. The calculation of a solution sequence $\hat{y}_t$, $t=1,\ldots,T$ for given x-values begins with the specification of initial conditions; then the model generates its own lagged endogenous variables as the solution proceeds. Thus in the case of first-order dynamics we have

$$f(\hat{y}_1,y_0,x_1,\alpha) = 0,$$
$$f(\hat{y}_t,\hat{y}_{t-1},x_t,\alpha) = 0,\ t = 2,\ldots,T.$$

Adjustments and interventions may need to take account of the model's dynamics. For example, a residual adjustment held at a constant level typically has a cumulative effect, and fixes designed to achieve a constant deviation in an endogenous variable typically vary over time. To illustrate, we return to a simple linear equation

$$b(L)y_t + c(L)x_t = u_t, \qquad (9)$$

where $b(L)$ and $c(L)$ are (scalar) polynomials in the lag operator, L. To compare a base solution $\hat{y}_t$ with an alternative solution $\tilde{y}_t$, subject to interventions δ_t or adjustments a_t, it is convenient to write the equation in explicit distributed lag form:

$$\tilde{y}_t = -b(L)^{-1}\ c(L)\ (x_t + \delta_t) + b(L)^{-1}a_t.$$

The dynamic responses to δ_t and a_t vary according to the lag polynomial $c(L)$; in particular, if the adjustments a_t represent corrections for the specific composition of δ_t, as in the example on p. 107, then attention must be paid to $c(L)$ in their calculation. The pattern of the differences $\tilde{y}_t - \hat{y}_t$ in response to residual adjustments a_t is given by the expansion of $b(L)^{-1}$. For example, in the first-order case $b(L) = 1 - b_1L$ we have

$$\tilde{y}_t - \hat{y}_t = a_t + b_1a_{t-1} + b_1^2a_{t-2} + \ldots + b_1^{t-1}a_1,\ t = 1,\ldots,T.$$

Thus, if the adjustment is held constant, the two solutions increasingly diverge, although at a decreasing rate if the model is stable (that is, if $|b_1| < 1$). If it is desired to achieve a constant difference $\tilde{y}_t - \hat{y}_t = d$, say, then the required adjustments are $a_1 = d$,

$a_2 = a_3 = \ldots = d(1-b_1)$; if $b_1 = 1$, so that the dependent variable is in first difference form, an adjustment in the first period is all that is required. In the general case type 1 fixes are calculated in the manner discussed above, period by period, and, as illustrated by this simple example, the magnitude of the required adjustment usually varies over time.

The dynamic pattern of a type 2 fix in equation (9) reflects both $b(L)$ and $c(L)$. Writing $-b(L)^{-1}c(L) = \pi(L)$, where $\pi(L) = \pi_0 + \pi_1 L + \pi_2 L^2 + \ldots$, the analogue of equation (4), describing the relation between the required change in y and the perturbation in x over T periods, is

$$\begin{bmatrix} \tilde{y}_1 - \hat{y}_1 \\ \tilde{y}_2 - \hat{y}_2 \\ \\ \cdot \\ \cdot \\ \tilde{y}_T - \hat{y}_T \end{bmatrix} = \begin{bmatrix} \pi_0 & & \\ \pi_1 & \pi_0 & \\ \cdot & \cdot & \\ \cdot \quad \cdot & & \cdot \\ \cdot \quad \cdot & & \cdot \\ \pi_{T-1} & \pi_1 & \pi_0 \end{bmatrix} \begin{bmatrix} \delta_1 \\ \delta_2 \\ \\ \cdot \\ \cdot \\ \delta_T \end{bmatrix} \tag{10}$$

The solution for the vector $(\delta_1,\ldots,\delta_T)$ is given by inverting the coefficient matrix on the right-hand side, although its lower triangular structure indicates that a period-by-period solution is straightforward to calculate. Once again, however, the magnitude of the required perturbation varies over time, and in practice may exhibit considerable variation, if not instability, particularly when the impact effect of a perturbation is of opposite sign to the long-run response, or in various kinds of over-shooting models. When the magnitude and frequency of the required changes in a policy instrument appear implausible, alternative methods may be employed that trade off the exact achievement of the target against the desirability of a relatively smooth instrument trajectory, as discussed next.

Control techniques

The application of control theory to problems of macroeconomic policymaking has a long history, and recent control-theory literature has been principally concerned with optimal control. Here, an objective function is first specified, which is a scalar function of the values of the endogenous variables (targets) and policy instruments over the planning period. The optimal control problem is then to find the values of the policy instruments that, together with the resulting predicted values of the endogenous variables, minimise the objective function. The objective function may depend on the deviations of actual values of endogenous variables from their desired values, and on the trajectories of the policy instruments. Relative weights attached to terms of the first kind reflect the policymaker's priorities, as between inflation and unemployment, for example, or between consumption now and consumption later. Terms of the second kind may reflect institutional constraints on the extent to which certain policy instruments can be used, or the desirability of relatively smooth changes in instruments. In a linear model, with a quadratic objective function, optimal control theory gives a control policy in the form of a linear feedback rule; in the nonlinear case, a time series of policy instrument settings is obtained by numerical methods, conditional on exogenous variable trajectories.

In a simple one target-one instrument case the multi-period quadratic loss function may be written

$$w = \Sigma_{t=1}^{T} \{k_{1t}(\tilde{y}_t - y_t^{\star})^2 + k_{2t}(\Delta(x_t + \delta_t))^2 + k_{3t}\delta_t^2\},$$

where $y_t^{\star}$ denotes the target value of the endogenous variable and x_t the base-run value of the instrument. The k_2-coefficients indicate the relative cost of changing the instrument from one period to the next, and the k_3-coefficients the cost of departing from the base setting. Type 2 fixes are a special case in which such costs are absent, thus $k_{2t} = k_{3t} = 0$ in all periods, and a minimum loss of zero is achieved by attaining the target in all periods.

Model-consistent forward expectations

The treatment of forward expectations variables in a model-consistent manner, as discussed in the first section, introduces two further issues, namely the treatment of terminal conditions and particular aspects of experimental design.

First, in calculating a solution in which future expectations coincide with the model's forecasts, in the last period of the solution an expectation of a variable outside the solution period is required, which is usually achieved through the specification of a terminal condition. Two methods of setting terminal conditions are commonly employed. Conditions which attempt to approximate the stable solution path of the model by specifying constant levels or constant growth paths for the expectational variables do not raise any major problems for policy analysis, provided that the overall solution period is sufficiently long so that the results for the periods of interest are not sensitive to changes in the terminal date. Equilibrium conditions derived from prior knowledge of the model structure also require that the solution period is sufficiently long to avoid distortions to the results from the requirement that the model approaches its equilibrium at the terminal date, particularly if this equilibrium is remote from the solution values at intermediate points. In policy analysis in this latter case, it may be necessary to ensure that assumptions made are consistent with the terminal conditions of the model, or that the terminal conditions themselves are appropriately modified.

Secondly, experimental design questions arise in models with forward expectations, because it may make a difference whether the intervention is anticipated or unanticipated, and whether it is permanent or temporary.

Conventional backward-looking models react no differently to anticipated or unanticipated events. If the shock is anticipated in a model with forward consistent expectations, however, a change in behaviour prior to the actual shock might be expected. In general models do not allow for different reactions to anticipated/unanticipated shocks through the specification of individual equations, and differences emerge only in complete model solutions for appropriately designed experiments. Simulation of anticipated effects is typically achieved by introducing the perturbation at an intermediate point of the solution period, while solving over the whole period under consistent expectations. With anticipated shocks, some effects may be experienced in advance of the shock, perhaps up to one year ahead, in current models.

Permanent and temporary shocks have no differential impact in conventional backward-looking models during the period they are in force, but once a temporary shock is removed, such models tend back to the original steady state. This distinction in respect of the long-run response also applies in models with forward consistent expectations, but in addition they may react differently to a shock during the period in which it is in force, depending on whether it is known to be permanent or temporary. Forward-looking economic agents may anticipate the future removal of a temporary intervention, with effects on their current behaviour. Again, models typically do not distinguish different reactions to permanent or temporary stimuli through the specification of individual equations, and the difference between permanent and temporary shocks occurs through a complete model solution. It depends not only on the nature and role of the forward expectations variables, but also on the model's dynamic adjustment, since a protracted period of lagged adjustment following the ending of a temporary shock also has an impact on current behaviour through future expectations variables.

The policy environment

Although the examples that follow illustrate the simulation of single policy innovations, not complete packages, in practice additional assumptions about the general policy environment are invariably required. Some view must be taken of the accompanying stance of monetary and fiscal policy, and again this must be made explicit. In general, policy changes lead, directly or indirectly, to changes in the public sector borrowing requirement (PSBR), and different results may be obtained according to the way in which this is financed. The standard possibilities are that the change in the PSBR is accommodated by additional money creation (money finance), financed by the sale of government debt to the non-bank public sector (bond finance), or offset by a change in other elements of the PSBR, such as additional taxes (tax finance). Each may be adopted on its own, or some combination of these methods may be employed, for example, balanced money and bond finance. Policy in the foreign exchange market, and its relationship with monetary policy, must also be specified. More generally a statement of an overall stance of policy, such as that suggested by a nominal income target, might be relevant, which would require the specification of policy instruments and the way in which they adjust to ensure the achievement of such a target. In many cases, therefore, some modification of policy instruments other than those of immediate concern is necessary in order to retain the internal consistency of the overall policy stance. Then the sensitivity of the simulations to different policy environments may be of interest.

On a practical level many of the models contain an implicit overall policy stance, as a kind of base setting, and sometimes this is not easily modified. For example the NIESR model cannot be simulated under conditions of bond finance. In our first two examples we adopt these basic assumptions, which are those contained in the model proprietor's published forecast or standard simulation base, which is taken as the base run in most of our experiments. The assumptions (see Wallis *et al.*, 1987, for further details) are as follows. For two of the quarterly models (LBS,HMT) nominal interest rates are held constant, and for a third (NIESR) the real interest rate is held constant: this approximates accommodating monetary policy. In the LPL model, which is an annual model, any change in the PSBR is assumed to be financed in a balanced manner by money and bonds. This model also treats the money supply as exogenously determined by the monetary authorities, and fiscal policy as an adjustment to government spending that maintains a fixed ratio of the PSBR to nominal income: neither of these assumptions appears in the other models. In the two remaining models used as examples in this chapter (BE and CGP) interest rates are determined by a reaction function, which includes, *inter alia*, the exchange rate. The relevant financing assumption is then neither pure money nor pure bond finance. Our third example, described in the fifth section, focusses

Table 5.1 Gross domestic fixed capital formation by sector and type of asset 1986

£ million

	General government		Public corporations		Private sector	
		%		%		%
Vehicles etc	190	(2.8)	610	(10.7)	5817	(12.2)
Plant and machinery	1183	(17.9)	2458	(43.0)	19655	(41.1)
Dwellings	2239	(33.9)	288	(5.0)	9588	(20.1)
Other bldgs. & works	4728	(71.5)	2713	(47.4)	7543	(15.8)
Purchases less sales of land and bldgs.	−1732	(−26.2)	−351	(−6.1)	5189	(10.9)
Total	6608	(100)	5718	(100)	47792	(100)

Source: United Kingdom National Accounts 1986, Table 10.1
Note: Figures in brackets show proportion of total sectoral gross domestic fixed capital formation which is spent on each asset.

on exchange rate targets and requires alternative assumptions regarding the setting of some of the policy instruments in the models. In particular, modifications are made to the constant interest rate assumption in the HMT model and the reaction function in the BE model.

Housing investment

Our first example illustrates the problems that arise when a policy instrument is specified in sufficient detail that it can be directly perturbed, but important features of the transmission mechanism through which the instrument operates are not distinguished. It represents a kind of aggregation problem, in that the policy instrument under consideration is a particular component of an aggregate variable, but its influences on other variables are erroneously specified in the model to be no different from those of the aggregate. We describe how policy simulations can be conducted under more realistic assumptions.

The example is that of an increase in general government investment specifically directed towards housing. We consider its implications for imports, manufacturing output, and unemployment. The aggregation question arises in two parts, first whether housing investment is distinguished from other government investment, and second whether the different asset composition of government and private sector total fixed investment, shown in table 5.1, is acknowledged. From the summary of model characteristics in table 5.2, we see that

Table 5.2 Public sector investment instruments in seven models

Model	Exogenous public sector investment instruments identified in model	Distinction between public sector investment & total investment in the determination of imports	Distinction between public sector investment & total investment in the determination of manufacturing output
LBS	Housing; Non-housing	No distinction	No distinction
NIESR	Housing; Non-housing	No distinction	No distinction
HMT	Central govt; Local authority housing; Other local authority	Yes; Plant & M/c invest. given higher weight in determination of imports	Yes; Plant & M/c. invest. given higher weight in determination of mfg output
BE	Housing; Non-housing	Yes; e.g. non-residential private sector invest. given higher weight in determination of imports	Yes; e.g. non-residential private sector invest. given higher weight in determination of mfg output
CGP	Education; Health; Roads; Other social invest; Housing	Yes; different types of invest. disaggregated into demand for 39 industries, each with different import propensity	Yes; different types of investment disaggregated into demand for 39 industries
CUBS	Total govt; Roads	NA; imports not distinguished by model	NA; Mfg & non-mfg sectors not distinguished by model
LPL	Public investment not distinguished from total public expenditure	NA	NA; Mfg & non-mfg sectors not distinguished by model

although public sector housing investment is separately identified in five out of seven United Kingdom models, two of these five make no distinction between different categories of total fixed investment in the determination of imports and manufacturing output. In general, for each of these models, LBS and NIESR, the simulation results of an increase in government housing or non-housing investment are the

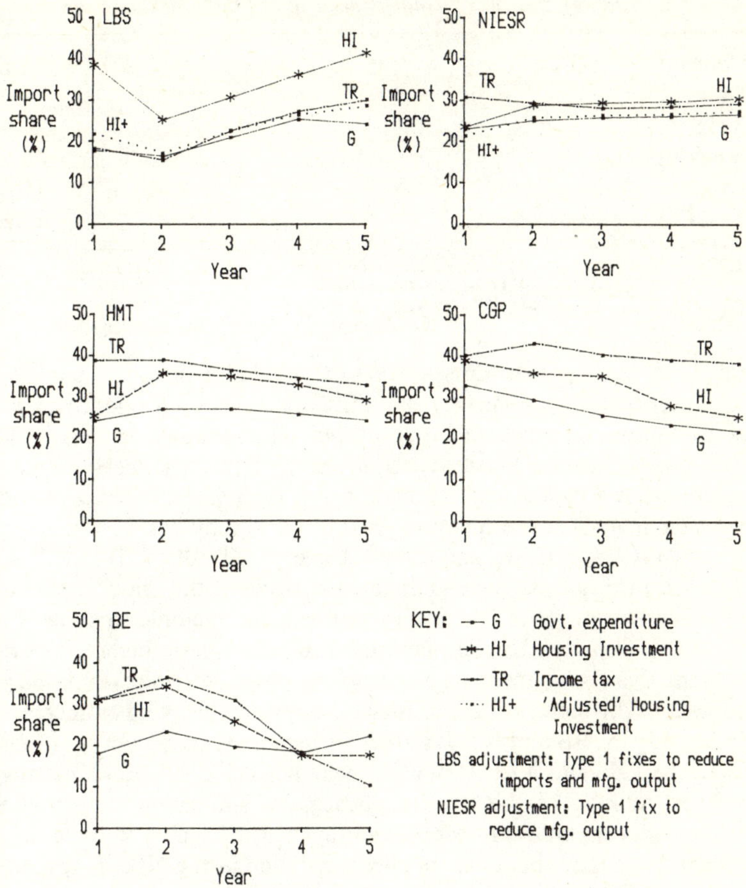

Chart 5.1 Marginal import shares – change in imports as a proportion of the change in total final expenditure for government expenditure, housing investment and income tax simulations

same, separate variables being identified mainly for forecasting purposes. These two models provide our principal illustrations.

Imports

We first present in chart 5.1 the change in imports as a percentage of the change in total final expenditure for an increase in housing investment compared with simulations of an increase in government current expenditure and a cut in income tax across five models.[1] The import content of the increase in total final expenditure is lowest

Table 5.3 Import content of final expenditure, 1979, %

Consumers' expenditure	21.2
Government consumption	11.0
Total fixed investment	29.9
Stockbuilding	38.6
Exports	25.6
Total final output	22.0

Source: Central Statistical Office, Input–Output Tables for the United Kingdom, HMSO, 1983.

for the government current expenditure simulation in all five models. This reflects the relatively low import content of government consumption, as given in input–output tables, shown in table 5.3. The cut in income tax leads to an increase in consumers' expenditure, with a higher import content, but the relative ranking of the housing investment simulation in this respect differs between the first two (LBS, NIESR) and the last three (HMT, BE, CGP) models. The last three all make some distinction between the import content of different categories of fixed investment, for example to allow for the fact that investment in plant and machinery has a higher import content than investment in construction projects, hence the import content of the increase in total final expenditure following an increase in housing investment is lower than for income tax cuts. On the other hand the LBS and NIESR models make no such distinction, and the relative ranking of the housing investment simulation reflects the higher import content of total fixed investment, shown in table 5.3, although we note the much smaller dispersion in the NIESR results.

In the LBS case, total imports of goods and services are determined by a composite domestic demand variable, which is constructed by weighting the main components of final demand according to their import content as in table 5.3, with total fixed investment treated as a single component. However its weight of 0.2992 is inappropriate for housing investment in particular and, given the different composition shown in table 5.1, for government investment in general. A more appropriate figure is 0.1442, the relative import content of primary inputs to the construction industry (Table F, 1979 Input–Output Tables); Davies and Metcalf (1985) argue that this is a more appropriate figure for public sector investment in general, given that spending is typically directed towards the construction industry. In table 5.4 we compare the results of the original housing investment simulation on the LBS model with those of an adjusted simulation which takes account of the lower import content of

Table 5.4 Simulations of increased housing investment on the LBS model (difference from base)

	Year	(1)	(2)	(3)	(4)
GDP (%)	1	0.47	0.66	0.43	0.62
	2	0.70	0.89	0.60	0.81
	3	0.76	0.94	0.66	0.86
	4	0.64	0.83	0.58	0.78
	5	0.47	0.68	0.44	0.64
Manuf. output (%)	1	0.41	1.18	0.24	0.44
	2	0.65	1.45	0.47	0.68
	3	0.70	1.46	0.58	0.73
	4	0.60	1.21	0.39	0.53
	5	0.44	0.91	0.15	0.29
Employment (000s)	1	37	45	38	47
	2	89	107	84	103
	3	137	156	126	148
	4	159	179	147	171
	5	160	181	151	174
Unemployment (000s)	1	−28	−35	−29	−36
	2	−67	−79	−64	−77
	3	−101	−113	−93	−108
	4	−112	−126	−104	−120
	5	−110	−124	−104	−120
Prices (%)	1	0.2	0.1	0.2	0.1
	2	0.9	0.5	1.0	0.6
	3	1.7	1.1	1.8	1.2
	4	2.5	1.7	2.6	1.8
	5	3.3	2.3	3.4	2.4
Imports (as % of change in total final expdt.)	1	38.4	21.4	40.2	21.7
	2	30.6	16.8	27.4	17.0
	3	30.6	23.0	31.7	22.6
	4	36.1	27.3	36.6	26.5
	5	41.3	29.2	41.2	28.6

Notes: Col.(1) – Increase in housing investment by £386 million per quarter. Col.(2) – as (1) but with residual adjustments to reduce imports, see Col.(1) of Table 5.A1. Col.(3) – as (1) but with residual adjustments to reduce manufacturing output, see Col.(2) of Table 5.A1. Col.(4) – as (1) but with residual adjustments to reduce both imports and manufacturing output, see Columns (1) and (2) of Table 5.A1.

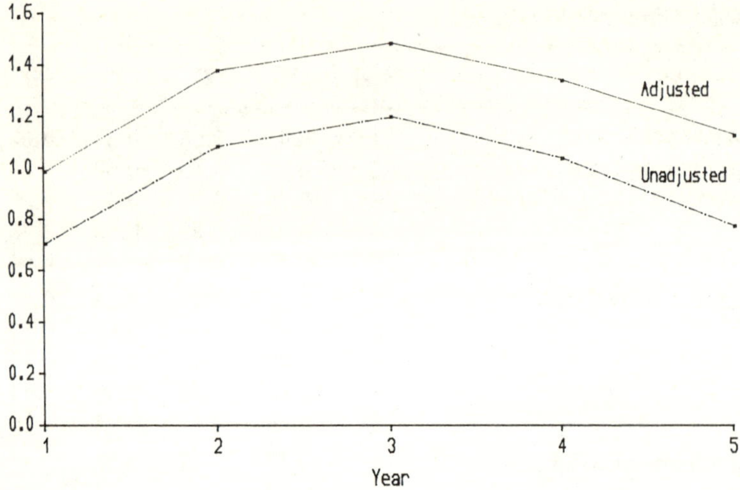

Chart 5.2 LBS model: housing investment multiplier – change in GDP as a proportion of the change in housing investment

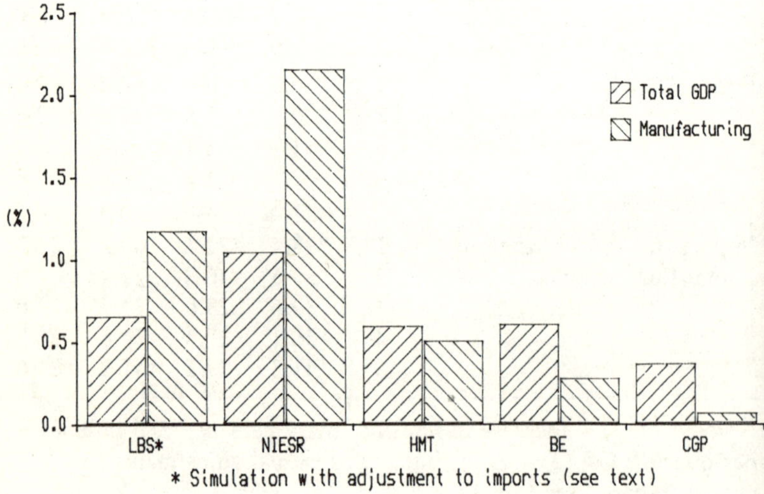

Chart 5.3 Composition of change in output following an increase in housing investment – change in output in first year, per cent

housing investment.[2] This adjustment has a significant effect on the overall macroeconomic results, lowering the import content of the change in total final expenditure and consequently raising the GDP multiplier by about 0.3, as shown in chart 5.2.

In the NIESR case it is more difficult to determine the appropriate adjustment to imports, because the weights on the various categories of final demand in the determination of imports are not directly based on their relative import content according to input–output data, as in the LBS case; rather, they generally take the value zero or unity (an exception being government current expenditure, which has a relative weight of one third in the determination of manufacturing imports). We present below an alternative adjustment, based on the relative impact of housing investment expenditure on the manufacturing and non-manufacturing sectors, which does have the effect of significantly reducing imports.

Manufacturing output

The major stimulus to the economy from additional housing investment might be expected to occur, at least initially, in the construction industry, which according to National Accounts definitions is classified as being outside the manufacturing sector. However, in both the LBS and NIESR models total fixed investment has a high weight, relative to other expenditure aggregates, in the determination of manufacturing output, with again no distinction being made between different categories of investment (see Wallis *et al.*, 1986, chapter 2 for a more detailed discussion of how the sectoral breakdown of output is determined). These high weights reflect the fact that investment in plant and machinery or vehicles tends to have a relatively large effect on the demand for manufacturing output; this is not the case, however, for housing investment. As a result, in both the NIESR and the import-adjusted LBS simulations of an increase in housing investment, the percentage change in manufacturing output is much greater than that in total GDP, as illustrated in chart 5.3. This does not occur in other models, where the differential impact on manufacturing of various categories of investment is acknowledged.

Alternative simulations may again be conducted on the LBS and NIESR models by applying a residual adjustment to manufacturing output to allow for the lower weight of housing investment in the determination of manufacturing output.[3] In the case of the construction industry, for each unit of final output the amount of value-added generated in manufacturing is 0.1355 (Table F, 1979 Input–Output Tables), and this is taken as the relevant coefficient for housing investment, rather than the weight of 0.386 used for

Table 5.5 Simulations of increased housing investment on the NIESR model (difference from base)

	Year	(1)	(2)	(3)
GDP (%)	1	1.05	1.14	1.13
	2	1.11	1.24	1.22
	3	1.10	1.25	1.22
	4	1.06	1.19	1.16
	5	0.98	1.09	1.06
Manuf. output (%)	1	2.16	1.66	1.64
	2	2.04	1.71	1.68
	3	1.85	1.57	1.53
	4	1.76	1.47	1.42
	5	1.62	1.30	1.25
Employment (000s)	1	81	91	90
	2	201	232	227
	3	302	361	352
	4	400	492	478
	5	499	628	608
Unemployment (000s)	1	−44	−46	−58
	2	−108	−112	−143
	3	−156	−163	−203
	4	−196	−210	−252
	5	−236	−258	−300
Prices (%)	1	0.1	0.1	0.1
	2	0.5	0.5	0.5
	3	1.1	1.1	1.2
	4	1.9	1.9	1.9
	5	2.5	2.5	2.5
Imports (as % of change in total final expdt.)	1	23.5	21.0	21.0
	2	28.6	25.3	25.3
	3	29.3	25.9	25.9
	4	29.6	26.3	26.3
	5	30.3	27.0	27.1

Notes: Col.(1) – Increase in housing investment by £386 million per quarter. Col.(2) – as (1) but with residual adjustments to reduce manufacturing output, see Col.(3) of Table 5.A1. Col.(3) – as 2 but with residual adjustments to increase the fall in unemployment, see Col.(4) of Table 5.A1.

aggregate investment in the models. In the LBS model the effect of this adjustment on aggregate variables is not substantial. It clearly has an impact on the allocation of the additional output and employment between the manufacturing and non-manufacturing sectors, but on comparing either columns (1) and (3), or columns (2) and (4), of table 5.4, we see that the effect on total output and employment is small.

In the NIESR model the effect on total output of this adjustment is slightly greater, in absolute terms, with an addition of just over 0.1 per cent to GDP (comparing columns (1) and (2) of table 5.5). As might be expected, the adjustment results in a reduction in manufacturing output growth, and although the percentage change in manufacturing output is still higher than the percentage change in GDP, the difference between them is much less marked. A further consequence of reducing the impact of additional housing investment on the manufacturing sector is a reduction in the import content of the change in total final expenditure. This occurs because the ratio of manufacturing output to total GDP is an explanatory variable in the equation for manufacturing imports. However, perhaps the greatest effect of the adjustment is on the employment response in the NIESR model, both aggregate and by sector, due to the marked differences in the properties of the labour market in the manufacturing and non-manufacturing sectors. In this model the long-run response of non-manufacturing employment to any change in output is very much higher than for manufacturing, the long-run elasticities of employment with respect to output in the two sectors being 5.7 and 1.5, respectively. This leads to the creation, by the fifth year of the simulation, of more than 100 thousand extra jobs as a result of the residual adjustment to manufacturing output (comparing columns (1) and (2) of table 5.5).

Unemployment

A further important distinction between the labour market responses of the manufacturing and non-manufacturing sectors in the NIESR model is that increases in non-manufacturing employment are much less effective in reducing registered unemployment than increases in manufacturing employment. In the long run the NIESR unemployment equation implies that every ten additional non-manufacturing jobs reduce registered unemployment by only two, whereas manufacturing jobs reduce registered unemployment on virtually a one-for-one basis (Trinder and Biswas, 1986). Thus adjustments which reallocate demand to non-manufacturing at the expense of manufacturing both raise the long-run employment response and also reduce the proportion of extra jobs which give a reduction in registered unemployment. However, this labour market response raises further questions, since it may be argued that additional jobs in the construction industry, which are typically full-time and male, are likely to be much more effective at reducing registered unemployment than is generally the case for other non-manufacturing jobs. We therefore conduct a further simulation on the NIESR model, with an additional residual adjustment that gives a greater fall in unemployment, assuming that extra construction jobs have an effect on registered unemployment more comparable to the effect of additional manufacturing rather than non-manufacturing jobs. Calculation of the appropriate magnitude of these adjustments rests on assumptions about the number of extra non-manufacturing jobs which arise in the construction industry.[4] The effect on the simulation results of introducing this further adjustment is shown in column (3) of table 5.5. The fall in unemployment by the fifth year of the simulation is 300,000, compared to a fall of 258,000 for the simulation with a residual adjustment to manufacturing output only, and a fall of 236,000 when no residual adjustments are made at all.

Concluding comments

In this example we show how adjustments might be made in order to allow for the different compositional effects of housing investment as compared with total fixed investment, which are not otherwise distinguished on the LBS and NIESR models. The results of the adjusted simulations on these models show a greater degree of consensus with the other models in certain respects, such as the share of imports in the change in total final expenditure and the relative impact on manufacturing output compared with total output. Such adjustments appear to be more important in producing greater consensus across models in terms of the relative ranking, on various criteria, of different policy instruments, rather than producing greater uniformity in the absolute results of any single policy simulation. This latter point is illustrated by the number of jobs created (thousands) in the fifth year of the housing investment simulation on each model, as follows:

LBS unadj	LBS adj	NIESR unadj	NIESR adj	CGP	HMT	BE
160	174	499	608	88	144	198

For both the NIESR and LBS simulations the additional adjustments do not improve the degree of consensus between the models. The

LBS employment response is still relatively high, and NIESR becomes even more of an outlier in this respect. The results of the LBS and NIESR simulations must therefore be explained in terms of the more general properties of the models. For example, it is a general feature of standard fiscal simulations on the LBS model that the employment generated tends to be high in comparison with the effect on other models – a result which can largely be explained by the greater responsiveness of the exchange rate in the LBS model (see Wallis *et al.*, 1987, chapter 2). In the case of NIESR, an important reason why it is such an outlier in respect of employment effects is the large long-run elasticity between employment and output in the non-manufacturing sector of 5.7. Given that the major part of the non-manufacturing sector is services, on *a priori* grounds we would not expect this elasticity to differ substantially from unity, a view which is confirmed by an examination of other models. If this view is correct then our adjustments which switch output from the manufacturing to the non-manufacturing sector, although implying a more plausible sectoral breakdown of the output effects, actually imply less plausible labour market effects! Further simulations to investigate the sensitivity of the results to this elasticity have not been performed, sensitivity analysis of this kind being outside the scope of the present chapter.

While macroeconomic models may not adequately capture the demand-side transmission mechanism through which an increase in public housing investment operates, as discussed above, a further deficiency in capital expenditure simulations may occur on the supply side. Changes in the level of housing investment, by their influence on the overall housing market, may induce changes in the efficiency of the working of the labour market, for example, by improving the mobility of labour. This, in turn, may induce changes in macroeconomic variables. The models considered here have no linkage between public sector housing investment and the rest of the housing market, and the problems of quantifying such effects in order to translate them into a set of model interventions are inevitably very formidable.

Finally we note that although attention has focussed specifically on a change in housing investment, the asset composition of fixed investment by general government is very different from other sectors of the economy (see table 5.1), and the same issues will need to be addressed in relation to *any* change in government fixed investment.

Incomes policy

In their econometric evaluation of labour market models Wallis *et al.* (1986) conclude that 'the effect of incomes policy on real wages

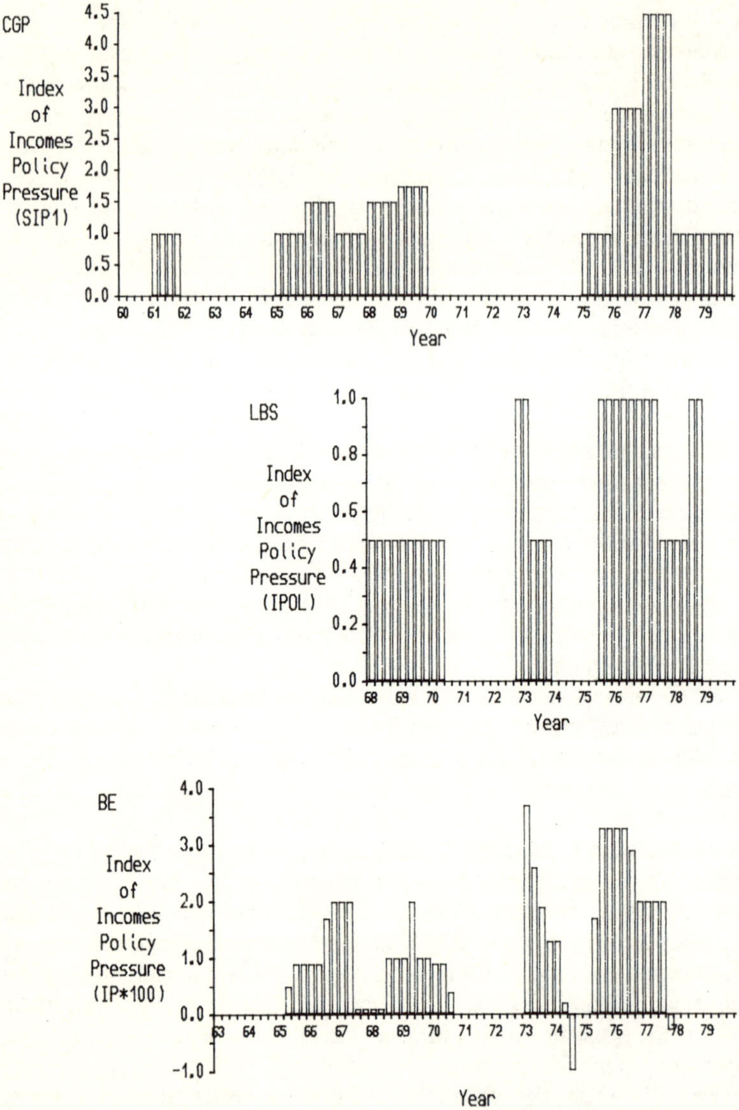

Chart 5.4 Incomes policy variables on three macro models

cannot be ignored'. Simulating an incomes policy, however, presents a number of inherent difficulties since there is no single generally accepted quantitative measure which summarises its impact on the macro economy. Although a particular incomes policy may be associated with a given nominal wage norm, the consequences of such a policy might be expected to depend on other factors such as the sanctions used to enforce the norm, the degree of support of employers and trades unions, and so on. Also the strength of incomes policy may not be well represented by the nominal wage norm, without reference to the going rate for wages that might exist in the absence of any restraint, nor to changes in wage earners' *real* standard of living. Despite these problems a number of attempts have been made to quantify a 'strength of incomes policy' index, (Lawson, 1981; Whitley, 1983, 1986), and some of the United Kingdom models include such a variable. We therefore begin by undertaking incomes policy simulations on two different models where such a variable can be directly perturbed, and discuss the difficulties of standardising the policy shocks across the models. We then consider simulating an incomes policy on a model where no incomes policy index exists. Nevertheless an index of this kind can be used to derive a set of model interventions on wages. This method of simulating an incomes policy yields a ready comparison between the strength of incomes policy implied by the model simulation and the strength of incomes policy over the historical past, and therefore provides an assessment of the plausibility of the model intervention. Finally we contrast this criterion for assessing the plausibility of an incomes policy simulation with more *ad hoc* approaches proposed in the past.

Perturbing an incomes policy variable

Variables to capture the effects of incomes policy are currently included in the wage equations of the LBS, CGP and BE models. An incomes policy can then be implemented in a full model simulation by perturbing this incomes policy index, as in previous studies with the LBS model (Breedon *et al.*, 1987) and the CGP model (Peterson and Turner, 1985). However, a problem arises in designing comparable simulations if the incomes policy index in one model cannot be expressed as a simple function of the index in another model. In chart 5.4 we plot the historical values of the CGP, LBS and BE incomes policy variables, and find that there is only a loose correlation among them. Differences between the three variables reflect the different methodologies used in their construction, and reflect an inevitable degree of subjective judgement in such calculations. In the CGP case the annual strength of incomes policy variable is constructed by examining the pressure on real wages implied by any wage norms and the extent to which reliance was placed on voluntary restraint or statutory powers (Lawson, 1981). The quarterly variable included in the BE model (Patterson *et al.*, 1987) is detailed in Whitley (1986) and is constructed using a similar approach. However, the LBS incomes policy variable is based on a

Table 5.6 Incomes policy simulation on the CGP and LBS models (difference from base)

Year	CGP	LBS
Unemployment (000s)		
1	−27	−12
2	−56	−51
3	−82	−80
4	−75	−77
5	−64	−36
6	−53	
Nominal wages (%)		
1	−2.8	−0.9
2	−4.9	−1.9
3	−6.6	−2.2
4	−5.3	−1.3
5	−4.4	−0.5
6	−3.7	
Prices (%)		
1	−1.1	−0.2
2	−2.3	−0.6
3	−3.6	−0.8
4	−3.6	−0.9
5	−3.5	−0.6
6	−3.2	

Note: CGP (LBS) simulation shows the effect of an increase in incomes policy pressure, variable SIPI is increased by 1.0 (variable IPOL is increased by 0.5) for the first three years of the simulation only, after which time the policy pressure is removed.

less elaborate methodology, and simply takes the values 0, 0.5 or 1.0.

In an attempt to design approximately comparable experiments on the CGP and LBS models we first regress the CGP index, IP_C, on the annual averages of the LBS quarterly index, $\overline{IP}_L$, over the period 1968–79, and obtain (t-ratios in parentheses)

$$IP_C = -\underset{(0.1)}{0.5} + \underset{(2.8)}{2.8}\,\overline{IP}_L \qquad R^2 = 0.44.$$

Thus an increase in the LBS index of 0.5 is broadly comparable with an increase in the CGP index of 1.0, and perturbations of these magnitudes are used in our simulations reported in table 5.6. Although there is much greater variability in the CGP index, we note

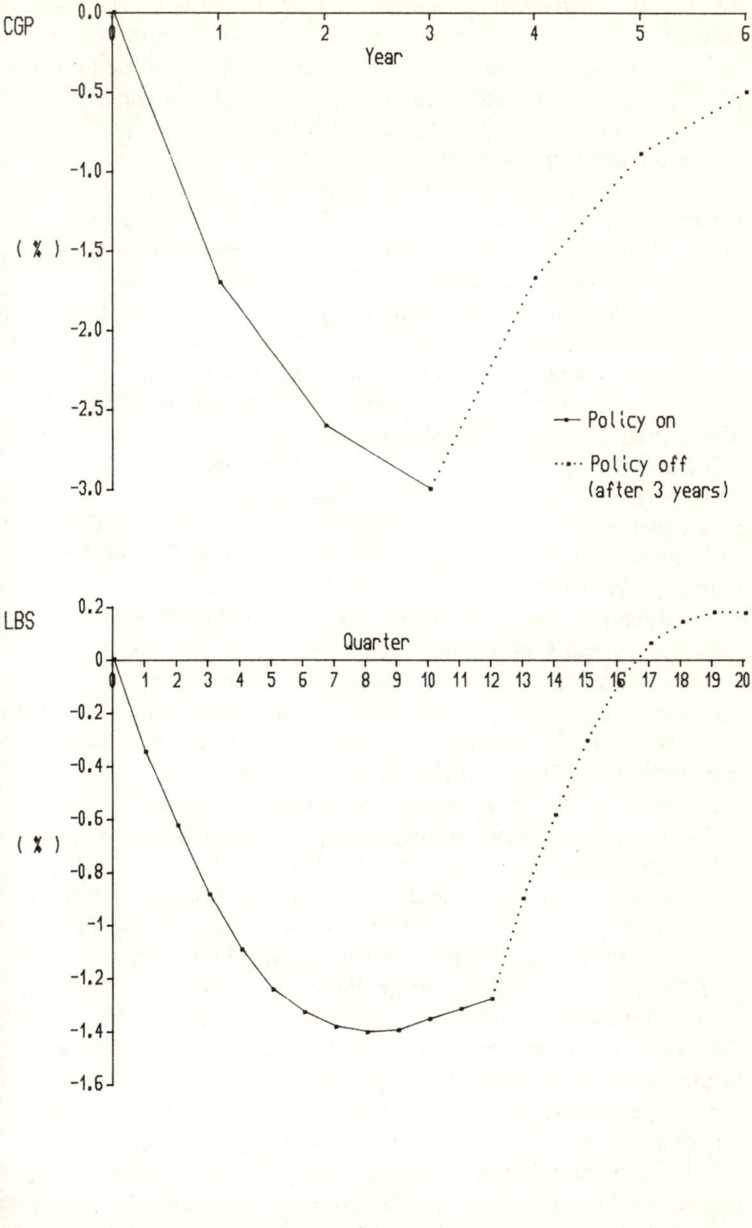

Chart 5.5 Effect of incomes policy on real wages – difference from base

that there are important episodes when the two indices similarly assume these values. Thus the CGP index takes values between 1.0 and 1.5 under the Wilson incomes policy in the late 1960s, and a value of unity towards the end of Labour policy in the late 1970s, both much less than the maximum values of 3.0 and 4.5 attained in 1976 and 1977. The LBS index has a value of 0.5 in the late 1960s and again in the late 1970s, attaining the value of unity in periods of maximum incomes policy pressure.

In the simulations the increased policy pressure is maintained for a period of three years and then removed, again achieving comparability with historical experience, as represented in chart 5.4. Then the behaviour of the economy, not only during the period of incomes policy but also following its removal, is of interest. During this policy-off period no further interventions are made so that the speed of any wage 'catch-up' depends on the rate of response of wages to any disequilibrium, as determined by the properties of the labour market in the respective models.

During the 'policy-on' period, the maintenance of a constant pressure of incomes policy tends to lead to a reduction in real wages by a constant amount below the base-run values in both CGP and LBS simulation results, once dynamic adjustment is complete (see chart 5.5). However, the two models differ in terms both of the speed of the dynamic adjustment of real wages and the magnitude of the reduction in real wages below their base values. In the CGP simulation real wages are reduced by more than 3 per cent below the base run after a period of three years. In the case of the LBS the adjustment is much quicker and the amount by which real wages are depressed is much less, with real wages settling at between 1.2–1.4 per cent below the base values after only five quarters.

The levels of nominal wages and prices are increasingly reduced below their base values in the policy-on period according to both model simulations. However this is less true of the rate of wage and price *inflation* (see chart 5.6). In the CGP simulation wage inflation is reduced by 2.8 percentage points in the first year, but by the third year the effect is reduced wage inflation of only 1.6 percentage points. This tendency for a diminishing effect on the rate of wage inflation is even more marked in the LBS simulation results. By the beginning of the second year wage inflation is reduced by about 1.5 percentage points, yet by the end of the third year there is a negligible effect on the rate of wage inflation.

Following the removal of the incomes policy pressure, real wages recover to their base values, although again the speed of adjustment is much quicker for the LBS compared with the CGP simulation. In the policy-off period, in both models there is a significant increase in

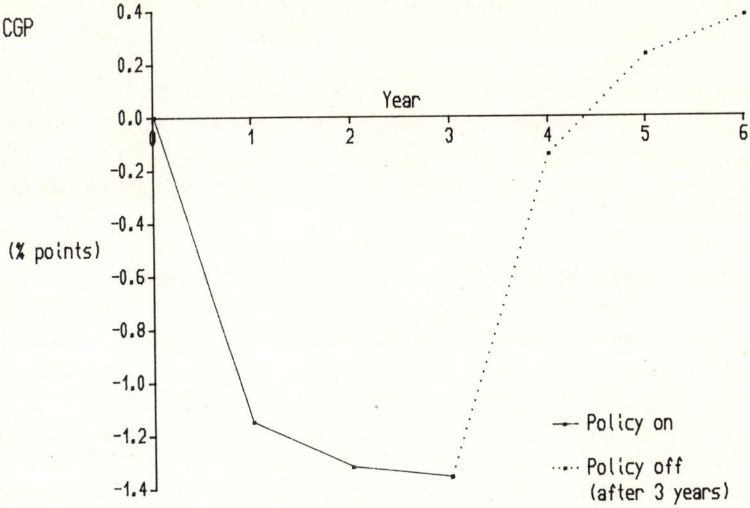

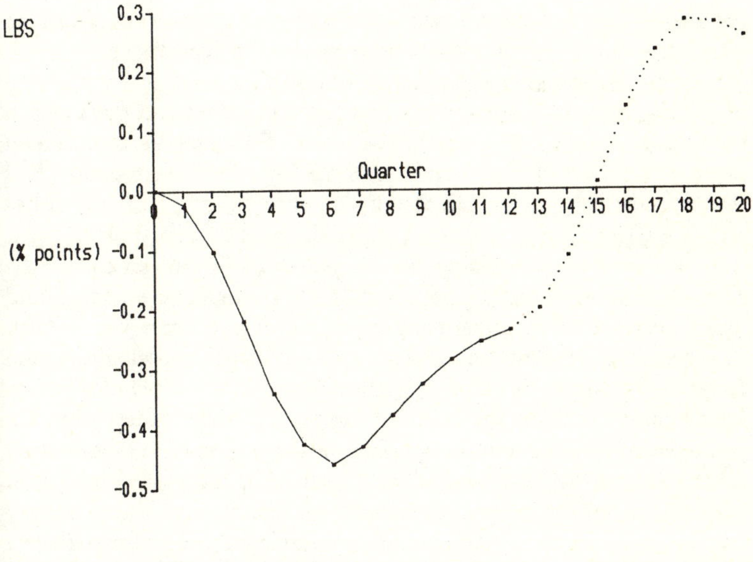

Chart 5.6 Effect of incomes policy on price inflation – difference from base, percentage points

the rate of wage and price inflation, over and above the inflation rate that would have been experienced in the absence of any incomes policy. However, although inflation is higher following the relaxation of policy, the *levels* of prices and nominal wages remain substantially below their base values. Partly as a result of the consequent real balance effects, as well as adjustment lags, in both models unemployment remains lower once the policy pressure has been relaxed, indeed the average reduction in unemployment in the policy-off period compares favourably with the average reduction in unemployment achieved in the policy-on period.

Simulating an incomes policy in the absence of an incomes policy index
We now consider how an incomes policy might be simulated on a model that includes no index of incomes policy pressure. A common procedure is to intervene directly in the determination of wages, either by means of residual adjustments to the wage equation or by formally exogenising wages. Problems remain, however, first in judging the appropriate magnitude of any residual adjustment to wages, unless an explicit justification for the intervention is given, and second in assessing the credibility of the results. In this respect we propose a method, based on the work of Lawson and Whitley discussed above, whereby changes in an incomes policy index which have some correspondence with relevant historical episodes can be translated into a set of model interventions on real wages.

Lawson and Whitley construct an index of incomes policy pressure in the framework of a real wage resistance equation and the Lawson index is the one used in the CGP model. This may be represented as $w_t = \pi(L)\ IP_t + \ldots$ where w is the log of real wages and IP is the incomes policy index. Then an incomes policy perturbation has a direct effect on real wages given by the π-coefficients, as in equation (10). For a given change in the policy index we can treat $\pi(L)$ IP as a missing term in another model's comparable equation and hence derive a set of adjustments of the form given in equation (10). However, we are now dealing with a simultaneous model and, as the Lawson equation is not a reduced form but includes other endogenous variables, the *ex post* effect on real wages differs from the value of the intervention, depending on the degree of feedback from other variables in the models. The adjustments therefore are *ex ante*. We can no longer reverse equation (10) and deduce the necessary change in the incomes policy index underlying a given change in real wages, since the latter additionally reflects the behaviour of other endogenous variables in the system. In our examples we assume an increase in the Lawson index of unity and augment the relevant equations of both the LPL and HMT models. The more straightforward

Table 5.7 Simulations of incomes policy on the LPL and HMT models (difference from base)

	Year	LPL	HMT *ex post* target	HMT *ex ante* target
Unemployment (000s)	1	−158	−10	−10
	2	−292	−83	−75
	3	−360	−187	−154
	4	−341	−268	−205
	5	−279	−282	−205
	6	−209		
Real wages (%)	1	−1.5	−1.8	−1.7
	2	−2.2	−2.7	−2.1
	3	−2.5	−3.1	−2.2
	4	−2.2	−2.5	−1.7
	5	−1.8	−1.6	−1.0
	6	−1.4		
Nominal wages (%)	1	−1.7	−2.7	−2.5
	2	−3.2	−5.5	−4.6
	3	−4.1	−7.7	−5.8
	4	−4.0	−8.0	−5.9
	5	−3.5	−6.9	−5.0
	6	−2.9		
Prices (%)	1	−0.2	−1.0	−0.9
	2	−1.0	−2.9	−2.5
	3	−1.7	−4.7	−3.7
	4	−1.9	−5.7	−4.2
	5	−1.7	−5.5	−4.0
	6	−1.4		

Note: Simulations show the effect of an increase in incomes policy pressure equivalent to an increase of 1.0 in the Lawson index maintained over the first three years of the simulation only, after which time the policy pressure is removed. See notes (5) and (6) for further details.

case is that of LPL where real wages are the dependent variable in the wage equation. Here we simply make residual adjustments which would imply an *ex ante* reduction in the level of real wages by 1.8, 2.7, and 3.1 per cent in the first three years respectively, making due allowance for equation dynamics.[5]

A feature of the results reported in table 5.7 is that the *ex post* reduction in real wages is less than the *ex ante* target reduction. Thus, for example, whereas a unit increase in the policy index would *ceteris paribus* reduce real wages by 3.1 per cent by year 3, in a full dynamic simulation on the LPL model, as a result of feedback from the rest of the model, the reduction in real wages is only 2.8 per cent. In particular the initial reduction in real wages brings about a substantial fall in unemployment, which in turn puts upward pressure on real wages through the tightening of the labour market. Although the increased incomes policy pressure on the LPL model leads to a reduction in unemployment that is much larger than in any of the other comparable model simulations, the effect on wage and price inflation is similar to the results from the LBS model. In particular, although there is a significant reduction in wage and price inflation during the policy-on period (averaging about 1.5 and 0.7 percentage points respectively), the policy has a progressively diminishing effect on inflation. This result is not surprising, given that in the long run the rate of inflation in the LPL model is entirely determined by the rate of monetary growth and the LPL simulation is carried out under an assumption of fixed monetary growth rather than accommodating money (fixed interest rates) as in the other model simulations. Although the LPL model is described as a new classical macro model the adjustment of real wages is comparatively sluggish, so that following the removal of policy pressure there is only a modest increase in inflation while much of the substantial reduction in unemployment remains.

Simulations on the Treasury model

A more difficult problem arises with the HMT model, where real wages are not determined directly by a single equation but by separate nominal wage and price equations. In order to derive the appropriate residual adjustments to nominal wages which imply the desired *ex ante* reduction in real wages, it is necessary to eliminate the potential feedback of the other variables in the price and wage equations, such as unemployment, demand and profitability. This is achieved by using a type 2 fix on the wage equation residual and eliminating the influences of these other variables by exogenisation. The derived set of adjustments are then used to generate a full model simulation incorporating all the feedbacks. The results are shown in table 5.7 under the heading *ex ante* target.[6]

These results can be compared with those derived using an *ex post* target for real wages, where the wage equation is deleted and nominal wages are used as an instrument to achieve the desired level of real wages, via a type 2 fix. This appears to be similar to the method used by HM Treasury (1985), although the policy mechanism is there left unspecified. These results are labelled *ex post* target in table 5.7. In both experiments an increase in policy pressure is applied over the first three years of the simulation and subsequently removed. In the *ex ante* case we observe a larger fall in unemployment than for either LBS or CGP (but not LPL) and a strong influence on wage and price inflation relative to LBS and LPL (but not CGP). Following the relaxation of policy pressure real wages respond sluggishly and the pick-up in inflation is only modest, while unemployment continues to fall.

Comparing the two HMT experiments in table 5.7, we note that where an allowance is made for the feedback from pressure of demand variables, the *ex ante* target reduction in real wages is not actually achieved *ex post*. Thus, for example, while a unit increase in the Lawson index would *ceteris paribus* imply that real wages were reduced by about 3.1 per cent after three years, the actual reduction in real wages achieved in the third year is only 2.2 per cent, as the fall in unemployment and increased company profitability influence real wages. The implicit strength of policy underlying the *ex post* case is therefore considerably greater than in the *ex ante* case, given that the target reduction in real wages is the same in both cases. A consequence of achieving a smaller reduction in real wages under the *ex ante* experiment is that the effects of the incomes policy on nominal wages and prices as well as unemployment are significantly reduced. The average reduction in nominal wage inflation during the 'policy-on' period is 1.9 percentage points in the *ex ante* case, as against 2.6 percentage points for the *ex post* experiment.

Concluding comments

In this section we review some methods of simulating an incomes policy. These methods focus on the direct consequences of restraining aggregate wages, and no assessment of the possible macroeconomic consequences which might arise from distortions to the labour market, for example due to the eroding of wage differentials for skilled workers, is attempted. Of the approaches considered, the most satisfactory case is where an appropriate incomes policy variable is specified in the model as an exogenous policy instrument and can simply be perturbed; questions of the possible endogeneity of policy have not been addressed. Where no such policy variable is included in the model, we suggest as a second best solution an interpretation of incomes policy which relates the strength of policy to its *ex ante* effect on real wages. This

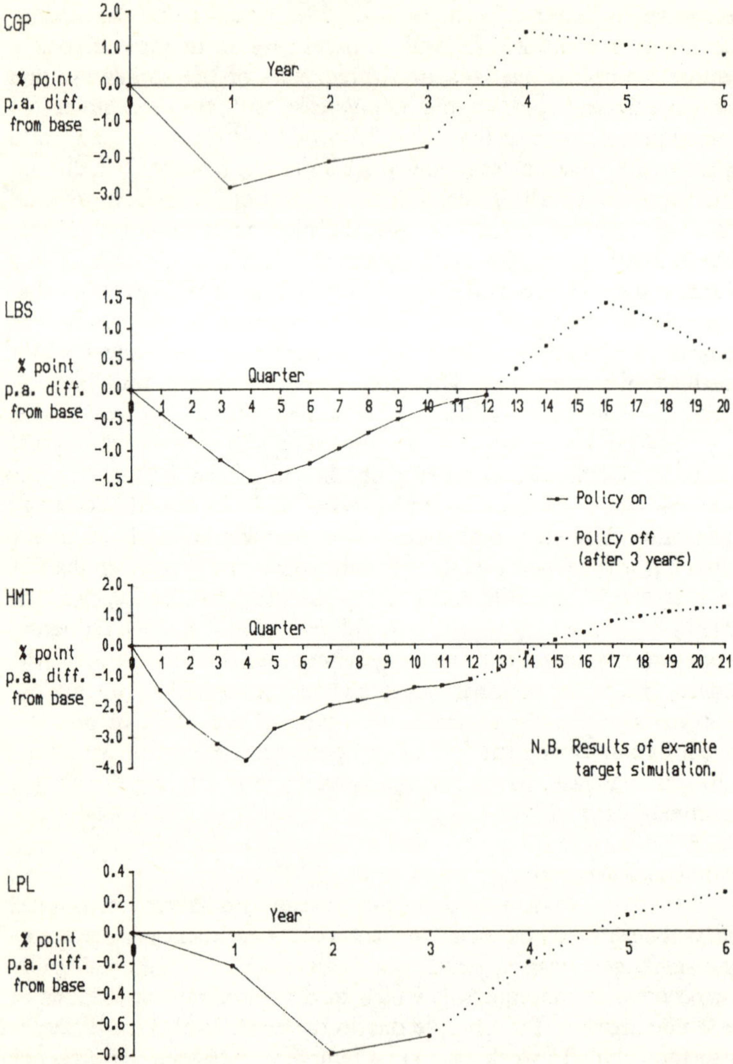

Chart 5.7 Effect of incomes policy on nominal wage inflation – difference from base, percentage points per annum

enables a series of model interventions on wages to be derived, *ex ante*, which are consistent with a given strength of incomes policy. Second-round effects, for example, tightening of the labour market, may cause real wages, *ex post*, to assume a different value. The duration and strength of the incomes policy implied by the model simulation can then be compared with an historical index to provide some assessment of the plausibility of the model intervention.

In the absence of such a framework the alternative may be to assess the plausibility of the model intervention by its *ex post* effects, either on the rate of nominal wage inflation or on the level of real wages. However, apparently contradictory conclusions may then emerge. For example, Surrey and Ormerod (1977), in their study on the NIESR model, judged policy by its impact on nominal wage inflation. Thus:

> . . . This near continuous 'policy-on' assumption is, however, in some respects deceptive. In each case the function of the policy is to provide a once-for-all safeguarding of a pause in the growth of net earnings such as is required for a successful devaluation: given this once-for-all effect and the associated reduction in inflationary expectations, succeeding stages of incomes policy hold the increases in money earnings close to the levels which we estimate would have taken place in the absence of a policy.

In contrast, our results described above, using real wages as a measure of policy, suggest that a constant pressure of policy may be consistent with a negligible effect on nominal wage inflation in the medium term (chart 5.7). The differences in findings could be due either to simulation methodology or to the choice of the underlying model. Such conflicts cannot be resolved, however, unless the exact nature of any off-model calculations, on which model interventions are based, is made explicit.

Exchange rate targeting

Exchange rate targets have received particular attention in the context of discussions of the European Monetary System (EMS), as some degree of exchange rate targeting is part of the overall design of this system. A full analysis of EMS is a complicated matter for the United Kingdom models, which in particular determine the average exchange rate across all major currencies rather than the average European rate or a particular European rate (for example, the Deutschmark) featuring in the EMS; issues of international policy coordination are also difficult to handle in single-country models. Accordingly, we restrict attention to exchange rate targets and the means by which they can be achieved, considering some of the methodological issues that arise. These issues are illustrated in one particular experimental setting, namely the reaction of the economy to an oil-price shock, and attention concentrates on the use of exchange rate targets alone, although an associated question is whether it is the real or the nominal exchange rate which is the target of policy (Artis and Miller, 1986). A reduction in the variability of exchange rates may produce benefits to trade, but this is not represented in the models; Williamson (1987) argues that such effects are likely to be very modest, and they are excluded from the analysis.

Simulation methodology

This example has two distinctive features. First, the standard approach of comparing a base run with an alternative policy simulation subject to a target exchange rate conveys little useful information if there is little divergence of the exchange rate from its desired target in the base run. What is more useful is a comparison of the response of the model to a common shock under alternative assumptions about exchange rate targets. Our illustrations involve the use of policy instruments to attain either a target nominal or a target real exchange rate in the face of a 20 per cent reduction in world oil prices. We consider different methods of targeting the exchange rate, specifically through short-term interest rates or foreign exchange intervention. These produce different effects on other key macroeconomic variables when used in any one model; moreover we find that certain designations of policy instruments cannot be used on some models. In general, targeting is accomplished by the use of a type 2 fix or by a simple optimal control approach, in each case using a single instrument.

Targeting via interest rates or foreign exchange intervention: HMT model

The HMT model is used with both nominal and real exchange rate targets achieved by use of short-term interest rates and action on foreign reserves using type 2 fixes.[7] The target values are given by the base-run trajectories of these variables. The results are summarised in table 5.8. With fixed interest rates and no foreign exchange intervention, a fall in world oil prices would lower the exchange rate and increase output for this model (see Wallis *et al.*, 1987, chapter 2). In contrast a targeted exchange rate (whether real or nominal) achieved by either intervention or interest rate policy delivers lower output, the decline being more marked when interest rates are used. However the price level rises after five years under an interest rate policy but falls under a policy of foreign exchange

Table 5.8 Exchange rate targets: responses to a 20 per cent fall in world oil prices

	Effects on					
	GDP (%)		Price level (%)		Unemployment (000s)	
	Year 1	Year 5	Year 1	Year 5	Year 1	Year 5
HMT						
No target	0.16	0.35	0.15	2.23	−4	6
Nominal exchange rate target						
Intervention	−0.14	0.14	−0.23	−0.33	65	74
Interest rates	−0.39	−0.65	−0.07	0.58	45	139
Intervention (optimal control)	−0.07	−0.25	−0.07	−1.40	14	68
Real exchange rate target						
Intervention	−0.20	−0.03	−0.28	−1.94	75	125
Interest rates	−0.44	−0.45	−0.08	−0.04	48	120
Exogenous nominal exchange rate	0.02	0.18	−0.16	−0.03	2	31
BE						
Standard interest rate response	0.19	0.49	−0.16	0.10	−6	−60
No interest rate response	0.22	0.38	−0.15	0.11	−7	−50
Nominal exchange rate targeted by interest rates	−0.04	−0.36	−0.27	−1.63	4	39

intervention. The dramatic scale of intervention on foreign exchange reserves necessary to achieve an exchange rate target using a simple type 2 fix as the oil-price shock hits the economy indicates the potential strain of policy. In general, investigation of the required movement in policy instruments can provide a guide to the plausibility of the policy. This cannot be assessed when the exchange rate is merely exogenised unless the implicit policy mechanism is fully specified. Moreover, by eliminating any possible response of other endogenous variables in the model to changes in the implied policy instrument the simulation results under exogenisation may be biased. In the case of HMT, exogenisation does produce a different impact on output and prices from that of simulations which explicitly incorporate changes in policy instruments. Thus comparing the results in table 5.8 for an exchange rate target achieved via interest rates with that derived

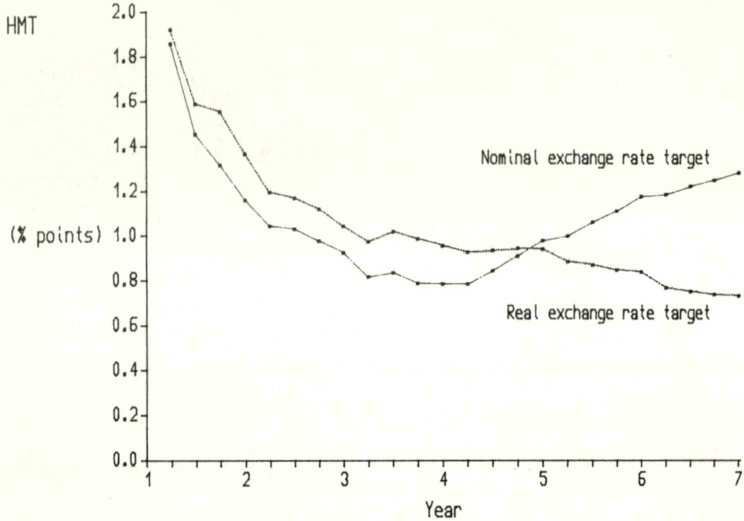

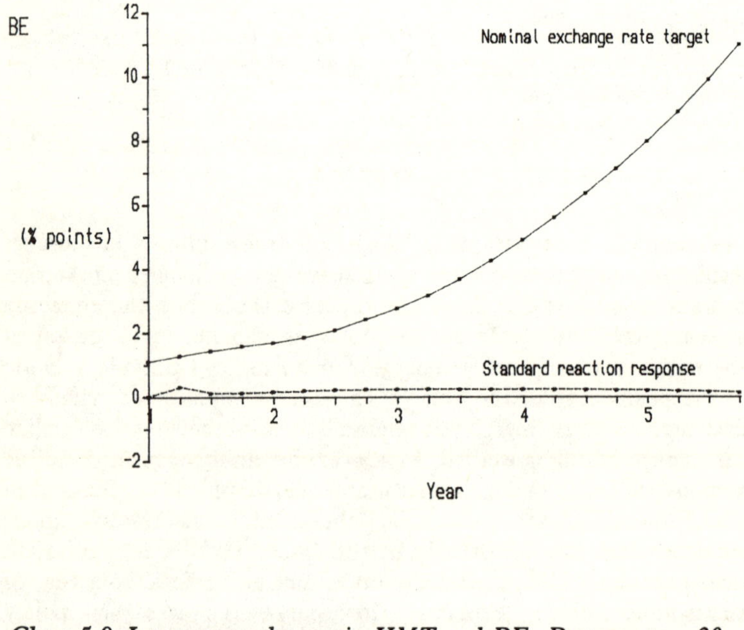

Chart 5.8 Interest rate changes in HMT and BE. Response to a 20 per cent fall in the world price of oil

from exogenising the exchange rate we observe a greater fall in GDP in the former. This arises as a result of the higher level of interest rates required to maintain the exchange rate and their (negative) influence on elements of final demand. Differences between nominal and real exchange rate targets show up mainly in the longer term where GDP responses are weaker under a real exchange rate target, given that this prevents some of the competitiveness changes that emerge under a nominal exchange rate regime.

It is possible to conduct simulations on the HMT model in such a way that the initial scale of intervention is less dramatic. This involves the use of optimal control, where instrument costs are explicitly incorporated but are allowed to become less important over time.[8] Allowing for instrument costs implies that the target exchange rate is not completely achieved, however. We find that a smoother path for intervention still requires a substantial scale of intervention, which may be possible only if the initial stock of reserves is particularly high. This supports the argument of Artis and Miller (1986) that the medium-term scope for intervention in order to target the exchange rate may be very limited. Although the plausibility of a foreign exchange intervention policy still appears in doubt when the rule for intervention is modified, the impact on other macroeconomic variables differs according to the nature of the intervention. Thus from table 5.8 we observe that a smoother profile of foreign exchange intervention results in a fall in GDP after five years but that immediate action on foreign exchange reserves results in a small increase. There is a more marked reduction in the price level also under the smoothed path of intervention. The sensitivity of the results to the exact specification of the objection function confirms previous results using optimal control in respect of another issue – namely the relationship between inflation and unemployment (Wallis *et al.*, 1987, chapter 3.3). Consequently, it is important that such details are reported along with the other assumptions used in policy analysis exercises.

Endogenous interest rates: BE model

The Bank of England (BE) model provides another example of nominal exchange rate targeting by the use of interest rates. In this model interest rates are not exogenous, as in the HMT model, but are determined by a reaction function which includes, *inter alia*, the exchange rate. We can therefore illustrate a number of different assumptions using this model. In the standard model which allows the interest rate to respond to both external and domestic pressures, an oil-price shock lowers the exchange rate and raises

GDP by similar amounts to HMT but has quite different effects on the price level and unemployment. The interest rate reaction function plays quite a small role in these responses. If the interest rate is assumed to be used in such a way as to solely target the exchange rate (thus eliminating other influences on the interest rate) the output and unemployment response to an oil-price shock is reversed and the magnitude of the effect on the price level is increased. A major difference between the two models arises in the response of the interest rate. In the HMT model interest rates are increased by 1.5 percentage points in the first year with a smaller effect after five years whereas a monotonic increase is required for BE, with interest rates 10 per cent higher after five years. Although an exogenous official financing variable is present in the BE model it has no effect on money supply, interest rates or the exchange rate, hence an illustration of exchange rate targeting by the use of this instrument is not possible with this model.

In the second section of this chapter it was noted that some of the models are not easily modified in respect of alternative policy rules. We have seen this to be the case for foreign exchange intervention in the BE model, but it also applies more generally to other United Kingdom models as discussed below.

Other models

The NIESR model includes forward-consistent expectations of the exchange rate and this, in principle, can incorporate the change in economic agents' expectations and hence in their behaviour that results from an announced change in policy regime. This feature is not included in either the HMT or BE model in their normal operating mode. However, interest rates cannot be formally used in the NIESR model to target the exchange rate, except by an interest rate response in the terminal period of the solution. In practice NIESR appears to use an off-model equation (NIESR, 1987a, p. 20) to derive a pattern for interest rates which delivers a constant or given exchange rate. However other variables which are endogenous in the formal model also enter this off-model equation and hence the augmented system is not necessarily internally consistent. In addition this methodology requires separate off-model calculations each time the exchange rate varies under any shock.

In the CUBS and NIESR models, an important internal linkage that is missing is the association between capital flows and the combination of interest rates and the exchange rate, and hence their contribution to the determination of the money stock. Thus the monetary effects of alternative exchange rate assumptions are not fully captured. The inclusion of this linkage would require further off-model calculations.

Concluding comments

In this example we consider the targeting of an endogenous variable, namely the exchange rate. Evaluation of this policy differs from standard simulation analysis in that assessment of the effects under additional shocks is required. Macroeconometric models of the United Kingdom do not usually contain explicit policy rules, but this form of policy analysis can be conducted on some models, without changing the endogenous/exogenous status of their variables, using type 2 fixes or optimal control. The results for HMT reveal the limited medium-term role for intervention compared with the use of interest rates to target the exchange rate. In comparison, however, interest rates are less powerful in achieving a given exchange rate target in the BE model than in the HMT model.

The simulation results reveal that the model outcomes are dependent on the way in which the exchange rate target is achieved. In particular it is shown that, where the exchange rate is simply exogenised, the impact on other model outcomes may be biased unless the implicit policy instrument has no influence on model variables other than through the exchange rate. In the absence of an explicit specification of the mechanism whereby an exchange rate target is achieved, the size of this potential bias cannot be evaluated.

Conclusion

The exercises presented in this chapter fall into two broad groups, which we believe encompass the majority of policy exercises currently undertaken or proposed using macroeconomic models. In the first, represented by the housing investment example, the models may appear adequate for policy analysis but in fact they are not, and some modifications to the transmission mechanism of the policy is required. In the second, represented by the incomes policy example, some of the models may appear inadequate for the purpose in hand, but amendments to the models may be possible. The common element in both groups is the need for a clear and unambiguous account of the nature of model modifications and the reasons for making them. A full statement of any adjustments and model alterations should be published, so that the results can be replicated and, more generally, so that the relative importance of the various elements of the calculations can be assessed, especially when different modelling groups present different estimates of the costs or benefits of a new policy. The supporting evidence underlying model interventions should always be described, and this chapter tries to indicate by its own example ways of recording such information in the hope that future policy analysis by others will do the same.

Estimating the effects of alternative policy actions is one of the principal uses of models, but different models, constructed for different purposes, and in accordance with different views of the economy, at different levels of aggregation, both sectoral and temporal, and with different relative weights on economic theory and statistical evidence, may give different estimates without the reasons for these divergences being well understood. Certain policy simulations may not be a good guide to understanding model differences if some of the differences in the results are merely due to simulation methodology. In many instances some of the policy choices have already been made and are incorporated in the structure of the model (for example, the method of financing any given budget deficit). In comparative questions it may be important to allow for such differences between models and consideration should be given to the consistency of the assumed policy rule and the remainder of the policy assumptions. A more complete assessment of increased housing investment, incomes policy and exchange rate targets would require examination of the sensitivity of the results to different policy environments, bearing in mind the internal consistency issue noted above. Distinguishing between underlying model properties and the effects of the simulation methodology typically requires simulation experiments under standardised conditions. These may be easier to design when some models are 'wrong' and others 'right'. In the face of an apparent consensus of results about the effects of a policy proposal, detailed scrutiny of the assumptions is still necessary, lest model differences are merely offsetting differences in experimental design. Differences in results are the norm, however. Their credibility rests on the credibility of the underlying assumptions, so these must be made explicit. Otherwise the profession will maintain its reputation for disagreement and the scope for constructive discussion will remain limited.

Table 5A.1 Residual adjustments used in housing investment simulations

	LBS		NIESR	
Quarter	(1) Imports (M)	(2) Manufacturing output (PRODMF)	(3) Manufacturing output (OMF)	(4) Unemployment (UNEMP)
1	−79.4	−0.694	−0.759	−3.4
2	−79.6	0.010	−0.759	−6.4
3	−79.9	0.009	−0.759	−9.0
4	−80.0	0.007	−0.759	−8.6
5	−80.1	0.005	−0.759	−8.6
6	−80.1	0.008	−0.759	−8.6
7	−80.4	0.014	−0.759	−8.6
8	−80.9	0.008	−0.759	−8.6
9	−81.2	0.004	−0.759	−8.6
10	−81.5	0.006	−0.759	−8.6
11	−81.8	0.006	−0.759	−8.6
12	−82.2	0.006	−0.759	−8.6
13	−82.6	0.004	−0.759	−8.6
14	−83.0	0.005	−0.759	−8.6
15	−83.4	0.006	−0.759	−8.6
16	−83.9	0.004	−0.759	−8.6
17	−84.4	0.003	−0.759	−8.6
18	−84.8	0.005	−0.759	−8.6
19	−85.4	0.005	−0.759	−8.6
20	−86.0	0.004	−0.759	−8.6
21	−86.5	0.002	−0.759	−8.6
22	−87.0	0.004	−0.759	−8.6
23	−87.6	0.005	−0.759	−8.6
24	−88.3	0.003		
25	−88.8	0.001		
26	−89.3	0.003		
27	−89.9	0.004		
28	−90.5	0.002		
29	−91.2	0.005		
30	−91.8	0.002		
31	−92.7	0.004		
32	−93.8	0.007		
Value at beginning of simulation	18,574	104.5	103.3	3,208.4

Note: We have only reported the results for the first five years of the simulations. However, as both the LBS and NIESR models incorporate forward-looking expectations, the adjustments must be maintained over the entire simulation horizon (32 quarters for LBS and 23 quarters for NIESR).

Table 5.A2 Additive residual adjustments to nominal wages (ERMF) used in incomes policy simulations on HMT model

Quarter	Ex-post target	Ex-ante target
1	−2.772	−2.703
2	−2.057	−1.870
3	−1.241	−1.039
4	−1.228	−0.898
5	−1.042	−0.717
6	−1.845	−1.251
7	−0.863	−0.458
8	−0.971	−0.584
9	−0.822	−0.423
10	−1.754	−0.964
11	−0.900	−0.568
12	−0.844	−0.526

Notes

1 The exogenous policy instruments representing public sector housing investment are *IHG* on the LBS model, *QDKLAD* on NIESR, *ILAD* on HMT, *IHG* on BE and *KGR*(5) on CGP. In each case the perturbation is £386 million per quarter, 1980 prices, this magnitude being chosen for comparability with other standard simulations.

2 In the LBS model the equation determining total imports of goods and services, *M*, is of the form $\ln M = f(\ln MDUM, \ln M_{-1},\ldots)$ where *MDUM* is a composite demand variable constructed as a weighted sum of United Kingdom expenditure components, with weights reflecting the 1979 input–output proportions of imports in final demand by expenditure category. Thus $MDUM = 0.2119\ C + 0.2992\ IF + \ldots$ where *C* is consumers' expenditure and *IF* is total fixed investment. We perturb *IF* by an amount δ, but identify this as public sector housing investment, so the relevant weight is 0.1442, and the appropriate residual adjustment to *MDUM* is $-0.155\ \delta$, as discussed in the second section. We take δ to be £386 million per quarter, 1980 prices. However in practice it is not possible to make a direct adjustment to *MDUM*, as it is only defined as a 'working variable', and instead a residual adjustment must be made to imports. Since total imports, *M*, are a dynamic non-linear function of *MDUM* the profile of the residual adjustments to *M* is determined as the difference between two single-equation runs. In the first run *IF* is perturbed by an amount δ per quarter; in the second by an amount $0.1442\ \delta/0.2992$ per quarter. The required residual adjustments to imports in a full model solution are given as the differences between the two single-equation solutions for *M*, quarter by quarter, and these are shown in column 1 of table 5.A1.

3 In the NIESR model manufacturing output, *OMF*, is determined as a weighted sum of United Kingdom expenditure components $OMF = (0.195\ C + 0.390\ IF + \ldots)/129.4$ where *C* is consumers' expenditure and *IF* is total fixed investment. We perturb *IF* by an amount δ, but identify this as public sector housing

investment, so the relevant weight is 0.1355, and the appropriate residual adjustment to *OMF* is $-0.2545\ \delta/129.4$ in each quarter, as discussed in the second section. We take δ to be £386 million, 1980 prices, giving a constant residual adjustment of -0.759, as shown in column 3 of table 5.A1.

The determination of manufacturing output in the LBS model is very similar except that the equation is coded as a proportionate rate of change:

$$\frac{OMF}{OMF_{-1}} = \frac{0.1979\ C + 0.3857\ IF + \ldots}{0.1979\ C_{-1} + 0.3857\ IF_{-1} + \ldots}$$

The profile of the adjustment to *OMF* is therefore determined as the difference between two single-equation runs. In the first run *IF* is perturbed by an amount δ per quarter; in the second by an amount $0.1355\ \delta/0.3857$ per quarter. The required residual adjustments to manufacturing output are given as the differences between the two single-equation solutions for OMF, quarter by quarter, and these are shown in column 2 of table 5.A1.

In the NIESR model the equation determining unemployment, *UNEM*, is

$$\begin{aligned}(1 - 0.851\ L)UNEM_t = {} & (-0.613 + 0.462\ L)EMPMF_t \\ & + (-0.469 + 0.4408\ L)\ (EMP_t - EMPMF_t) + \ldots\end{aligned}$$

where *EMPMF* is manufacturing employment, *EMP* is total employment and *L* is the lag operator. We perturb non-manufacturing employment by an amount δ_t, $t = 1,\ldots,T$, representing an increase in construction employment but assume that this has an effect on unemployment which is more characteristic of manufacturing employment. Then the appropriate residual adjustment, a_t, to *UNEM* is derived according to the example on p. 107 making additional allowance for equation dynamics, $a_1 = (-0.613 + 0.469)\delta_1$; $a_t = -0.144\delta_t + (0.462 - 0.4408)\delta_{t-1}$, $t = 2,\ldots,T$.

Next, an assumption about the number of jobs, δ, created in the construction industry is needed, since in the NIESR model the construction industry is not separately identified. According to the 1979 Input–Output tables (Table F) for an increase in construction output about 55 per cent of value-added is generated within the construction industry with the remainder originating in the industries supplying inputs (either directly or indirectly) to the construction industry. We therefore assume that an increase in housing investment of £386 million per quarter leads to an increase in construction value-added of $386 \times 4 \times 0.55 = 850$ per annum (£million, 1980 prices). Using an average labour–(net) output ratio of 80 workers per £million value-added (derived from figures taken from the 1986 National Accounts, Table 1.13 and the September 1987 Employment Gazette, Table 1.2) and assuming that this is equivalent to the marginal labour–(net) output ratio, this implies an increase in employment in the construction sector of approximately 70,000. This may well be an underestimate, since any second round effects which boost construction are neglected.

A further complication arises from the fact that in the NIESR model simulation it takes at least three quarters before there is an increase of 70,000 in the non-manufacturing sector as a whole. We therefore assume an increase in construction employment of 24,000 and 48,000 in the first two quarters, and the appropriate residual adjustments are then given as

$$\begin{aligned}a_1 &= 24 \times -0.144 = -3.4 \\ a_2 &= (48 \times -0.144) + (24 \times 0.0212) = -6.4 \\ a_3 &= (70 \times -0.144) + (48 \times 0.0212) = -9.0 \\ a_t &= 70 \times (-0.144 + 0.0212) = -8.6,\ t = 4,\ldots,T.\end{aligned}$$

5 In the LPL model 'actual' real wages, *ZRW*, are determined by a non-linear dynamic equation. The appropriate (additive) residual adjustments sufficient to produce an *ex ante* reduction in wages of p_t per cent, are taken as the wage residuals generated in a single-equation type 1 fix, with the values of p_t being given by $p_t = \Sigma_{i=1}^{t} 1.8^{0.5(i-1)}$ $t = 1,2,3$; $p_t = 0$ for $t > 3$. The residual adjustments to *ZRW* derived in this way are −0.0221, −0.0035 and −0.0040 in years 1 to 3 respectively.

In the LPL model 'equilibrium' real wages, *ZVW*, are distinguished separately from actual real wages, *ZRW*. However since the incomes policy is only temporary no adjustment to *ZVW* is necessary.

6 In the HMT simulation which has an *ex ante* target a type 2 fix is used to achieve the target reduction in real wages with an additive fix on nominal wages as the instrument, but exogenising all other variables which enter into the determination of wages and prices (variables *WPF, UMNF, ES, UMNFW, CBIC, SAC, NSOP, DNSOI, UKIP, UKTP, SAVIC, NODIV, Y, YOG, YPU, PTFE, UKCP, RX, OCR, YPNIR, NIS, UMFMA, EPROM, WPM, UMGMA*). The resultant set of additive residuals to nominal wages are then used in a final simulation in which wages and prices are fully endogenous. As manufacturing acts as a leading sector in the HMT model both the real wage target and the residual adjustments are applied to earnings in manufacturing (*ERMF*).

In the *ex post* experiment only one simulation is required and here a type 2 fix is applied to the residual on money wages in order to achieve the real wage target, with all other influences on wages and prices incorporated.

As the Lawson index is annual the target adjustments (which are identical in both experiments) are given in Note 5 above but for use in the HMT model these have to be interpolated into quarterly adjustments (p_t) using a log-linear approximation where p_t is given by:

$$\begin{aligned} p_t &= 0.85 \ln 3.78\, t && t = 1,\ldots,8 \\ p_t &= 2.90 + (t - 8) \times 0.10 && t = 9,\ldots,12 \\ p_t &= 0 && t > 12 \end{aligned}$$

7 In the current software the iterative procedure used to determine δ_t requires an estimate of the coefficient, λ, in the linear approximation $\delta_t = \lambda(\tilde{y}_t - \hat{y}_t)$. These values are 714 for foreign exchange reserves (*RESOS*) and 1.0 for short-term interest rates (*RSHRT*).

8 Specification of the objective function: HMT model

	Desired value	Weight
Target		
Nominal exchange rate	Base trajectory	1.0
Instrument		
Change in official reserves (*RESOS*) £m	0	0.4×10^{-7}*
Damping term		
Level of official reserves (*FCRESV*) £m	Base trajectory	0.4×10^{-7} 1987 Q2
		0.1×10^{-9} 1987 Q3–1993 Q1

Simulation period 1987 Q2–1993 Q1

*indicates equal priority of 1 point of the exchange rate to £5000m of foreign exchange reserves.

6 The Impact of Monetary Policy on Inflation: Modelling the UK Experience, 1978-86*

David Mackie, David Miles and Christopher Taylor

For about a decade monetary policy has been formulated with the prime intention of bringing down inflation. The purpose of this chapter is to use a model-based methodology to explore the policy's effect. The first part sketches the theoretical background, paying some attention to the role of econometric macromodels in informing policy. The core of the chapter lies in the second part, which describes a set of counterfactual simulations using the Bank of England macroeconomic model.

Theoretical background

Some prior considerations

The idea of a stable link between the stock of money and the general price level has a long history. It was implicit in some 16th Century writings, it was hinted at by Smith and Hume, more fully exploited by Ricardo, and received explicit statement in the well-known Fisher equation some seventy years ago:

$$MV = PT \tag{1}$$

This promoted the identity between money and transactions flows to the status of a behavioural equation by postulating (long-run) constancy for V, the transactions velocity of circulation. Given several further postulates – the 'neutrality' of money (that is, that T, the real value of transactions, is independent of M, the stock of money, being determined in the long run solely by population,

* The views expressed are those of the authors, and not necessarily those of the Bank of England. The authors would like to thank a number of colleagues at the Bank for helpful comments: in particular, D.G. Barr, P.G. Brierley, G.P. Dunn, J.S. Flemming, A.R. Latter, I.M. Michael, G. Midgley and J.B. Wilcox. In addition S.J. Butcher provided technical assistance with the model simulations. The authors are responsible for any errors which remain.

technology and the stock of capital) and price flexibility – the Fisher equation implies that P can be fixed by the authorities if they can control M, at least in the medium to long term. The theory has of course been subject to serious challenges of various kinds over the years: that velocity is not constant, being dependent in part on interest rates and in part on institutional and technological change in the financial system, among other factors; that many prices are not very flexible, so that money may influence real transactions or output, at least in the short/medium term; and that money is hard to measure or control, especially if made an instrument of policy. Some now go as far as to argue that for practical purposes money cannot be controlled in an economy like that of the United Kingdom with highly developed and internationalised financial markets. All this is familiar. And yet there was, beginning in the late 1960s, a remarkable renaissance of belief in the efficacy of monetary policy in this and other countries.

Economic modellers have participated in this renaissance, and yet it cannot be claimed that they have found it, at least technically, a rewarding experience. There is some inclination to blame their difficulties on theoreticians. This is no mere buck-passing. There seem still to be major theoretical problems in tying down the links between money and the price level. It is perhaps indicative of these intellectual problems that in the most familiar theoretical model of the whole economy – the Arrow-Debreu general equilibrium model – there is no role for money.

Perhaps it is not surprising, then, that workable macroeconomic models which attempt to describe the evolution of money, aggregate output and economy-wide prices will not usually be derived from a theoretical model of general equilibrium.[1] Empirical macromodels involving money are often felt to lack a rigorous theoretical basis. Such models of the macroeconomy have, however, been found useful in informing policy. For even if economic theory may not provide a very firm foundation for such models, empirical investigation often can, at the very least, give an indication of where hypotheses are seriously misleading. This is a rather limited and modest role for large econometric models to play. It is also a much less ambitious role than we suspect many modellers, and perhaps policymakers, have thought in the past that models could play.

It may be instructive to consider why a reappraisal of the role of models has occurred. Over the past decade economists' faith in their ability to build models which could be used to formulate an optimal policy, in order to maximise some objective function deriving from government (or from the model proprietors), has been severely shaken. The complexity of the information needed to construct a discretionary, counter-cyclical policy had already been emphasised in the 1950s and 1960s (see in particular, Phillips, 1954, 1957, Baumol, 1961, Friedman and Schwarz, 1963 and Friedman, 1968). In practice, the disastrous inflation and, to a lesser extent, growth performance of many western economies in the 1970s probably did more at the time to undermine faith in the reliability of macromodels as tools with which to formulate discretionary policy. At the same time a new wave of theoretical objections to such policies appeared which, in different ways, depended on considering the private sector's reactions to macro policies (see Lucas, 1976, Kydland and Prescott, 1977, and Barro and Gordon, 1983). Even the minimalist, Popperian role which it is suggested with more confidence that models can play – identifying seriously misleading theories of how the economy works – makes major demands on modellers' abilities. For identifying misleading or unhelpful models often takes time, whereas when faced with new situations policymakers usually cannot wait several years to adapt policy. In such an uncertain environment both the design and evaluation of policy are particularly difficult. Despite these problems it is still generally accepted that a macroeconomic policy of some kind is needed, if only to provide a nominal anchor for the economy. For without some policy in the sense of a preconceived pattern of actions involving monetary, fiscal or exchange rate instruments, it is generally impossible, at least in theoretical models of the whole economy and probably too in the real world, to tie down the price level. Monetary policy over the past ten years or so has been designed precisely with that objective in mind, as the Chancellor of the Exchequer said clearly in his 1984 Mais Lecture.[2] This represents a considerable departure from much of the previous postwar era, during which monetary policy was largely subordinated to fiscal policy in the pursuit of a high and rising level of activity.

Policy instruments

In considering the ways by which monetary policy affects the economy, in particular the aggregate price level, one should perhaps begin by recalling what instruments of monetary control are now considered by the authorities to be effective. Not only has policy to be implemented in an environment of uncertainty, it is also the case that the range of effective monetary instruments used for its implementation has narrowed considerably over the past ten years, so that policy now operates in essence through the short-term interest rate, as the Governor of the Bank explained in his 1987

Mais Lecture.[3] Financial markets have become increasingly competitive and boundaries between institutions that formerly provided different services have broken down. Direct controls, or other instruments, which differentially affect institutions providing services which are close substitutes, are likely to prove both ineffective and distortionary. Influencing the price of funds to all institutions is both more effective and impinges in a less discriminatory way. Movements in the cost of money also have a significant impact upon the exchange rate, which has been larger since the abolition of exchange controls. Hence the importance of short-term interest rates over which the authorities enjoy a good measure of control. (In recent years the process has worked through setting the rate at which eligible commercial bills are purchased from the discount houses.) The authorities' influence over longer-term rates, which works through funding policy, is held to be much less than that over short-term rates.

Direct controls over the banking system, such as the supplementary special deposits scheme (the 'corset'), have also come to be regarded as at best rather ineffective in controlling the sources, as opposed to the symptoms, of excessive monetary growth and at worst highly damaging to the efficiency of the financial system through causing large-scale disintermediation away from the banking system. Such controls were abandoned in 1980. Foreign exchange market intervention, which might be considered a tool of monetary policy, has obvious and quite narrow practical limits. This is especially true for one country acting alone. In many circumstances the size of capital flows through the exchange markets today makes the scale of intervention needed to sustain some shift in rates from non-intervention market levels infeasible. Exchange controls, like direct controls over the banking system, have also come to be seen as distortionary and largely ineffective and were abolished almost ten years ago.

The rationale of policy

The policy approach of the past dozen or so years has adopted one or more monetary aggregates as central intermediate targets. Policy has also attached growing weight to the level and rate of change of the exchange rate while relying increasingly on short-term interest rates as the primary control instrument.

There are three main reasons why economists have thought setting monetary targets desirable for controlling inflation. First, if the relation between money, its opportunity cost and nominal income (which in the absence of quantity rationing can be seen as the key elements in the demand for money) is fairly stable, then under further, but not implausible, conditions a stable path of nominal income can be implemented by setting money targets. The money targets would be set taking into account a desired path of nominal income and the rate of growth of money which the money demand relation suggests is consistent with that path. Interest rates might be used as the instrument to achieve the money target. Since interest rates will have a negative impact on the growth of nominal income and a further direct negative price effect on money demand, moving interest rates in response to deviations of money from target should prove to be stabilising; growth of nominal income in excess of the desired rate causes money to grow above target and will trigger interest rate rises which can be expected to reduce the growth in income.

A critic might point out that a policy of directly targeting nominal income is more efficient than setting an intermediate (money) target: directly targeting nominal income should avoid the problem of mistakenly changing interest rates in response to noise from the money demand equation which is unrelated to the path of income. In practice both lags in the relation between money and income and the much speedier publication of money as compared with income figures (together with the proneness of the latter to revision) may make setting intermediate money targets preferable. Consider the lags between income and money. In the short term individuals may hold wealth increases in money and only slowly spend (eventually a large proportion of) it on goods and services. In this case money is a leading indicator of income. Even if money and income are only contemporaneously linked, if money is measured more often than income (as it is in the United Kingdom) it can give information on income developments which would allow the authorities to react more rapidly to deviations from the prescribed nominal path. These characteristics of monetary aggregates, the relatively short measurement lag and their role as leading indicator, are also shared by the exchange rate. Indeed, there is no delay in the measurement of the exchange rate whilst there is a lag between changes in the rate and any impact on money income.

The path of money and the level and rate of change of the exchange rate may, for either of these reasons, give more information on trends in nominal income than do data on nominal income itself. Whether the path of money does give useful information depends also on the accuracy with which the parameters of the money demand equation can be measured. This last point is crucial and is considered in more detail below.

As a counter-inflationary policy, designed to reduce an initially high rate of inflation, targeting money will, however, ultimately be effective only if the consequent reduction in the growth of nominal income generates lower inflation rather than lower real output. A key element of monetary policy under the MTFS has been that by announcing a credible, non-accommodating policy, agents will respond by moderating price and wage increases. The effectiveness of such a policy depends crucially on its impact upon inflation expectations which in turn depends on the private sector believing that the authorities are serious about not accommodating inflation. This leads to the second point about monetary targeting; the now much-analysed notion of policy credibility.

If a policy of monetary targetry is both understood and credible, it is likely to influence expectations in such a way as to have some counter-inflationary effect. It was thought that monetary targets promised well in terms of comprehensibility since, on the face of it, it should be possible to detect deviations of money from targets accurately and with little delay. It was acknowledged that to build up credibility could, however, be more difficult. Ultimately, credibility is best achieved by attaining over a period of time the aim of policy: first reducing, and subsequently stabilising, price inflation.

A third reason, or rather set of reasons, for using monetary targets as a means of controlling inflation, was that the alternative policies were held to involve more serious problems. In principle, there are as many ways to control nominal variables as there are nominal prices. Counterinflation policy had in the past tended to focus on trying to fix, or at least influence, one or more of three key prices; nominal wages, the exchange rate and interest rates.

There is not space here to review the arguments for and against incomes policies; there would now probably be a wide measure of agreement among economists that experience in the 1970s cast strong doubt on the ability of both statutory and voluntary incomes policies (even when accompanied by dividend and price controls) to control wages and prices in the longer term. Poor design and implementation of the policies may have been contributory factors.

It was noted above that some advantages of a policy of setting intermediate money targets hold, in principle, equally for a policy of exchange rate targeting. It does seem that the exchange rate could provide an anchor for domestic wages and prices, although the problem of determining the appropriate rate is formidable. (On the links between interest rates, the exchange rate and the ultimate goals of policy see Flemming, 1987). The authorities have over the past year given more weight to keeping sterling stable, as is well known. However, a policy which focussed only on the exchange rate would ignore the extra information on likely income and price trends contained in monetary aggregates, just as a policy which focussed on monetary aggregates risks ignoring the information in the foreign exchange markets. Clearly the exchange rate does not give an absolute guide to the pressures on wages and prices. That this is not just a point of theory is shown by the fact that there are periods when domestic economy conditions and exchange rate pressures point to very different policy responses; and the record does not suggest a consistent domination of one indicator by the other. The behaviour of the exchange rate should, then, be assessed in the context of a wide range of indicators of monetary conditions, and *vice versa*. For, in an uncertain and changing world, the stance of monetary policy is not measured perfectly by the actual rate of growth of money relative to the target. At the same time the impact of changing interest rates upon income will be crucial in determining how large a change in rates is needed to bring money back on target, but is not known with certainty. Empirical evidence incorporated in the various major econometric models of the United Kingdom economy suggests that the key channel through which interest rate changes affect income is via the exchange rate. Thus, given the uncertainty about the size of the impact of an interest rate change on income, it makes sense to monitor as well the major intermediate link in the chain, the exchange rate itself: one may be very uncertain of the size of the change in competitiveness induced by a change in interest rates, but less unsure about the impact of any movement in competitiveness upon nominal incomes. In practice, therefore, monetary targets and exchange rate targets may be more like complements than substitutes, especially when the uncertainty and noise in the economic system is significant.

Interest rate setting without reference to the money stock or exchange rate was the third counter-inflation policy alternative mentioned above. Either real or nominal rates may be targeted but in either case there are serious objections. If real interest rates are chosen as intermediate targets, the rate of inflation becomes indeterminate; any rate of inflation is consistent with any particular real interest rate target. If a nominal interest rate target is set the stability of the policy rule is open to doubt; positive inflation shocks which, other things being equal, might be expected to put upward pressure on nominal rates, lead to an easing of policy. This is perverse and destabilising.

Implications for macromodels

Such are some of the main prior considerations underlying the approach to monetary policy over much of the past decade. They are neither very contentious nor profound: some nominal anchor is needed to tie down the rate of price inflation; the levels of nominal income and various measures of the stock of money are, in the longer term, positively linked; expectations are crucial and for this reason a policy that is easy to understand and verifiable will be more likely to be credible and the transition to lower inflation less painful; to create credibility in the policy it is necessary to persevere with a non-accommodatory stance to inflation. The difficult problems in formulating monetary policy arise because of major uncertainties over the form of the key relations in the real world. It is unfortunate, though not accidental, that these key relations – between money and income, between income and interest rates, between interest rates and exchange rates and between future expectations and current and past outturns – are all hard to model.

Although this may sound ultra pessimistic, it is not meant to be. The implication is that policymaking has to be conducted in an environment where the structure of the economy is known only very imperfectly. Indeed, modellers, like policymakers, tend only to become aware of their ignorance about the structure of the economy with a time lag. The picture we have of the economy is one that is both changing and out of date, and this suggests that counter-inflationary policy needs to evolve, and also provide for contingencies. But this raises an important problem, namely the conflict between the flexibility of a monetary (or any other) policy and its credibility.

Consider a real world example. At the outset of the MTFS a target range was set for £M3 (hereafter referred to as M3), a fairly broad measure of the stock of money. The usefulness of such an intermediate target, and the wisdom of moving interest rates mechanically so as to try to hit it, depends on the stability, or at least predictability, of the relation between the target and nominal income or prices. In the past three years there have been major institutional changes which have had dramatic effects on M3 velocity. Shifting attention to the narrower M0 aggregates, within the overall policy of considering a range of indicators, was a sensible response to these developments. The link between M0, money income and interest rates has remained a reasonably close one. The problem is that shifting emphasis from one aggregate to another when the relegated money stock has grown much more rapidly than its target rate can look very much like abandonment of the non-accommodating policy. The effect upon expectations and upon jump variables which depend upon them (most obviously the exchange rate) can be damaging. Monetary policy has therefore to evolve in order to keep pace with structural changes but it must do so in a cautious, well-publicised and explicable way. Credibility need not be sacrificed when policy evolves, provided that a convincing explanation can be given for the change. Indeed, the credibility of the Government's anti-inflation policy appears to have suffered no damage when M3 was dropped as a target, in the 1987 MTFS, because such explanations were readily accepted.

It has been argued that policymaking when the true model of the economy is not known is hard. The appropriate reaction to financial developments depends on how these are interpreted; and because of uncertainty about how the world works, interpretation is difficult. Whether a build-up in liquidity is likely to prove inflationary, as might occur in certain cases if buffer stock theories of money demand are true, or rather represents some long-term portfolio shift which is unconnected with expenditure on non-financial assets, is crucial. There is a vast amount of relevant information which could be used to illuminate the issue. Macromodels provide an integrated picture drawn from aggregate economic statistics. At the other extreme, the central bank may well have detailed micro information on where heavy lending or depositing took place: it may even know the individual economic agents concerned and their alleged motives. This combination of highly aggregate and highly disaggregated information is regularly discussed at policy meetings at the Treasury and Bank. Trying to fit them together is generally a test of ingenuity. The difficulty is to avoid attaching too much weight to what is sometimes no more than anecdotal information, while realising that the financial system is too complex and evolves too quickly for its essentials to be captured fully by econometric models. One reaction to such difficult informational problems would be that econometric models have little to contribute to the formulation and evaluation of monetary policy. The rest of this chapter attempts to illuminate that issue by showing how a large econometric model may be used to assess the contribution of monetary policy to the reduction in inflation in recent years.

A model-based exercise

Introduction

This part of the chapter describes an exercise which uses the Bank of England's quarterly macroeconomic model of the United Kingdom economy to analyse the behaviour of inflation over the period 1978–86 (see Patterson *et al.*, 1987, for a fuller account of the Bank model). It considers the influence of various policy and exogenous factors on the rate of inflation, concentrating in particular on the model's assessment of the contribution monetary policy may have made to the reduction of inflation over the period. (See the next sub-section for a discussion of the choice of period.)

The methodology of such historic counterfactual exercises has been discussed elsewhere (see, for example, Bank of England, 1981, Artis *et al.*, 1984, and Saville and Gardiner, 1986). Essentially the exercise involves returning each of the policy and exogenous variables to a trend or neutral path and allowing the model to determine a counterfactual path for inflation conditional upon the various assumptions made. The difference between this counterfactual case and actual history (referred to as 'the base') is decomposed in stages to identify the effects of the individual variant factors.

It has been argued on many occasions that conventional large-scale macroeconomic models are not appropriate tools for such counterfactual analysis because the response of the economy to a policy or exogenous shock will depend not only on the nature of the shock, but also on agents' expectations of future states of the world, which will themselves be influenced by the shock (see Lucas, 1976). The Lucas critique seems particularly relevant to this exercise since, with the announcement of monetary targets, the government began to give considerable weight to the notion that expectations are important and that the authorities could, by announcing their intentions well in advance, lower the costs involved in reducing inflation.[4]

Another possible problem with exercises of this sort concerns the size of the shocks which are being administered to the model. Sims puts it as follows: 'the rational expectations critique is only a special case of a more general cautionary note – statistical models are likely to become unreliable when extrapolated to make predictions for conditions far outside the range experienced in the sample' (Sims, 1982, p. 122). It may well be that the parameters of the model are unstable, not only for reasons related to the Lucas critique, but also because the equations may only represent local approximations to the 'true' functional form. We believe that, with certain notable exceptions, the Bank model is reasonably good at explaining the consequences of small disturbances in many of its exogenous variables. However, the shocks the model is subjected to in this exercise are far from marginal and we have considerably less experience of how well the model performs in such circumstances. Furthermore, these exercises are run without any explicit intervention (except in the case of short-term interest rates, as explained below), other than where necessary to enable the model to solve. Consequently the results are highly dependent on the properties of the model, and are valid only in so far as those properties are accepted as reasonably representative of actual behaviour.

Given all these qualifications, the results should be regarded as telling us as much about the model as the real world. The present chapter does not produce all the evidence on which to base a judgment of the difference between the two. They are put forward here essentially as an illustration of the uses to which a large macroeconomic model may be put (which is after all the theme of the present book), and not in themselves as a definitive assessment of policy.

Choice of period, and assumptions

The period 1978–86 was chosen because it comes close to capturing the important change in the monetary policy regime which is believed to have taken place, as described earlier. It is a moot point when exactly the new regime began. Some might put it at 1976, when monetary targets were formally announced; others might prefer 1980, when the MTFS was introduced. We opted for 1978 in part as a compromise between such views, but mainly because it comes closest to the timing of the uncapping of sterling in the autumn of 1977. This more than any other was the point at which monetary policy became 'serious', in the sense of being freed from an exchange rate override.

The counterfactual case for comparison is what we estimate would have happened if the stance of policy had not changed from that existing and had the rest of the world been 'on trend'. A number of important and difficult practical questions arose in defining 'unchanged policies' and selecting the appropriate values for monetary variables for the counterfactual case, as will be explained. The choices made were inevitably matters for judgement. An element of judgement was also needed in selecting values for the other exogenous variables which are explored in the counterfactual: in particular those representing unchanged fiscal policy and trend or normal behaviour of activity and prices outside the United Kingdom. World activity and prices, treated as exogenous in the Bank model, were returned to trend rates of growth based, in the main, on the experience of the past two decades. It is difficult to decide what constitutes a trend rate of growth for these variables because the experience of the 1970s was so different from that of the 1960s. Averaging the growth rates over the whole period represented a compromise. The world oil price, also exogenous, was treated differently from the other world prices in that it was maintained at a constant level relative to the world price of manufactured exports. The purpose of such adjustments is of course that they enable an assessment of the influence of external developments in activity and prices on the path of United Kingdom inflation.

Unchanged fiscal policy involved making assumptions regarding taxes and public expenditure. *Ad valorem* indirect tax rates were held constant at 1977 Q4 values while the effective rates of other indirect taxes were held broadly constant by indexing specific duty rates to inflation and by maintaining local authority rates as a fixed proportion of consumers' expenditure. National Insurance contribution rates and personal sector direct tax rates were held constant and tax allowances and earnings limits were indexed to the price level. Public sector current and capital expenditure were both set to grow at 2 per cent a year, the assumed potential growth rate of GDP.

Measuring the stance of monetary policy

The selection of an appropriate counterfactual path is particularly difficult when it comes to monetary policy since there is no simple way of measuring monetary stance. As noted earlier, the instruments of monetary policy have evolved considerably since the early 1970s, an important change being the replacement of an array of direct controls affecting monetary growth by greater reliance on market instruments, principally short-term interest rates. In choosing the particular model variable(s) that can best characterise unchanged monetary policy in the counterfactual case, it is necessary to bear in mind how the thrust of policy has actually been transmitted in recent years. This suggests that the exercise might concentrate on real or nominal short-term interest rates, but they are not necessarily the sole or best measure to use. Other exercises have used a number of definitions of unchanged or neutral monetary policy. The studies by Worswick (1981) and Budd (1981) both define monetary policy in terms of nominal interest rates and the real exchange rate,[5] that is, their definition of neutral monetary policy holds nominal interest rates at some level below their historical path and the nominal exchange rate is manipulated to maintain either a constant (Worswick) or trended (Budd) real exchange rate (defined in terms of relative price competitiveness). Artis *et al.* (1984) define monetary policy in terms of the nominal interest rate although, because changes in nominal interest rates are not able to explain fully the behaviour of the exchange rate over this period in the models they use, they do go on to consider the role of the real exchange rate. In contrast to these exercises, Saville and Gardiner (1986) define neutral monetary policy in terms of relative real interest rates (United Kingdom rates relative to overseas rates). The variety in these approaches perhaps suggests that the measurement of monetary policy stance should depend in part on the structure of the macroeconomic model being used and the likely channels of influence.

The main instrument of monetary policy in the Bank model is the short-term interest rate and there are two main channels from interest rates to inflation.[6] The first channel is via the exchange rate. A change in the exchange rate will have a direct effect on import prices and also indirect competitiveness effects on manufacturers' margins. For example, a decline in the sterling value of competing manufactured goods is assumed to put downward pressure on United Kingdom manufacturers' domestic and export margins. In addition, importers' margins also decline in response to lower prices in the United Kingdom. Given the difficulty experienced in trying to model the exchange rate econometrically, the Bank model employs several alternative equations for determining the nominal effective exchange rate and these differ in their responsiveness to interest rate changes.

The second channel from interest rates to inflation is via activity. There are direct interest rate effects on several components of demand including manufacturing investment, residential investment, consumption of non-durables and manufacturers' stockbuilding. In addition, there are indirect effects via the mortgage market where mortgage lending influences the consumption of durables and residential investment. Activity in turn impinges on inflation in two ways; firstly, it influences earnings via a Phillips' curve mechanism and secondly, it affects manufacturers' profit margins via rates of factor utilisation, an increase in employed factor utilisation rates tending to raise manufacturers' margins. In addition, changes in interest rates affect the income of surplus and deficit sectors which may influence expenditure and there are also liquidity and wealth effects, notably on consumers' expenditure and stockbuilding. The Bank model does not have a well developed transmission mechanism from interest rates via monetary aggregates to inflation mainly because it is very difficult to model the financial decisions of the main sectors in the economy, for reasons touched on at the beginning of this chapter. So it is not appropriate in this exercise to define monetary policy in terms of the monetary aggregates. Instead, given the structure of the Bank model, monetary policy is defined here in two alternative ways: in terms of the real exchange rate and in terms of real interest rates.

The 'real exchange rate' case

In an economy characterised by quickly adjusting financial markets and slowly adjusting product and labour markets one could argue

Table 6.1 Real exchange and interest rates: 'real exchange rate' case

	1978	1979	1980
Counterfactual			
Real exchange rate[a]	69.5	69.5	69.5
Real short-term interest rate, %[b]	–2.2	–5.4	–6.8
Historic base			
Real exchange rate[a]	73.0	84.3	100.0
Real short-term interest rate, %[b]	0.3	0.8	0.1
Major six real interest rate, %[b,c]	0.2	0.6	0.6

[a] Historic 1980 = 100.
[b] Defined with reference to consumer price inflation.
[c] Unweighted average.

that, in the absence of any changes in the structure of tastes or technologies or other major shocks, the most important influences on the real exchange rate are monetary and fiscal policy. It is likely that the announcements of tighter monetary policy beginning in 1976, and the policy adjustments initiated then, together with the uncapping of sterling in 1977, were sufficiently credible to contribute to the large appreciation of the real exchange rate that started about then. The election of a new government in 1979 committed to reducing inflation as one of its main priorities, and the subsequent introduction of the MTFS, will have made a further contribution.[7] It is, however, very difficult to assess how much of the appreciation of the real exchange rate from 1977 to 1981 was a consequence of the announcement and implementation of tighter monetary policy and how much was due to other factors such as fiscal policy and North Sea oil. One extreme is to assume that the entire appreciation of the real exchange rate was due to the tightening of monetary policy. This extreme case involved defining unchanged (or accommodating) monetary policy in the counterfactual as a constant real exchange rate (measured in terms of normalised relative unit labour costs), set at its average of 1973–7 (69.5).

It would have been desirable to obtain the constant real exchange rate by manipulating the nominal short-term interest rate, with the nominal exchange rate determined endogenously. However, because of the absence of an optimal control facility in the model it would have been difficult to calculate the appropriate nominal interest rate path in this way. Accordingly, we simply assumed that the nominal

1981	1982	1983	1984	1985	1986
69.5	69.5	69.5	69.5	69.5	69.5
−3.3	−4.0	−4.5	−5.1	−3.8	−2.0
103.7	99.6	94.1	95.2	99.3	95.1
2.9	3.2	4.7	5.1	6.8	6.8
4.0	4.4	4.2	5.1	4.1	4.6

interest rate remained constant at its starting level (7.6 per cent, the average of 1977). This turned out to imply a counterfactual real interest rate of *minus* just over 4 per cent on average between 1978 and 1986. We assumed that this would be broadly consistent with a real exchange rate averaging just below 70. This assumption is supported by the results in table 6.4, where a constant real interest rate of −3.5 per cent implies a real exchange rate averaging just over 73. The results with monetary policy defined in this way are given in tables 6.1 and 6.2.

As can be seen, the counterfactual real exchange rate was considerably lower than the historic rate throughout, while the counterfactual real interest rate (based on the model's inflation projection) remained consistently negative, well below the historic United Kingdom rate, and well below the average of equivalent rates in the six other major industrial countries. It can be argued that the size of the adverse international differential against sterling raises questions about the plausibility of the counterfactual case. Given the constant real exchange rate, it implies a substantial and rising real yield gap between sterling and foreign currency assets, at least on an *ex post* basis. The same would be true on an *ex ante* basis if the constant real exchange rate induced a corresponding profile of expectations about future rates. Those who put a lot of weight on currency real yield equalisation as an equilibrium condition in exchange markets might find such a gap, persisting for so long, hard to swallow.

An alternative course would have been to assume a constant small (or zero) real interest rate differential. We decided against such

Table 6.2 Monetary policy defined in terms of the real exchange rate and nominal interest rates: effects on consumer price inflation

	1978	1979	1980
Counterfactual inflation	*9.8*	*13.0*	*14.4*
Monetary policy	−0.2	−1.3	−4.1
Real oil prices	−0.1	−0.2	0.9
Other world prices	−0.1	0	1.1
World activity	0	0	0
Government expenditure	0	0	−0.1
VAT	0	1.0	2.8
Other indirect taxes	−0.7	−1.0	−0.6
Direct taxes & NI	0.5	2.0	1.8
Historic base inflation	*9.2*	*13.5*	*16.2*

Notes: (1) Unchanged monetary policy is defined as a constant real exchange rate at 69.54 and constant short-term interest rates at 7.632 per cent. (2) The top and bottom lines show annual percentage

alternatives in part because they implied, when taken in conjunction with inflation rates in the counterfactual, implausibly high levels of United Kingdom nominal interest rates (much higher than historical rates) in what was intended to represent an accommodative policy stance; and in part because international yield parity should not be expected to hold in an unchanged policy regime (which would retain, for example, exchange controls); it certainly did not do so in the decade before 1978, at least *ex post*.[8]

While use of an alternative United Kingdom counterfactual interest rate would have affected the other results somewhat, it would not have changed them radically in a case where the real exchange rate is fixed, given the interest rate properties of the model. The top line in table 6.2 shows what the model calculates inflation would have been had monetary and fiscal policy been unchanged as defined above, and had the world variables grown at the imposed trend rates. The bottom line shows the actual historic path of inflation. The intermediate lines decompose the difference between the counterfactual and the base and attribute it to the various factors under consideration; that is, monetary policy, real oil prices, other world prices, world activity, government expenditure, VAT, other indirect taxes and direct taxes and National Insurance. Inflation settles down in the counterfactual to around 10–12 per cent a year, comprising world inflation at around 6 per

1981	1982	1983	1984	1985	1986
10.9	*11.6*	*12.1*	*12.7*	*11.4*	*9.6*
−7.5	−9.2	−9.0	−7.3	−5.3	−3.7
1.5	1.1	0.4	−0.3	−0.5	−1.3
1.6	1.7	1.1	0.8	−0.3	−3.4
0	−0.2	−0.4	−1.3	−1.4	−0.5
−0.1	−0.4	−0.7	−0.4	0.2	0.3
2.5	1.4	0.5	0.5	1.2	1.5
1.4	2.4	1.3	0	−0.7	−0.1
1.1	0.2	−0.2	0.1	0.7	1.3
11.4	*8.6*	*5.1*	*4.8*	*5.3*	*3.7*

changes. The intermediate lines show percentage point deviations from the counterfactual.

cent a year in local currency terms and a nominal exchange rate depreciation of around 6 per cent a year. Given the way in which prices and wages are determined in the model, maintaining a constant real exchange rate ensures that any inflation differential between the United Kingdom and the rest of the world is perpetuated indefinitely.

The second line indicates that, according to the model, the tightening in monetary policy around 1977 (as defined above) exerted downward pressure on inflation throughout this period. The effect of monetary policy is assessed by returning the nominal exchange rate and nominal short-term interest rates to their historic paths, leaving the other factors as in the counterfactual. Thus the model suggests that had monetary policy not been tightened inflation would have been higher throughout by the amounts in the second line. For example, in 1982 the rate of inflation would have been just over 9 percentage points higher than actual (at almost 18 per cent a year rather than 8½ per cent).

According to the model the appreciation of the nominal exchange rate, relative to the counterfactual case, amounting to about 50 per cent in 1981, put downward pressure directly on import prices. This effect was reinforced by indirect competitiveness effects on manufacturers' margins, as the model adjusts margins to partially offset changes in competitiveness. Furthermore, the appreciation of the real exchange rate initially depressed domestic activity, which put downward pressure on prices via the Phillips curve mechanism and contributed to a further reduction in manufacturers' margins through a decline in employed factor utilisation rates.

As mentioned earlier the effects attributed to monetary policy here could be considered to be an upper bound of the possible effects since all of the exchange rate appreciation is attributed to changes in monetary policy. The role of oil prices is considered explicitly later but no attempt is made to distinguish between the effects of monetary and fiscal policy on the real exchange rate. Hence, these results will tend to understate the role of fiscal policy if a tightening of fiscal stance in this country leads to an appreciation of the real exchange rate.[9] In fact, over this period monetary and fiscal policy have been closely linked via the MFTS and the results in the second line might be more appropriately interpreted as an upper bound of the effects of the MTFS working via the exchange rate.

Other factors in the real exchange rate case

Turning to the other factors analysed in table 6.2, the third line suggests that real oil prices exerted downward pressure on domestic inflation at the beginning and end of the period, but upward pressure from 1980–83. (Note that the oil price does not, here, affect the exchange rate.) The effect in this line is calculated by returning real oil prices to their historic level but based on the counterfactual level for the world price of manufactured exports. Hence the 'other world prices' line includes, in addition to non-oil price effects, a nominal oil price effect due to the change to world manufactured export prices.[10] The fourth line suggests that other world prices have exerted mainly upward pressure on United Kingdom inflation, although towards the end of the period the large declines in real commodity prices since 1984, and the general decline in world inflation, begin to have a significant downward impact on United Kingdom inflation, which becomes strong in 1986.

The analysis suggests that neither world activity nor government expenditure have had a very large effect on inflation over this period.[11] For example, the combined effects of the counterfactual paths for world activity and government expenditure add around a cumulative 4¾ per cent to the level of United Kingdom consumer prices by the end of 1986.

In the Bank model all indirect tax changes are passed on completely by firms in the form of higher prices, so the effects of changes in indirect taxes on inflation are almost certainly overstated. According to the model the increase in VAT in 1979 not only affected the price level but also increased the rate of inflation throughout, as domestic wages responded and a wage–price spiral was set in motion. The model has a strong tendency to generate wage–price spirals once either wages or prices receive a shock. This is due not only to the dynamic structure of the wage and price equations themselves but also to important linkages between manufacturing real earnings and labour demand. For example, an increase in real earnings in the Bank model will decrease the demand for labour (with given output) as firms substitute capital for labour, and the subsequent increase in actual labour productivity puts further upward pressure on real earnings since the manufacturing earnings equation uses a moving average of actual labour productivity as a proxy for trend labour productivity. This interaction between real earnings and labour demand is an important mechanism that generates wage–price spirals in the model. In addition, the model's responsiveness to an inflationary shock is increased further by the manner in which certain indirect taxes are modelled; that is, as a function of consumers' expenditure in current prices.

Regarding other indirect taxes, the rates set for duties on hydrocarbon oil and alcohol and tobacco exerted downward pressure on inflation in the first three years since they were not indexed to keep pace with inflation, which they do in the counterfactual. The upward pressure on inflation from other indirect taxes in 1981–3 comes about in almost equal proportions from specific duties and local authority rates.

Turning to changes in direct taxes, the exercise suggests that they have exerted a small amount of upward pressure on inflation in the first few years mainly on account of the increase in employers' National Insurance contributions towards the beginning of the simulation period which, in the Bank model, are passed on completely by firms as higher prices. This almost certainly overstates the impact since firms may respond to higher labour taxes by resisting upward pressure on nominal earnings rather than by raising prices. There is a direct link from personal sector direct taxes to earnings in the model since the manufacturing earnings equation contains a retentions ratio term, although the effect is fairly weak. However, despite cuts in the basic rate of tax over this period the historic path of the retentions ratio term has not been higher than in the counterfactual throughout, since changes in National Insurance rates and allowances have, in certain years, offset the effects of basic rate cuts.[12]

The 'North Sea oil' variant

As mentioned previously, it seems likely that the appreciation of the real exchange rate from 1977 to 1981 was influenced by certain non-monetary factors, among which North Sea oil may have been specially important. North Sea oil may have exerted two kinds of influence. The first relates to the now widely recognised endowment effect. The existence of the North Sea oil endowment was undoubtedly known in the early 1970s, but both its scale and value remained highly uncertain and it may not have begun to influence the real exchange rate substantially until later in the 1970s, when oil output grew rapidly. Secondly, there is likely to have been a direct effect on the exchange rate from the large rise in the real oil price (around 87 per cent) which occurred between 1978 and 1980. Unfortunately, the size, and possibly even the direction, of any such effect is highly uncertain, because the United Kingdom's self-sufficiency in oil cannot be regarded as permanent. Accordingly, the endowment effect of a change in the oil price will depend on the future profile of oil production and consumption, and the discount rate used to estimate the present value of the oil reserves (Bank of England, 1986). Despite these considerations, most modellers assume a positive relationship between the value of the oil endowment and the real exchange rate and this is the assumption made here.

To analyse the possible importance of North Sea oil a simulation was performed which allows the real oil price directly to influence the real exchange rate with an elasticity of 0.3.[13] That could be considered a fairly high value for this elasticity (see Powell *et al.*, 1985) and so the results could represent an upper estimate of the likely effects of North Sea oil and hence a lower bound for the effects of monetary policy. By considering only changes in the real oil price and making no allowance for any increased perception of the pre-1978 value of the North Sea reserves, we may be guilty of ignoring the first of the two effects discussed above.

The results of this simulation are given in table 6.3. In 1981, the level of the real exchange rate in the base is about 50 per cent above the level in the counterfactual, and almost half of this appreciation is attributed to the real oil price.[14] There is, of course, a sizeable appreciation of the nominal exchange rate relative to the counterfactual, attributed to the rise in the oil price, the effect of which is to produce the somewhat counter-intuitive result that the 1979 oil price shock actually put downward pressure on United Kingdom inflation (which becomes quite powerful after two years) because the effects of the resulting exchange rate appreciation on domestic prices outweigh the direct effect of the oil price increase. Furthermore, declines in the real oil price beginning in 1985 are calculated to have put upward pressure on United Kingdom inflation since then because they are associated in the model with an exchange rate depreciation.

The effect of monetary policy is calculated by returning the nominal exchange rate from the level implied by the behaviour of the real oil price to its historic path. In addition, nominal interest rates are returned to their historic path. Compared with the results in table 6.2, this variant attributes a much smaller cumulative downward effect on the consumer price level to monetary policy, although still an important one (that is, some 29 per cent by 1986, compared with 48 per cent in table 6.2). The effects in tables 6.2 and 6.3 are comparable in the early years, but thereafter monetary policy loses roughly half its influence to oil prices, until 1986 when the picture changes. The reason for the reversal in 1986 is that the recent large decline in the real oil price is associated in the simulation with a large depreciation in the exchange rate so that moving the exchange rate from that counterfactual level to the historic base level is larger than previously, thus attributing more of an effect to monetary policy.

Tables 6.2 and 6.3 present the decomposition of differences between the counterfactual and historical paths for inflation only. However, the plausibility of these results clearly depends on a wider group of characteristics from the counterfactual simulations. In fact, the corresponding results for output, unemployment, and the current balance, among other key items, in no case looked highly implausible. This suggests that the model was standing up well to the strains of an exercise which would have been a severe test for any large econometric model.

One such set of results for the 'North Sea oil' variant is presented, without intervention, in an appendix table (table 6A.1) along with the historic base values. While the counterfactual numbers there are felt to present a reasonably consistent picture of the real economy, we would not put a lot of weight on the output or unemployment figures because we believe that the model does not capture well the detrimental effects of inflation on output or activity; for example, fixed investment and underlying productivity growth might have been lower in the counterfactual world, were the model able to incorporate the numerous inhibiting effects that high inflation probably has on investment planning. If so, such shortcomings would mean that the model may also understate the less direct and longer-run inflation-reducing effects of a non-accommodative monetary policy, while capturing the direct effects of a high exchange rate reasonably well. But we have no ready way

Table 6.3 Monetary policy defined as in table 6.2, but with oil price effects: effects on consumer price inflation

	1978	1979	1980
Counterfactual inflation	*9.8*	*13.1*	*14.5*
Real oil prices	0	−0.1	−0.9
Monetary policy	−0.3	−1.5	−2.4
Other world prices	−0.1	0	1.1
World activity	0	0	0
Government expenditure	0	0	−0.1
VAT	0	1.0	2.8
Other indirect taxes	−0.7	−1.0	−0.6
Direct taxes & NI	0.5	2.0	1.8
Historic base inflation	*9.2*	*13.5*	*16.2*

Note: See note 2 to table 6.2

of assessing this set of questions within the present ambit of the model. Accordingly these results should be treated with particular caution.

It is moreover important to appreciate that table 6.A1 does *not* enable an assessment of the impact of a change of policy stance on the economy. It summarises the model's estimate of what the full counterfactual simulation would have looked like, assuming unchanged United Kingdom policy, and the other exogenous factors on trend. Its purpose is to provide corroboration for the counterfactual results.

The 'real interest rate' case

It was decided to explore an alternative definition of unchanged monetary policy concentrating on the level of real short-term interest rates instead of the real exchange rate. As is well known, there are serious problems in defining and measuring real interest rates since they involve agents' expectations of future nominal interest rates and the rate of inflation.[15] Because of the nature of the Bank model we have had to define the real interest rate in a backward-looking manner which must be only a crude approximation of what real interest rates actually were.

This approach to measuring unchanged monetary policy involved the nominal exchange rate being determined endogenously by the model, so the estimated effect of changes in monetary policy in this approach are critically dependent on the specification of the

1981	1982	1983	1984	1985	1986
11.0	*11.6*	*12.2*	*12.8*	*11.4*	9.7
−2.2	−4.3	−5.0	−4.2	−2.0	+1.2
−3.9	−3.8	−3.7	−3.5	−3.8	−6.3
1.6	1.7	1.1	0.8	−0.3	−3.4
0	−0.2	−0.4	−1.3	−1.4	−0.5
−0.1	−0.4	−0.7	−0.4	0.2	0.3
2.5	1.4	0.5	0.5	1.2	1.5
1.4	2.4	1.3	0	−0.7	−0.1
1.1	0.2	−0.2	0.1	0.7	1.3
11.4	8.6	*5.1*	*4.8*	*5.3*	*3.7*

exchange rate equation. The exchange rate equation used in this exercise has the real exchange rate as a function of differential real interest rates (the difference between domestic and overseas), the real oil price and the real current account balance.[16]

The choice of the precise counterfactual value for the real interest rate under this approach raises further difficult issues. United Kingdom real short-term interest rates, measured on a backward-looking basis, changed considerably during the 1970s, becoming heavily negative at times of exceptionally high inflation; forward-looking rates were probably a good deal less volatile, although one cannot be sure by how much. There is a question how far such rates can be taken to represent unchanged monetary stance, and whether some more conventional value, perhaps representative of a 'neutral' policy stance, reflecting the relative stance of policy in other countries (where real rates became substantially positive after 1980, as table 6.1 shows) might not be preferable.

Any solution must be somewhat arbitrary. One course was to adhere to the approach adopted for other key variables in the exercise by choosing as the counterfactual value the rate that prevailed around the *beginning* of the period, that is, the average historic rate seen during 1977–8 (−3.5 per cent). This implies a counterfactual stance of monetary policy that is exceptionally relaxed by historical standards, although less so than such a measure would imply during the mid-1970s. It also implies that the historic stance tightened after 1977–8, when the United Kingdom real interest rate

Table 6.4 Counterfactual exchange and interest rates: 'real interest rate' case

	1978	1979	1980
Real short-term interest rate, %[a]	−3.5	−3.5	−3.5
Real exchange rate	69.8	76.9	86.5
Counterfactual nominal exchange rate	79.8	82.4	87.9
Historic nominal exchange rate	81.5	87.3	96.1

Note: Historical values of real exchange rate and interest rates are in table 6.1.

rose considerably in relation to the starting level, as table 6.1 showed. The resulting counterfactual exchange rates were as in table 6.4.

Whether this particular choice of counterfactual gives a realistic measure of the change in the thrust of policy is again a matter for judgment. It is open to the same kind of objection arising from interest parity considerations as was mentioned in relation to the interest rate assumption in the constant exchange rate case. Indeed the present assumption is perhaps more vulnerable to such criticism, in that the protracted post-1980 decline in the counterfactual real exchange rate here lowers the relative yield on sterling assets.[17] In view of these considerations, several alternative values were explored for the counterfactual real interest rate, as reported later.[18]

For the purpose of this part of the exercise, nominal short-term interest rates in the counterfactual were at whatever level was necessary to ensure the chosen counterfactual real interest rate. Overseas real interest rates were kept at their historic level throughout. The results for the counterfactual real interest rate of −3.5 per cent are given in table 6.5.

Counterfactual inflation in this case turns out to be lower after 1978 until the middle of the period, when it accelerates sharply to reach rates that exceed those at the start. Much of the difference between the counterfactual and the base is accounted for by the influence of VAT and direct taxes, which assume a surprisingly important role in this simulation. Some light is shed on these results by comparing the real exchange rate and real interest rate counterfactuals. Initially inflation is lower in table 6.5 than in table 6.2 owing to a higher nominal exchange rate which is itself a

1981	1982	1983	1984	1985	1986
−3.5	−3.5	−3.5	−3.5	−3.5	−3.5
80.9	73.9	68.1	65.5	68.2	69.0
81.4	75.5	67.3	58.7	55.7	53.3
95.0	90.5	83.3	78.7	78.2	72.8

[a] Defined with reference to consumer price inflation.

consequence of higher differential real interest rates. In fact, differential real interest rates are less negative in the present case through most of the period (compare tables 6.4 and 6.1), and this puts upward pressure on the nominal and real exchange rate.

In addition the use of a real exchange rate equation in this part of the exercise means that any reduction in the United Kingdom price level will itself lead to upward pressure on the nominal exchange rate. This illustrates a problem in using an equation for the real exchange rate when analysing price shocks. We can write the exchange rate equation as:

$$\frac{P_d \cdot}{P_w} e = f(\underset{+}{R}, \underset{+}{P_o}, \underset{+}{BAL})$$

where *e* is the nominal effective exchange rate, *R* is the differential real interest rate, P_O is the real oil price, *BAL* is the real current account balance, P_w is the level of world prices and P_d is the level of domestic prices. The signs of the partial derivatives are shown below the arguments. Any shock which puts upward pressure on domestic prices relative to world prices will tend to put downward pressure on the nominal exchange rate, which in turn will put further upward pressure on domestic prices and so on. Thus the effects of the various shocks tend to be amplified by movements in the nominal exchange rate and as a consequence some of the results in table 6.5 look somewhat implausible. This applies especially to the strength of the inflationary effect attributed to differences between actual and counterfactual rates of tax and of National Insurance.

The effect of monetary policy is calculated by returning the

Table 6.5 Monetary policy defined in terms of real interest rates: effects on consumer price inflation

	1978	1979	1980
Counterfactual inflation	*9.7*	*12.3*	*11.5*
	(6.2)	(8.8)	(8.1)
Monetary policy	−0.1	−0.4	−0.8
Real oil prices	0	−0.2	0.5
Other world prices	−0.1	−0.1	0.7
World activity	−0.1	0	−0.1
Government expenditure	0.1	−0.1	−0.1
VAT	0	1.0	3.0
Other indirect taxes	−0.8	−1.1	−1.0
Direct taxes & NI	0.5	2.1	2.5
Historic base inflation	*9.2*	*13.5*	*16.2*
	(9.5)	(14.3)	(16.5)

Notes: See note 2 to table 6.2. In the counterfactual case the real short-term interest rate (the short-term interest rate relative to

short-term nominal interest rate to its historic path. With the stance of monetary policy defined in this way the model suggests that policy exerted progressively more downward pressure on inflation through the period, as the historic real interest rate increased in almost every year since 1978.

Table 6.6 presents the results of running the exercise with several alternative counterfactual levels of United Kingdom real interest rates and an alternative measure of inflation. If the counterfactual level of the real interest rate is set at zero (with reference to the non-oil GDP deflator) then monetary policy exerts less downward pressure on inflation over this period but the broad pattern of the effects is the same. A similar result applies *a fortiori* if the real interest rate is set at a positive 2 per cent. Downward pressure on inflation takes a long time to come through in these cases because actual real short-term interest rates are not consistently above the counterfactual measures until after 1980. This illustrates the difficulty in using a single measure as an indicator of the stance of monetary policy, for between 1979 and 1981 other indicators were signalling that monetary policy had been tightened significantly. It also suggests that backward-looking real interest rates are not a very reliable indicator of the stance of monetary policy over this period. Defining unchanged monetary policy in terms of constant *nominal* interest rates (at 7.6 per cent), with the real exchange rate endogenously determined, gives an impact for monetary policy

1981	1982	1983	1984	1985	1986
5.5	*5.7*	*6.8*	*10.5*	*13.3*	*13.5*
(2.0)	(2.3)	(3.3)	(7.0)	(9.8)	(10.0)
−1.8	−3.7	−5.8	−9.1	−13.6	−16.1
0.5	−0.4	−1.5	−2.5	−3.0	−3.3
0.7	0.1	−0.7	−0.7	−1.2	−3.4
0.2	0.4	0.8	0.3	0.7	1.5
−0.4	−1.1	−1.6	−1.6	−1.6	−1.9
3.4	3.3	3.2	4.0	5.6	6.4
0.7	1.8	1.3	0.7	0.6	1.3
2.6	2.5	2.6	3.2	4.5	5.7
11.4	*8.6*	*5.1*	*4.8*	*5.3*	*3.7*
(14.3)	(11.9)	(9.8)	(9.8)	(12.2)	(10.5)

consumer price inflation) is kept at −3.5 per cent. The nominal short-term interest rate is shown in parentheses.

Table 6.6 Estimated effects on consumer price inflation of monetary policy using alternative counterfactual real interest rates

	(1)	(2)	(3)	(4)	(5)
1978	−0.1	0.1	0.1	0.2	−0.1
1979	−0.4	0.2	0.2	0.4	−0.3
1980	−0.8	0.1	0.1	0.5	−0.8
1981	−1.8	0.2	0.1	0.8	−1.5
1982	−3.7	−0.6	−0.4	0.5	−2.9
1983	−5.8	−1.5	−1.3	−0.2	−4.7
1984	−9.1	−3.1	−2.8	−1.5	−6.8
1985	−13.6	−7.1	−5.0	−4.7	−9.1
1986	−16.1	−10.2	−6.6	−7.3	−9.9

Notes:
(1) Real short-term interest rate kept at −3.5 per cent, measured with reference to consumer prices.
(2) Real short-term interest rate kept at 0 per cent, measured with reference to the non-oil GDP deflator.
(3) Real short-term interest rate kept at 2 per cent, measured with reference to consumer prices.
(4) Real short-term interest rate at 2 per cent, measured with reference to the non-oil GDP deflator.
(5) *Nominal* short-term interest rate kept flat at 7.63 per cent.
All columns show the percentage point deviation in consumer price inflation from setting nominal interest rates at their historic base level as compared with their relevant counterfactual level.

Table 6.7 Monetary policy defined in terms of real interest rates: effects on consumer price inflation with shocks administered independently

	1978	1979	1980
Monetary policy	−0.1	−0.5	−0.7
	(−0.1)	(−0.4)	(−0.8)
Real oil prices	0	−0.2	0.4
	(0)	(−0.2)	(0.5)
Other world prices	−0.1	−0.2	0.7
	(−0.1)	(−0.1)	(0.7)
World activity	−0.1	0	−0.1
	(−0.1)	(0)	(−0.1)
Government expenditure	0	−0.1	−0.2
	(0.1)	(−0.1)	(−0.1)
VAT	0	0.9	3.1
	(0.1)	(1.0)	(3.0)
Other indirect taxes	−0.8	−1.2	−1.2
	(−0.8)	(−1.1)	(−1.0)
Direct taxes & NI	0.5	2.1	2.5
	(0.5)	(2.1)	(2.5)

Notes: See note 2 to table 6.2. Figures in brackets are from table 6.5.

which is between the −3.5 per cent and the 0 per cent real interest rate cases in terms of cumulative effects on the price level.

In the real exchange rate simulations discussed earlier, once the exchange rate has been exogenised, the results do not depend on the order in which the effects of each shock are removed from the counterfactual. However, this is not true when the exchange rate is endogenous. Hence, the results in table 6.5 do depend, to some extent, on the order in which the effects are analysed. The sensitivity of the results to changes in the ordering was assessed by repeating the exercise with each shock administered independently and the subsequent model run was compared to the base. In this case obviously no counterfactual is constructed. The results are presented in table 6.7 with the effects from table 6.5 in parentheses. Table 6.7 suggests that while the magnitudes of some of the results are dependent on the ordering, the broad conclusions from table 6.5 are unchanged.

1981	1982	1983	1984	1985	1986
−1.2	−2.6	−3.7	−5.1	−7.5	−9.4
(−1.8)	(−3.7)	(−5.8)	(−9.1)	(−13.6)	(−16.1)
0.4	−0.9	−2.3	−3.4	−4.3	−4.6
(0.5)	(−0.4)	(−1.5)	(−2.5)	(−3.0)	(−3.3)
0.7	0.1	−0.7	−0.7	−1.4	−3.9
(0.7)	(0.1)	(−0.7)	(−0.7)	(−1.2)	(−3.4)
0.3	0.4	0.8	0.3	0.6	1.6
(0.2)	(0.4)	(0.8)	(0.3)	(0.7)	(1.5)
−0.4	−1.3	−1.9	−2.0	−2.1	−2.5
(−0.4)	(−1.1)	(−1.6)	(−1.6)	(−1.6)	(−1.9)
3.6	3.4	3.6	4.5	6.0	7.0
(3.4)	(3.3)	(3.2)	(4.0)	(5.6)	(6.4)
0.6	1.6	1.2	0.5	0.4	1.0
(0.7)	(1.8)	(1.3)	(0.7)	(0.6)	(1.3)
2.6	2.5	2.6	3.2	4.5	5.7
(2.6)	(2.5)	(2.6)	(3.2)	(4.5)	(5.7)

Other factors influencing inflation

There are a number of other factors not analysed above which have probably had an effect on inflation over this period, the most important of which are likely to be changes in behaviour brought about by the new policy environment. Perhaps the most important factor to be considered is trend labour productivity. Actual labour productivity in manufacturing grew by around 4 per cent a year on average in the 1960s, 2.2 per cent a year in the 1970s and 5.6 per cent a year in the 1980s.[19] There has been considerable recent discussion about trend productivity (see, for example, Harvey *et al.*, 1986, Muellbauer, 1986, and Spencer, 1987). While there is some dispute about whether there has been an increase in trend productivity in the 1980s, there is no doubt that there was a very marked amount of labour shedding in the manufacturing sector during 1979–81. Evidence for this is contained in the single equation residuals for the labour demand schedule on the Bank model.

This labour shedding led to large increases in actual labour productivity and possibly to large declines in unit labour costs relative to what they would otherwise have been. One way of obtaining an estimate of the importance of the labour shakeout is to run the model with zero residuals on the labour demand schedule and examine the effect on inflation. This also gives an assessment of the effect on actual labour productivity being above the trend rate assumed in the equation throughout the 1980s. The results suggest that, had there not been a labour shakeout and assuming that wages did not increase in response to higher productivity, inflation in most years would have been up to one percentage point higher than it was. However, the upward pressure on prices in this simulation is slightly offset by an effect attributable to different employed factor utilisation rates. With more labour employed in the simulation relative to the level of output, employed factor utilisation rates are pushed below the base and this puts downward pressure on producers' margins and hence prices. This effect is quite powerful because of the size of the labour shakeout. It might be considered unrealistic that margins respond in this manner, and accordingly the simulation was repeated with employed factor utilisation rates constrained to the base. As would be expected, this constraint means that the effects of the labour shakeout on inflation are estimated to have been a little higher in almost every year.

Conclusions

The exercises reported have sought to show how a large econometric model may be used to explore the main influences on inflation since the important policy shifts of the late 1970s. The limitations of such exercises must be borne in mind: the results are dependent not only on the counterfactual definitions used but also on the structure of the model; and when simulations involve large and growing divergences from base levels, as here, the ability of coefficients in the model equations to portray real-world responses is increasingly open to question. Subject to these caveats, the analysis suggests that monetary and fiscal policy have both had an important influence on inflation over the past few years, although determining the magnitude of the effects is very hazardous. The variation in the results as between different counterfactuals provides some indication of the large ranges of uncertainty involved and serves as a reminder that the results should be treated with great caution.

One result suggested by the counterfactuals is that exogenous 'world' developments, with the notable exception of oil price changes, have not contributed systematically to lowering United

Kingdom inflation during the period. This does not mean that the influence of external factors has been negligible. The impact of non-oil world prices has been adverse overall because of the sharp increase in commodity prices which occurred in the late 1970s and early 1980s. The more recent decline in commodity prices only begins to have an effect from 1985. In contrast, there is a suggestion that changes in the real oil price since 1978 have contributed a marked disinflationary effect overall, if the exchange rate is assumed to respond to changes in the real oil price, although this too changed recently. This is a distinctly counterintuitive result in a period which saw a very large rise in oil prices in its early years; it depends of course on the assumed relationship between the real oil price and the real exchange rate. It must be stressed that although that relationship does not seem unreasonable in relation to views widely expressed by informed commentators, it is not firmly based on empirical evidence.

If the model numbers are taken at face value, the relatively direct impacts of fiscal changes seem not to have been helpful in reducing inflation overall. Restraints on public expenditure and changes in 'other' indirect taxes had comparatively small net effects overall, whereas the effects attributed to VAT changes are estimated to have been clearly inflationary, as have the combined effects of changes in direct taxes and National Insurance contributions. An important feature here seems to have been the short-run influence of employers' labour taxes, the inflationary effects of which have more than offset the disinflationary effects of income tax reductions. We are inclined to discount the larger estimates of the inflationary impact from these sources shown in table 6.5.

The tentative conclusion that fiscal changes have not on balance helped reduce inflation applies only to the effects that can be picked up in the Bank model. Such a conclusion is not inconsistent with the view that fiscal policy in its totality has helped to reduce inflation during the period through the role it played in supporting monetary policy via the MTFS. We suspect that this influence has operated principally through the contribution that smaller public sector deficits will have made to lowering inflation expectations and sustaining the real exchange rate; but there is no way in which such influences can be assessed using the Bank model because its structure has no formal links between the overall fiscal stance, inflation expectations, and/or the exchange rate.

All the simulations suggest that the strong exchange rate was an important factor tending to reduce inflation, and are consistent with the view that the move to a non-accommodating monetary stance in stages between 1976 and 1979 played a large and decisive role in reducing inflation, principally through its impact on the exchange rate. Upper and lower bounds for this impact were given in tables 6.2 and 6.3, and the implied answer is somewhere in between. This conclusion depends heavily on the assumption that monetary policy, or more broadly the MTFS, was an important influence in causing the real exchange rate to appreciate well above its average 1973–7 level, and to keep it from subsiding as rapidly as it might otherwise have done. We would put less weight on the later set of simulations that focus instead on the real interest rate, despite the fact that the short-term interest rate has become increasingly the major instrument of monetary policy, because we distrust the powerful nominal exchange rate–price linkages implied by adopting a real exchange rate equation in these simulations. Nevertheless, these later simulations do provide a degree of corroboration for the earlier ones, in that they also suggest that tighter monetary

Table 6A.1

	GDPO growth (% pa)	Unemployment (mn)	Inflation (% pa)
Real economy: the historic base			
1978	3.5	1.23	9.2
1979	3.2	1.14	13.5
1980	−2.7	1.45	16.2
1981	−1.6	2.27	11.4
1982	1.7	2.63	8.6
1983	3.1	2.87	5.1
1984	3.2	3.00	4.8
1985	3.7	3.11	5.3
1986	2.9	3.19	3.7
Real economy: 'The North Sea oil' variant			
1978	4.1	1.21	9.8
1979	5.4	0.90	13.1
1980	0.7	0.75	14.5
1981	4.1	0.74	11.0
1982	3.4	0.37	11.6
1983	2.2	0.32	12.2
1984	2.0	0.51	12.8
1985	4.7	0.65	11.4
1986	4.6	0.52	9.7

[a] Output per man hour in manufacturing.

policy was in due course responsible for much of the fall in inflation, whichever of a range of counterfactual interest rate values is chosen.

Some support for these conclusions can moreover be drawn from the finding, after examining other possible causes, that no other factor appears to be capable of explaining nearly as much of the large fall in inflation that took place during the period.

The foregoing may serve to illustrate some of the pitfalls and difficulties of using a large model for policy evaluation, especially in the monetary/financial area. It should be stressed that the exercises were done with minimal intervention and are therefore highly model-dependant. It is felt that much can be learned from such work, both about improving the model and about how it can be used. Such work is of course only one element among many that go into the assessment of policy.

Productivity[a] (% pa)	PSBR as a % of GDP	Current account as % of GDP	Nominal exchange rate	Real exchange rate
0.7	5.04	0.58	81.5	73.0
1.2	6.47	−0.36	87.3	84.3
−0.7	5.12	1.27	96.1	100.0
5.8	4.24	2.43	95.0	103.7
4.7	1.77	1.42	90.5	99.6
7.5	3.88	1.04	83.3	94.1
4.7	3.19	0.40	78.7	95.2
3.2	2.14	0.83	78.2	99.3
2.9	0.63	−0.29	72.8	95.1
1.0	5.73	0.16	79.3	69.4
1.8	6.35	0.04	74.0	69.4
0.1	5.17	3.29	68.6	69.4
5.5	4.89	5.00	63.8	69.4
1.5	1.63	4.56	60.7	69.4
4.2	2.61	4.84	56.3	69.4
4.1	2.06	5.45	50.3	69.4
5.1	1.10	6.22	47.5	69.4
3.4	−2.06	6.17	46.9	69.4

Notes

1 Douglas Gale (1983), in a book which attempted to provide insights for monetary economies in a rigorous way, concludes: 'The best current research into macro related issues produces exciting theory but . . . it produces little of use to people who make the decisions'.

2 Rt Hon Nigel Lawson, MP, 'The British Experiment', Fifth Mais Lecture delivered at the City University Business School, Centre for Banking and Finance, 18 June 1984 (HM Treasury, Press Office).

3 Rt Hon Robin Leigh Pemberton, 'The Instruments of Monetary Policy', Seventh Mais Lecture delivered to the City University Business School, Centre for Banking and Finance, 13 May, 1987 (see also Leigh-Pemberton, 1987).

4 For a discussion of how the Lucas critique might be overcome, see Wallis (1980) and Hall (1987b). This requires the model to be solved in a forward-looking manner with appropriately defined expectations variables. Unfortunately, this is not feasible with the current Bank model.

5 The introductory text covering the Worswick and Budd articles states that monetary policy is defined as changes in real interest rates. However, this is represented in practice by actual differences in the minimum lending rate from a level of 11½ per cent.

6 For a fuller discussion of the structure of the Bank model and the effects of interest rates see, respectively, Patterson *et al.* (1987) and Easton and Patterson (1987).

7 The important 'news' for markets in 1979 may have been as much the rejection of expansionist policies which might have displaced the previous government's non-accommodative stance, as the acceptance of new non-accommodative policies.

8 A further option, to meet efficient markets arguments, would have been to adjust overseas real interest rates to give, say, a constant real differential in favour of United Kingdom rates at or close to its starting level. There would then be another column in the tables to show the effects attributable to overseas real interest rates. In a counterfactual based on a constant United Kingdom real exchange rate, as here, the implications of this option for inflation would be zero, or virtually so. In a counterfactual based on an endogenous United Kingdom exchange rate, described later, the rate of inflation under this option would be lower than that shown, because the constant yield differential would have meant a higher path for sterling. However, the effects attributed to United Kingdom monetary policy would be unaffected in either case.

9 In contrast with the conventional view of the United States economy, which has argued that a tightening of fiscal policy would lead via lower real interest rates to a lower dollar.

10 This follows from the exogeneity of world prices and the oil price in the model. If the world prices were made to depend partly on oil prices, larger effects on United Kingdom inflation would be attributed to them, and less to non-oil prices.

11 This ignores any influence that either may have had on the real exchange rate via expectational or confidence effects. In principle, any influence that public expenditure cuts contributed to reducing inflation will be included in the second column (that is, under 'monetary policy'). This qualification also applies to effects of tax changes, discussed below.

12 All the effects reported are clearly dependent on the structure of the model and as such as susceptible to the criticism that they illustrate the model's properties as much as the true effects of the various changes. The sensitivity of the results was examined by replicating the exercise with an alternative set of earnings equations based on Mackie (1987), which admittedly suffer from the same instability property as that described earlier. The results are affected to a small extent but the broad conclusions remain unchanged.

13 Thus, a 10 per cent increase in the real oil price leads to a 3 per cent increase in the real exchange rate. In this simulation only the *ex ante* effects of changes in the real oil price are allowed to affect the exchange rate; that is, second round effects from domestic prices to the exchange rate are suppressed.

14 This seems consistent with official estimates at the time which attributed about one third to one half of the strength of sterling in the 1979–81 period to North Sea oil. See HM Treasury (1981), page 131.

15 For a discussion of the conceptual and practical difficulties see Bank of England (1983).

16 The exchange rate equation is based on Hall (1983) and is thus similar to the equation used by Saville and Gardiner (1986). However, in adapting the equation for use on the Bank model, the definitions of some of the variables have been changed.

17 Even so the problem is acute only in the three years 1981–3, when the real United Kingdom rate of return available to foreigners was some −11 per cent a year, whereas they could earn over +4 per cent a year at home (see table 6.1).

18 As noted earlier, objections based on efficient market arguments could alternatively be met by adjusting overseas interest rates to give a rational-seeming differential with United Kingdom rates, but the impact attributed to United Kingdom monetary policy would be unaffected. Admittedly, the counterfactual/historic inflation gap would be different, so that the proportionate contribution of United Kingdom monetary policy to the gap would be different, but not radically so.

19 These figures are output per head in manufacturing for the periods 1963–9, 1970–79, 1980–86.

Comment on Chapter 6

John D. Whitley

This chapter follows in the tradition of counterfactual policy exercises conducted on macro models, earlier examples being Artis *et al.* (1984) and Saville and Gardiner (1986). It raises some questions about these exercises in general and some in respect of the particular approach adopted in the Bank exercise.

The first point is a particular one. Given the emphasis assigned to the role of expectations over this period by many commentators, it is disappointing that the Bank's analysis can throw no light on this. Although the effects of exchange rate expectations can be thought to be implicitly included, the influence of expectations on quantity variables such as stockbuilding and employment are not. Yet these are often regarded as leading features in the recession of 1980–1 (Buiter and Miller, 1983).

The usual approach in counterfactual exercises of this type is to set paths for the policy variables simulation which are 'neutral' or reflect 'unchanged policies'. A common assumption is that of unchanged tax rates and trend government spending for neutral fiscal policy and constant interest rates for neutral monetary policy.

However, it is important that the fiscal and monetary policies are mutually consistent. This requires the explicit consideration of the government budget constraint. In the Bank study there is the assumption that any change in the PSBR is fully funded by debt sales but this funding is additionally assumed to be possible at the prevailing interest rate.

In the Bank study it is assumed that a neutral monetary policy either consists of a predetermined constant real exchange rate or alternatively a constant real interest rate (achieved by appropriate changes in nominal interest rates). The results are sensitive to the choice of monetary policy stance and one might draw quite different qualitative conclusions regarding the timing of the impact of monetary policy on inflation as well as in its overall effect.

Of particular interest is the approach adopted in the first definition of monetary policy stance, that is, a constant real exchange rate. As the Bank find it impractical to target the exchange rate by an exogenous policy variable within the model, the assumption made is to exogenise relative normalised unit labour costs directly but with constant nominal interest rates. Since no explicit link is specified between monetary policy and the exchange rate, several problems arise.

Firstly, although an outside observer may be able to replicate the Bank's exercise, he or she cannot investigate the effects of alternative monetary policy stances in respect of the real exchange rate since the implicit model relating monetary policy to the real exchange rate is not fully elucidated.

Secondly, even though the Bank exercise may result in the same real exchange rate as that obtained when a policy instrument is explicitly included in the model, the effects on other variables of interest, and in this instance inflation, may well be different. As an example consider the use of interest rates to achieve an exchange rate target. Interest rates do have effects on other variables in the Bank model, including inflation. The Bank use constant nominal interest rates but there is no way of knowing whether these are consistent with the chosen value of the real exchange rate.

If such a potential bias is to be removed it is necessary in the Bank's case that the implied monetary policy instrument, if it is other than interest rates, should have no impact on the macroeconomic aggregates other than through the exchange rate. But, as we note above, we have no way of assessing whether this is so in the absence of a specified link between monetary policy and the exchange rate.

Third, exogenisation may bias the calculation of the relative effects of monetary and fiscal policy. The Bank approach is to calculate a model solution under neutral policy paths and then derive the individual policy effects by removing the neutral assumption for that particular policy. Thus to calculate the role of monetary policy the model is simulated when all policy instruments other than monetary policy are set at neutral values and those for monetary policy are set at historical values. The impact of monetary policy is then derived by contrasting this simulation with that where all policy variables are in their neutral setting. This is the so-called integral approach and can be contrasted with the piecemeal approach, where each policy element is simulated directly, rather than derived as a residual. This is recognised in table 6.7 in respect of the constant real interest rate definition of neutral monetary policy although the statement that this does not apply to the exogenous real exchange rate case is misleading. This arises because the integral approach assumes that the policies are independent yet this is not true of the Bank *model* where both fiscal and monetary policy influence the real exchange rate. The order of calculations therefore matters in this case. If we start with counterfactual monetary policy with its assumption of an exogenous real exchange rate, then add counterfactual fiscal policy, it is clear that fiscal policy can have no further effect on the real exchange rate, but if we reverse the order and start with fiscal policy we (correctly) include the real exchange rate effects of fiscal policy and hence do not overestimate the real exchange rate contribution of monetary policy. The consolation in the Bank case is that the qualitative conclusions are not severely affected although the magnitudes differ and, as the Bank recognises, the inflation effects might be best viewed as arising from the MTFS in general rather than monetary policy alone.

In general, as is acknowledged in the chapter, one may learn more about the models from these exercises than about the conduct of economic policy. In order to have confidence in the policy results we need to be convinced that the model can explain history itself – not by including estimation residuals *ex post* which guarantee this (although the scale of these residuals may be informative) but by evidence from *ex ante* model forecasts. For example the Bank model attributes a strong role to oil prices on the exchange rate and hence the fall in oil prices in 1986 does have important effects in explaining inflation in their exercise. However several independent forecasters experienced model failure at this time as the fall in oil prices had a far wider effect on the exchange rate and inflation than the models would have predicted (Wallis *et al.*, 1987). The role of oil prices on the exchange rate has since been revised down in these models showing that forecast failure does provide useful information about the relevance of the model to the real world. Similarly the introduction of forward consistent expectations in some of the quarterly models (LBS, NIESR) in recent years has often been justified in terms of explaining forecasting failures around 1980. Faced with the situation where different models attribute different effects to policy in recent years (for example, contrast the results with the Liverpool model in this volume) a necessary condition for evaluation of the conflicting results is some information about how well history itself was explained. Only then can we start to focus on the relative effects of alternative policies derived from the models.

Chapter 6 is to be welcomed as a contribution to the policy evaluation area. It is useful in outlining some of the problems involved in setting a neutral monetary policy stance. It shows that the behaviour of the real exchange rate may have been very important to the development of the United Kingdom economy in the early 1980s but, given that the behaviour of the exchange rate is difficult to explain over this period, it cannot quantify the relative contributions to exchange rate changes and hence inflation. But the suspicion, gained from reading this chapter, is that the MTFS was responsible for a large degree of the appreciation of the real exchange rate and this is an important finding which deserves further investigation.

Comment on Chapter 6

Simon Wren-Lewis

The main part of this chapter presents and analyses some interesting simulations of the Bank's macroeconomic model. As a prelude, the authors present a 'theoretical background'. I found this first part of the chapter worrying in a number of ways. The first point to make is that there is no necessary connection between the two parts of the chapter; while the latter deals with monetary policy in terms of levels of interest rates and exchange rates with little or no reference to money, the first section is concerned with targeting the money stock. The absence of any linkage is unfortunate, partly because it would have been useful in this context to have a theoretical and empirical account of the transmission mechanisms in the Bank's model. However, even on its own terms, I had serious reservations about the arguments in this initial section.

The main part of the first section deals with the rationale for money supply targets. It gives three; that controlling money may stabilise GNP, that it enhances policy credibility, and finally the familiar TINA: there is no alternative. I would question whether any of these three played a critical role either *ex ante*, in bringing about the adoption of monetary targets, or *ex post*, in explaining their continuing (but diminishing) appeal.

The first rationale takes us back to Poole's well-known comparison of the merits of interest rate and money control in stabilising GNP. A key parameter in this analysis is the variance of the money demand equation, and the larger this is the less sensible is monetary targeting. One general lesson we can probably draw from a decade of monetary targets is that the error term on most money demand functions is not even stationary because of periodic financial innovation, often induced by control itself. Even if we are able to model such shifts in the demand function, its variance is likely to be large because of the buffer stock characteristic of money. This chapter attempts to turn this problem into a virtue, by noting that a buffer stock may be a useful leading indicator. While this may be true, using money as an indicator for policy, say as one argument in a feedback rule for interest rates, it is quite different from using money as *the* intermediate target. It does not normally make economic sense to attempt to fix a buffer stock.

The issue of policy credibility has nothing intrinsically to do with targeting money, and of course targets that are not met or move in mysterious ways hardly enhance credibility. As for TINA, chapter 6 in fact gives one very good alternative, exchange rate targets, and says nothing in favour of monetary targets as opposed to exchange rate targets or zones. The authors in fact suggest that both variables may provide useful signals to guide monetary policy. This seems fairly uncontentious, but such an eclectic approach is a far cry from a policy (the original MTFS) designed to achieve a fixed path for a monetary aggregate.

Moving to the main part of the chapter, we should note that the scope of the study goes beyond that of looking at the effects of monetary policy. Simulations are also presented looking at the impact of various fiscal policy changes, and external events. The Bank should be commended, both in using its model in an exercise of this type and, of equal importance nowadays, allowing the results into the public arena. In discussing the simulation results the authors address the key issues in a clear and interesting way.

The first problem the authors have to grapple with is the definition of a 'neutral' monetary policy to compare actual policy with. As already noted, definitions in terms of monetary aggregates are eschewed in favour of definitions involving interest rates and exchange rates. In the Bank's model, the latter seems to do most of the work in terms of inflation. The authors note that conjunctions of interest rate and exchange rate paths may be inconsistent, and in one section they attempt to achieve consistency by using an exchange rate equation.

While the chapter discusses most of the relevant issues here, things might have been a little clearer if two conceptual points had been clarified at the outset. The first concerns the way the various simulations that lead from history to the full counterfactual have been split up. The dividing lines here can be drawn for analytical convenience, or to produce consistent plausible scenarios. For example, it is interesting to divide the external changes into activity changes and price changes and look at their effects separately, but in reality changes in world activity would have induced price changes and so each individual simulation is not a realistic self-contained entity. If the authors were after analytical convenience, as their treatment of the world simulations suggests, then it would also have been useful to split up the effects of interest rate and exchange rate changes. If, alternatively, each simulation is designed to be realistic, then the treatment of world interest rates needs to be addressed, which brings in the second point.

One dominant feature of the external environment over the period was the sharp tightening of monetary policy led by the United States. As table 6.1 shows, United Kingdom real rates did little more than follow world rates up in the early 1980s. In this situation, any definition of a neutral or unchanged monetary policy independent of world developments seems to be extremely problematic. With this in mind, one possibility the authors might have explored is to define monetary policy in terms of the interest rate changes required to produce a roughly constant real exchange rate at a level consistent with long-run current account equilibrium.

Turning to the simulations themselves, it would have been helpful to have had a little more quantitative information on the characteristics of the transmission mechanisms in the monetary policy simulations. One of the advantages in using a structural model is that it provides information on output, unemployment, real wages, the current account and so on, which, apart from being of interest in their own right, help in assessing the plausibility and influences behind the inflation effects. The authors seem to be on dubious ground when they appear to suggest that the inflation effects are somehow more soundly based than the model's output for these other variables. Certainly the figures presented in Appendix 6.1 are striking, and immediately raise further questions about the model's results and properties. One fairly easy calculation that might have been illuminating here would have been to calculate the expression for the NAIRU implied by the model's wage and price equations. As both direct and indirect taxes seem to be below historical levels in the counterfactual, this may have tended to reduce both the NAIRU and inflation in these simulations.

7 Wealth Targets, Exchange Rate Targets and Macroeconomic Policy*

Andrew Blake, David Vines and Martin Weale

Introduction

Objectives of policy: price stability and national wealth

It is generally accepted that any sensible economic policy should contain an element designed to suppress inflation, although there is considerable disagreement about the appropriate policy with which to achieve this end. Among the various suggestions are monetary targets, money GDP targets, a fixed nominal exchange rate and incomes policy. In this chapter we assume that the counter-inflationary element of macroeconomic policy is represented by a money GDP target. Meade first proposed this some years ago (Meade, 1978, Vines, Maciejowski and Meade, 1983) and it now appears that money GDP plays at least some part in official policymaking.

However, we argue that money GDP should not be the sole aim of economic policy. Policymakers face an understandable temptation to control inflation through policies which reduce inflationary pressures by raising current living standards at the expense of future living standards. We advocate the use of a target value for national wealth to be used concurrently with a target value for money GDP, as a means of preventing this.[1]

We seek here to demonstrate how financial policy rules (that is, fiscal and monetary policy) can be designed which both steer money GDP to a target value and keep national wealth close to a target value. We shall see that if wages are strongly indexed to prices, and thus if real wages are sticky, the temptation for the authorities to buy out inflation at the expense of wealth will be much increased. For example, if real wages are sticky, a real

* This research has been supported by the Centre for Economic Policy Research, the Department of Applied Economics of Cambridge University, the Economic and Social Research Council, Glasgow University and the Houblon-Norman Fund, through the award of its Fellowship to Martin Weale. James Meade has provided invaluable guidance for the work described here.

exchange rate appreciation will be attractive as a means of reducing inflationary pressures, despite the fact that it reduces both domestic and foreign investment. We seek to design policy rules which will avoid such difficulties, and argue that the appropriate structure for these rules is determined by the structure of the economy, in particular by the extent of wage–price indexation observed in the labour market.

Intermediate targets and policies: monetary targets and exchange rate targets

Our chapter has a second objective. Intermediate targets can provide a useful guide for short-term policymaking. Movements in the money stock have at times been used as a guide to indicate the appropriate setting of the short-term interest rate. However, more recently, the use of the money stock as an intermediate target has become less popular. This is partly a consequence of the practical difficulties of monetary control. It is also partly because the use of the money stock as an intermediate target has led policymakers to set interest rates at levels which have had undesirable and unintended effects on the exchange rate.[2]

Increasingly the exchange rate has been adopted as an intermediate target of policy. This need not necessarily imply that policymakers aim to stabilise exchange rates at levels fixed either in nominal or in real terms. A more flexible use of the exchange rate as an intermediate target can be achieved if a rule is specified indicating how this target is to be set. Within such a context the operation of monetary policy requires another set of rules (that is, for the interest rate and for foreign exchange market intervention) in order to guide the actual exchange rate to its target value. Our second aim is to describe the use of the exchange rate as an intermediate target in this fashion.

Thus the policy rules to be studied here examine the pursuit of targets for money GDP and national wealth when: (i) the exchange rate target is not fixed but follows a 'closed loop' feedback rule; (ii) monetary policy steers the exchange rate to its target; and (iii) fiscal policy is also used.

Outline of the chapter

First we discuss these issues using an analytic model. The model is presented in the second section after which we discuss the required steady state instrument movements in response to exogenous shocks. The fourth and fifth sections take up dynamic adjustments and the stability of control and this is followed by an analysis of comparative advantage of fiscal and monetary policy. All this analytic work demonstrates the profound impact that wage indexation has on policy options.

The second part of the chapter is empirical. We quantify the investigations using responses from a model of the United Kingdom economy which we have built from version 7 of the National Institute model. First we take up the issue of comparative advantage in this model and then we present sets of fully-blown empirical rules designed to control money GDP and national wealth, and to keep the exchange rate close to its intermediate target level. We do this for two different sets of assumptions about wage indexation.

Summary of conclusions

Our major conclusion concerns the crucial importance of the structure of the labour market for the operation of all of: the exchange rate target, monetary policy, and fiscal policy. We show that different types of policy rules must be designed, depending on whether wages are indexed or unindexed, at least on the basis of the plausible assumption which we make, that fiscal fine-tuning has be to carried out by variation in tax rates.[3] Our work implies that even a moderate degree of wage indexation would make it impossible to operate Williamson's system of exchange rate target zones (Edison *et al.*, 1987).

A subsidiary conclusion concerns the role of expectations formation. In common with other modellers over the past ten years we have taken the Lucas critique seriously. Thus the analytical work which follows assumes either regressive or 'rational', that is, model-consistent, expectations in financial markets. This allows us to investigate whether the formation of expectations is of major importance in policy design. In our empirical work we allow for the possibility of forward-looking model-consistent expectations formation in the determination of all of: the exchange rate (which influences trade flows and prices), human capital (which influences consumption), the rate of interest on consols (which also influences consumption) and the stock market valuation ratio (which influences investment and consumption). In addition a simple form of model-consistent expectations is allowed for in wage fixing. We find that policy rules can be found which perform satisfactorily independently of whether expectations are model-consistent or regressive. This issue, we conclude, is not nearly as important as that of wage indexation in influencing the design of appropriate policy rules.

We also have a methodological conclusion. We suggest that much insight into policy design on large empirical macroeconomic models is provided by small analytical representations of them. We show that analysis, on small algebraic models, of first, steady state instrument movements; second, stability; and third, comparative advantage of instruments, is very revealing. It provides a useful guide when choosing the structure of simple control rules to regulate an actual economic model.

The analytic model

The formation of macroeconomic policy will be examined using an expanded version of the Dornbusch (1976) model.[4] The model is one in which stock effects are neglected despite their undoubted importance; investment behaviour is modelled in a very simple way; no role exists for foreign exchange intervention and the model does not incorporate any proper production function. Nevertheless the model does allow us to explore the effects of attempting to stabilise prices by means of either monetary or fiscal policy and in the context of an exchange rate target. The model's dynamic structure does not allow us to explore some of the issues which can be considered using short-term models (Aizeman and Frenkel, 1985 for example). However to be set against this is the fact, to which we attach very considerable importance, that the model allows us to consider issues such as steady state outcomes and the stability of different policies, as well as some short-term responses.

Right at the beginning we make a very helpful simplification. In our analytic model we specify the counter-inflation policy target in terms of a designed price level. We have argued elsewhere for the importance of a money GDP target. Nothing presented below is intended to detract from the argument that a money GDP target may be useful, and our empirical work makes use of such a target. However, for the purpose of obtaining a simple understanding of the workings of our system, and in particular its dynamics, it is helpful to express counter-inflation policy in terms of the price level rather than in terms of money GDP.

Policy objectives

There is a target path, $p^\star$, for the level of the domestic (factor cost) output prices, p. It is sometimes convenient to express this as equal to the original price level, p_0, augmented over time by the target inflation rate, $\dot{p}^\star$. Prices are measured in logarithms, thus we may write $p^\star = p_0 + \dot{p}^\star t$.

There is also a target, $i^\star$, for the level of national investment, i.[5] We measure i as the logarithm of investment expenditures, in units of gross domestic product. i includes both domestic investment and foreign investment (the latter is equal to the surplus on the current account of the balance of payments).

The labour market

Wage rates, w, are assumed to respond to excess demand in the labour market, to price inflation and to changes in the rate of tax. Prices and quantities are measured in logarithms with the base value of log prices set at zero. Thus we write

$$\dot{w} = \bar{\beta} + \beta_1(l^d - l^s) + \beta_2(\dot{p} - \eta\dot{a}) + \beta_3\dot{s} + \beta_4 p \qquad (1)$$

where $\bar{\beta}$ is a constant and l^d and l^s represent labour demand and labour supply respectively. a is the real exchange rate, measured in units of foreign currency per unit of domestic currency, adjusted for inflation in domestic output prices, so that a fall in a represents a real depreciation.[6] The (pre-tax) price of consumption on goods is $p - \eta a$ (and its rate of change is $\dot{p} - \eta\dot{a}$) since it is assumed that a fraction η of spending is directed towards imports.

In this equation we do not distinguish the effects of direct taxes from those of indirect taxes. It is widely argued that the inflationary consequences of indirect tax changes are much stronger than are those of direct tax changes. This is a phenomenon which we would not wish to rely on for purposes of economic management, because we suspect that any systematic attempt to exploit it would result in labour market behaviour changing so that it was no longer true.

p is the 'core' rate of inflation, and is exogenous. We do not in this analytical section consider mechanisms by which the core rate may be brought into equality with the actual rate of inflation.[7] Instead we assume here that the core rate of inflation is the same as the government's inflation target.[8] Thus we write

$$p = p^\star \qquad (2)$$

Homogeneity of degree 1 of wage inflation with respect to price inflation requires $\beta_2 + \beta_4 = 1$ and we also assume this from now on.

A simple labour supply curve is specified

$$l_s^s = \bar{l}_s + \beta_5(w - (p - \eta a)) - \beta_6 s \qquad (3)$$

where $\bar{l}_s$ is a constant. We abstract from shifts in the supply curve over time, due, for example to the growth in workers' aspirations.[9] We do not embody any intertemporal substitution effects in this supply curve.

In addition to the labour supply and labour demand curves, an embryonic short-run production function may be embodied in the assumption that labour demand is proportional to output, y. We abstract from productivity growth.[10] This gives

$$l^d = y + \bar{l}^d \qquad (4)$$

Equations 1, 2, 3 and 4 combine to produce a Philips curve augmented by a response of wages to price changes and to a target level of the real wage adjusted for tax effects.

$$\dot{w} = \bar{\beta}' + \beta_1 y + \beta_2(\dot{p} - \eta\dot{a}) + \beta_3\dot{s} + \beta_4 p^{\star}$$
$$- \beta_1\beta_5(w-(p - \eta a)) + \beta_1\beta_6 s \qquad (5)$$

where $\bar{\beta}'$ is a constant. This wage equation is typical of the wage equations found for the major European countries (Layard and Nickell, 1985).[11] It implies that the factors influencing wage inflation may be split into four: first, core inflation; second, demand-pull pressures caused by a high level[12] of y; third, cost-push pressures caused by a depreciated level of the real exchange rate and a high level of taxes; and fourth, cost-push pressures caused by a falling real exchange rate and a rising tax rate. We call the first set of cost-push factors 'long-run cost-push', and the second set 'short-run cost-push'.

In passing we may note an important dynamic implication of the two sets of cost-push pressures. The upward cost-push pressure on wages of a high level of tax is greater during the process of raising the tax (when both the long-run and short-run cost-push pressures are present) than it will be during the subsequent period in which the rate of tax is stabilised at the higher level (when only the long-run cost-push pressures are present). Similarly the upward cost-push pressure on wages of a lower real exchange rate is greater during the period in which the real exchange rate is falling than it will be subsequently when the real exchange rate has stabilised at the new lower level.

Output

Output is demand-determined and is represented by a simple IS curve

$$y = \bar{\gamma} - \varkappa(\gamma_1 r + \gamma_2 a + \gamma_3 s - j) \qquad (6)$$

where $\bar{\gamma}$ is a constant. y is measured as the deviation of the logarithm of output from its initial level. γ_1, γ_2 and γ_3 represent the 'impact effects' on demand, as a proportion of the level of output, of changes in r, a and s respectively; j is real government spending, measured in deviations from its initial proportion of the initial level of output. $\varkappa$ is the Kahn-Keynes multiplier which augments all these impact effects on demand in the usual way. (Care is needed here in the choice of units and proportions because the model is log-linear). We abstract from any trends in the constant $\bar{\gamma}$, or in government spending.

Prices

The price of domestic output is set by a markup, $\bar{m}$ on unit labour costs, $w - \bar{l}^d$; it is assumed that there are no imported raw materials. In logarithms we write

$$p = \bar{m} + w - \bar{l}_d \tag{7}$$

National investment

National investment, i, is the sum of home and foreign investment. It plays no role in the dynamics of the model but, since the economy is assumed to have a target for the level of investment, it is essential to consider its determinants. A real interest rate term γ_1 represents the effects of that variable on domestic investment, while terms in the real exchange rate and in output are included as a consequence of their effects on the net foreign balance. The coefficient $\bar{i}$ is a constant; we abstract from any trend in this.[13]

$$i = \bar{i} - \gamma_1 r - \gamma_2 a - \eta y \tag{8}$$

The financial markets

It is assumed that there is perfect substitutability between home and foreign assets, so that the expected rate of change of the real exchange rate depends only on the gap between the home and foreign real interest rates

$$\dot{a}^e = r_f - r \tag{9}$$

There is a simple LM curve which could be used in the model, showing the relation between nominal income, the nominal interest rate $(r + \dot{p})$ and the money stock, m

$$m = y + p - \epsilon(r + \dot{p}) \tag{10}$$

If a monetary target were to be adopted then this equation would play a crucial role as the determinant of interest rates in the short term and the price level in the long term. However, in the examples which we consider in detail, an interest rate rule is used. In such circumstances the LM curve is an appendage required solely for the sake of completeness. It is true the LM curve is important because the proportion of outstanding government debt in the form of money affects the amount of interest the government has to pay and therefore the budget deficit. However the present model does not show the effects of that deficit on interest payments, and therefore the extent to which the national debt is financed by non-interest-bearing rather than interest-bearing debt has no effect on the behaviour of other variables.

Expectations

We consider two naive assumptions about the formation of expectations in the foreign exchange markets. The easiest approach is that of model-consistent expectations. This assumption is very simply

$$\dot{a}^e = \dot{a} \tag{11a}$$

The assumption of model-consistent expectations is often regarded as an approximation to the slightly more realistic assumption of rational expectations.

The alternative expectational assumption which we consider is that of regressive expectations. Depreciation of the real exchange rate in one period is expected to be followed by appreciation in the next period. In the limiting case of continuous times, this reduces to

$$\dot{a}^e = -\phi_1 \dot{a} \tag{11b}$$

Expectations are not fulfilled except in the steady state, when $\dot{a} = 0$.

A common alternative form of regressive expectation depicts the real exchange rate as expected to return gradually to some long-run steady-state level, rather than (as here) being expected to reverse the direction of its present change. However, such a form is not suitable for simulating in our model since it requires the identification of a long-run steady-state exchange rate. (We were in any case reluctant to make the assumption, in our regressive expectations model, that the long-run steady-state real exchange rate was easily identifiable.) But the present formulation has the feature – arguably a disadvantage – that, with regressive expectations, the real exchange rate only responds gradually when the model is shocked.

Open loop dynamics and the policy problem
After substitution we may express the behaviour of the 'open-loop' (that is, uncontrolled) economy equations in terms of the policy instruments, r and s, and the exogenous constants.

The first of these equations, for price inflation, comes from equations (5) and (7). After substitution for output from the IS curve, we find[14]

$$\dot{p} = \bar{\beta}' + \beta_1[\bar{\gamma} - \varkappa(\gamma_1 r + \gamma_2 a + \gamma_3 s - j)] + \beta_2(\dot{p} - \eta\dot{a}) + \beta_3\dot{s} + \beta_4 p^\star - \beta_1\beta_5(w-(p - \eta a)) + \beta_1\beta_6 s.$$

Noting that $w - p = \bar{l}^d - \bar{m}$ (from equation (7) we may re-express this, after grouping terms, as

$$\dot{p} = \bar{\alpha} - \alpha_1\varkappa\gamma_1 r - (\alpha_1\varkappa\gamma_2 + \alpha_5\eta)a - (\alpha_1\varkappa\gamma_3 - \alpha_6)s - \alpha_2\eta\dot{a} + \alpha_3\dot{s} + \varrho^\star \tag{12}$$

where $\bar{\alpha} = [\bar{\beta}' + \beta_1(\bar{\gamma} + \varkappa j) + \beta_1\beta_5 (\bar{m} - \bar{l}^d)]/(1-\beta_2)$; $\alpha_i = \beta_i/(1 - \beta_2)$, $i = 1, 2, 3$; $\alpha_i = \beta_1\beta_i/(1 - \beta_2)$, $i = 5, 6$. The coefficient on $p^\star$ is unity, because of homogeneity with respect to price inflation in the wage inflation equation (that is, because $\beta_2 + \beta_4 = 1$). A depreciating real exchange rate causes upward cost-push pressure on prices, as does a low level of the real exchange rate. The latter also causes demand-pull pressure through its effects on the trade balance. A rising tax rate causes upward cost-push pressure on inflation, as does a high level of the tax rate. But the latter also causes downward demand-pull pressure and thus the direction of the effect of the level of the tax rate on inflation is ambiguous. A high real interest rate obviously dampens inflation, for a given level and rate of change of the real exchange rate, by means of demand-pull influences.[15]

The second equation shows the rate of appreciation of the real exchange rate. In the case of model-consistent expectations equations (9) and (11a) imply that

$$\dot{a} = r_f - r \tag{13a}$$

whilst for the case of regressive expectations equations (9) and (11b) imply that

$$\dot{a} = -(r_f - r)/\phi_1 \tag{13b}$$

Finally the equation for the level of national investment may be written, after substituting the IS equation into (8), as

$$i = \bar{i}' - \gamma_1[1-\eta\varkappa]r - \gamma_2[1-\eta\varkappa]a + \eta\varkappa\gamma_3 s \qquad (14)$$

where $\bar{i}' = \bar{i} - \eta[\varkappa\bar{j} + \bar{\gamma}]$. We make the standard assumption that $\eta\varkappa < 1$. This implies that import leakages cannot be large enough to reverse the direction of influence on national investment of the negative impact effect of the real interest rate on domestic investment. It also ensures that, provided the Marshall-Lerner condition holds, as is implied by $\gamma_2 > 0$, a real depreciation has a positive effect on the trade balance. Higher taxation increases national investment because it reduces imports.

The policy problem addressed in the analytic part of the paper may now be stated formally. It concerns the use of the two policy instruments s and r so as to obtain from equations (12) to (14) the desired outcomes $p^\star$ and $i^\star$ for the two policy objectives of the price level and national investment.

The steady state of the real economy

The solution

Before considering the way in which the price level might be stabilised, it is helpful to consider the consequences of such stabilisation. The logic of adopting this particular order is to reinforce the vital point made by Meade and Vines (1987) that the steady state of the real economy is independent of the control rules which are adopted. We also show that this steady state is independent of the inflation target.

A steady state is defined as

$$p = p^\star \qquad (15a)$$

$$i = i^\star \qquad (15b)$$

$$\dot{a} = 0 \qquad (15c)$$

Equation (15c) immediately implies, together with (9) and (11a,b), that $r = r_f$ in the steady state; this follows from our assumption of perfect capital mobility. Equation (15a) implies that $\dot{p} = \varrho^\star$[16] which then leads to (16a); equation (15b) may be written as (16b):

$$0 = \bar{\alpha} - \alpha_1\varkappa\gamma_1 r_f - (\alpha_1\varkappa\gamma_2 + \alpha_5\eta)a - (\alpha_1\varkappa\gamma_3 - \alpha_6)s \quad (16a)$$

$$i^\star = \bar{i}' - \gamma_1[1-\eta\varkappa]r_f - \gamma_2[1-\eta\varkappa]a + \eta\varkappa\gamma_3 s \quad (16b)$$

Equations (16) can be used to find the steady-state values of s_∞ and a_∞. They are

$$s_\infty = [\bar{\alpha}\gamma_2(1-\eta\varkappa) + (\alpha_1\varkappa\gamma_2+\alpha_5\eta)(\bar{i}^\star-\bar{i}') + \alpha_5\eta\gamma_1(1-\eta\varkappa)r_f]/\Delta \qquad (17a)$$

$$a_\infty = [\bar{\alpha}\eta\varkappa\gamma_3 - (\alpha_1\varkappa\gamma_3-\alpha_6)(\bar{i}^\star-\bar{i}') - (\gamma_1\alpha_1\varkappa\gamma_3-\alpha_6\gamma_1(1-\eta\varkappa))r_f]/\Delta \qquad (17b)$$

where $\Delta = \alpha_1\varkappa\gamma_2\gamma_3 + \alpha_5\eta^2\varkappa\gamma_3 - \alpha_6\gamma_2(1 - \eta\varkappa)$

The expression Δ will be positive unless the upwards long-run cost-push effect of an increase in the tax rate, α_6, is so large as to outweigh the downward demand-pull effect $\alpha_1\varkappa\gamma_3$ by enough to offset the other term. We describe an economy with these abnormal properties as 'very long-run cost-push'. We note that if α_5 is large, that is, if the real exchange rate has powerful cost-push effects, then the chance of the economy being very long-run cost-push is reduced.

Chart 7.1 illustrates this. The $i^\star$ line shows combinations of s and a consistent with equation (16b) such that national investment remains at its steady state value $i^\star$. It is upward sloping. The $p^\star$ line shows combinations of s and a consistent with equation (16a) such that inflation remains at its steady-state value. If $\alpha_1\varkappa\gamma_3 > \gamma_6$ then it is downward sloping. An increase in the long-run cost-push effect of a tax increase, γ_6, causes this line to rotate in a clockwise manner, for example, from as in (a) to as in (b). If γ_6 becomes bigger than $\alpha_1\varkappa\gamma_3$ but Δ (defined above) remains positive, then the line is upward sloping but steeper than the $i^\star$ line (case (c)). Finally if $\gamma_6 > \alpha_1\varkappa\gamma_3$ and if Δ is negative then the line is upward sloping and flatter than the $i^\star$ line (case (d), the very long-run cost-push case). We will find below that in our empirical model the economy is far from being very long-run cost-push – indeed that case (a) is the most relevant.

The solutions s_∞ and a_∞ are obtained where the two lines intersect. Notice that the steady-state solutions are independent of the inflation target, because homogeneity is assumed.

Steady state comparative statistics

We now comment on how the required steady-state values for a and s change as a result of three shocks.[17]

An increase in inflationary pressure shifts the $p^\star$ line to the right. Chart 7.1 shows that s_∞ and a_∞ both rise in all the cases except when the economy is very long-run cost-push (that is, except when Δ is negative). Except in that case, taxes are raised to counter the inflationary pressure through a reduction in output y and the real

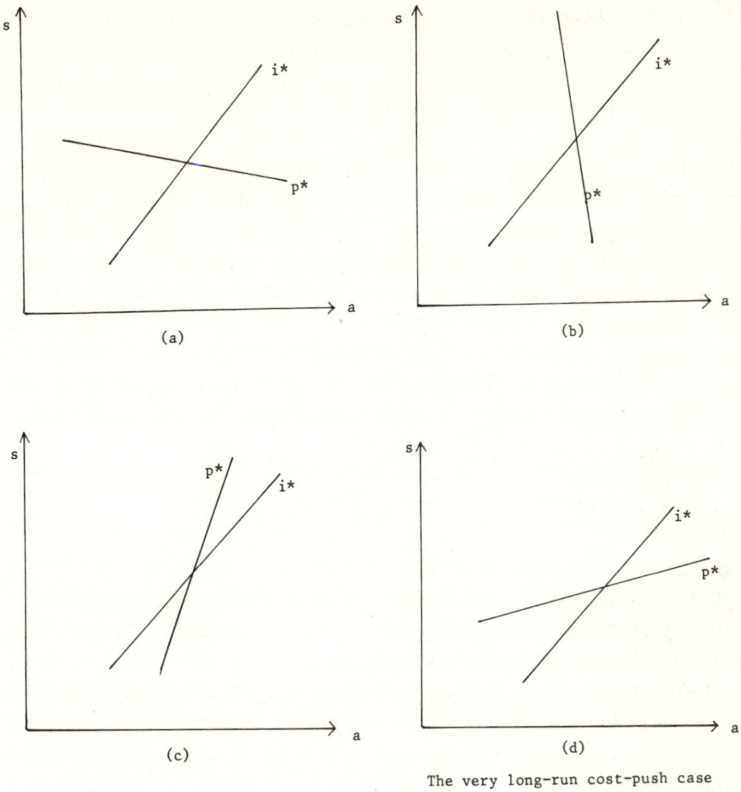

Chart 7.1 The steady-state relationship between the instruments and targets

exchange rate can be appreciated because imports fall. This is true even in case (c): a 'free lunch', with lower taxes, higher output and a depreciated exchange rate, is only possible in case (d). As already noted, this case does not appear to be empirically relevant.

An increase in the investment target shifts the i^* line to the left. In cases (a) and (b) taxes are cut to improve the trade balance and the exchange rate is depreciated, to counteract the effect of lower activity on inflation. In case (c) taxes are still raised, but the effect of this on inflation is now positive, and the real exchange rate must be appreciated to offset this. In the 'very long-run cost-push' case a 'free lunch' is again possible: taxes are cut and the exchange rate depreciated.

A rise in the foreign interest rate shifts both lines to the left, since it depresses investment, output and inflation. In cases (a) and (b) a real exchange rate depreciation is required to make good the fall in investment. If α_5 were zero so that this devaluation had no long-run cost-push effect on inflation, then taxes would not need to be changed: the fall in output and inflation would have been corrected by the depreciation. However, with positive α_5 taxes need to be increased. In cases (c) and (d), as is by now familiar, these outcomes can be reversed.

This analysis makes clear that the steady-state values of the tax rate and the real exchange rate are uniquely determined by the target for investment and the requirement that inflation should have settled at its steady-state rate. If the economy is homogenous of degree one, then the steady state of the real economy and so the levels of the policy instruments are not themselves affected by the rate of inflation.

The policy framework

Four types of inflation control

The model allows us to consider four possible types of counter-inflationary policy. The first policy is that of monetary targets. The nominal money stock is allowed to grow at the target rate of inflation and the interest rate is determined by inverting (10). The second approach also uses monetary policy as the route to keeping prices growing on their target path. However, as discussed in the introduction, an intermediate target is established for the exchange rate, with reference to the level of prices. The home interest rate is then set with reference to the gap between the actual and target exchange rates. The remaining approaches to maintaining price stability rely on fiscal policy: either government spending or the tax rate is varied so as to stabilise inflation. In this section we discuss some of these alternative methods of disinflation.

A monetary target

The use of monetary targets in an open economy results in a system very similar to that described by Dornbusch (1976). It is now well documented that disturbances to international capital markets or shifts in the velocity of circulation will, in a regime with a fixed money stock, lead to fluctuations in the real exchange rate and disturbances to output even though there may be no inflationary pressure. We can see no advantages in such a system compared with one in which the interest rate is used explicitly for counter-inflationary purposes. It has been much discussed elsewhere and we do not consider it further.

An exchange rate target

The main route by which monetary policy achieves inflation control in an open economy is through the exchange rate. There therefore seems to be an advantage to expressing anti-inflationary monetary policy in terms of an exchange rate target and an interest rate rule. In our analytic model we write

$$a^\star = a_\infty + k_1(p - p^\star) \qquad k_1 > 0 \tag{18a}$$

This implies that the real exchange rate target is appreciated above its steady state level if prices are above their target level. (Note that the special case of $k_1 = 1$ corresponds to fixed nominal exchange rates.) Interest rate policy now becomes subordinated to the attainment of this target exchange rate in a manner discussed below. At the present stage it is simply assumed that monetary policy is used so as to ensure that the exchange rate reaches its target $a^\star$, where, with $k_1 > 0$, this target is used for inflation control.

This formulation assumes that the authorities know a_∞ and can use this information in the setting of $a^\star$. We do not assume this in our empirical work, but to do so here greatly simplifies our analytic investigation.[18]

A tax rate rule

A third approach is to set the tax rate with reference to the deviation of prices from their desired level. In our analytic model we write

$$s = s_\infty + k_2(p - p^\star) \tag{19a}$$

This implies that taxes are set above their steady-state level whenever prices are above target.

This formulation assumes for simplicity that the authorities know s_∞; we do not assume this in our empirical work.[19]

A public expenditure rule

Public expenditure can be used as an alternative fiscal instrument, giving the fourth means of price stabilisation. For the purposes of this paper it can be treated in the same way as the tax rate. The only major difference is that we assume that the cost-push effects of both the level and rate of change of public expenditure (α_3 and α_6) are zero.

A number of factors govern the choice between taxes and public expenditure as the fiscal instrument. The use of government spending faces problems of inflexibility. Taxes are generally thought to be more flexible.[20] The main disadvantage with the use of taxes for control purposes is that indirect taxes have a direct cost-push effect on the market price of consumption goods: a tax increase designed to suppress inflation by reducing demand may in fact make it worse. Although direct tax changes do not affect prices in the same way, the Lucas critique suggests that wage bargainers would adjust their behaviour so as to respond to direct tax changes in the same way as to indirect tax changes. To rely on the use of income tax as a means for fiscal control would be likely to run into the same sort of cost-push problems as would arise with an indirect tax. Our subsequent analysis is set out in terms of the tax rate. We can then infer the results which would be found if government spending were used instead, by setting $\alpha_3 = \alpha_6 = 0$.

The fiscal-monetary mix

None of the options outlined above are sufficient to close the system. If monetary policy is used for counter-inflationary purposes, some principle is needed for the setting of fiscal policy. If, on the other hand, fiscal policy is used to suppress inflation, some guidance is needed to indicate an appropriate monetary state.

We assume in our analytical model that the 'spare' policy instrument is set in a manner which ensures that the investment target is achieved in the steady state. In fact it may be desirable to use this missing policy instrument actively in order to damp down disturbances; indeed in our empirical work discussed below this is done. However, the dynamic model presented here would become intractable if any attempt were made to extend it in this way, and we do not make any such attempt.

Thus, if the real exchange rate intermediate target is used for disinflation, and if it is assumed that the level of real government spending is exogenous, then the tax rate is set to ensure that the investment target is met. The appropriate tax rate is given in equation (17a).

$$s = s_{\infty} \tag{18b}$$

If fiscal policy is used for disinflation, then we assume that a target real exchange rate, consistent with the desired investment target, is adopted. The required target value is given by equation (17b)

$$a^{\star} = a_{\infty} \tag{19b}$$

Specification of interest rate policy

Target values for the real exchange rate have been specified in three of the four policy rules: it is now necessary to indicate how monetary policy should respond when the actual real exchange rate is away from its target. In any real world environment there would be two arms to monetary policy, foreign exchange intervention and interest rate setting. However, by making the simplifying assumption that there is perfect substitutability between home and foreign assets, any role for intervention is lost. And so it remains to consider only the setting of the interest rate. An obvious suggestion is to adopt a high real interest rate when the real exchange rate is below its target, and a low real rate when the real exchange rate is above its target. If the domestic real interest rate is also set with reference to world real interest rates then an appropriate simple rule is

$$r = r_f + \theta(a^\star - a) \qquad \theta > 0 \tag{20}$$

We use just such a rule in our analytical model. In our empirical work, the use of integral control means that it is possible to specify a control rule without explicit reference to the foreign rate of interest, and so the structure is slightly different.

Why investigate decoupled control rules?

In order to investigate stability with our simple analytic model it is necessary to restrict the system to be second-order. As a consequence we make the following assumptions which have already been noted. When the active exchange rate target rule is used to stabilise prices, the tax rate is assumed to be set permanently to s_∞. On the other hand if an active fiscal rule is used to stabilise prices, the target real exchange rate is assumed to be set to α_∞. In both cases interest rate policy is used as in (20). In neither case is there any dynamic feedback from the level of investment to the policy instruments.

We are now equipped to compare the dynamics of two regimes: (a) monetary disinflation using a target exchange rate (with s constant at s_∞); (b) fiscal disinflation (during which $a^\star$ is constant at a_∞).

The reader may doubt the relevance of such decoupled regimes in which one instrument is exclusively assigned to the control of one target. We perform these investigations for two reasons. Firstly, other people propose assignments. It is apparently a view of H.M. Treasury that inflation control should take place as in regime (a), with the fiscal instrument only being adjusted for 'longer-term structural reasons' (that is, in pursuit of a wealth target?). By contrast Edison *et al.* (1987) have advocated regime (b), with the real exchange rate being kept at or near a_∞. Our investigation means that we can compare the dynamics of their proposed assignments. Secondly, this investigation also gives preliminary indications concerning appropriate system design for our more complex empirical investigations (where we do not confine ourselves to decoupled designs).

The dynamics of adjustment

The dynamic system into which we insert our control rules for the purpose of this dynamic analysis is a subset of the full system described in equations (12) to (14). We need only consider the evolution of prices (12) and of the real exchange rate (13a or 13b). The investment equation (14) can be ignored.[21] Our aim is to investigate whether this system will converge to the steady-state trajectory.

Model-consistent expectations

Taking first the case of model-consistent expectations we substitute for r from (20) and obtain

$$\dot{p} = \bar{\alpha} - \alpha_1 \varkappa \gamma_1 [r_f + \theta(a^\star - a)] - (\alpha_1 \varkappa \gamma_2 + \alpha_5 \eta) a - (\alpha_1 \varkappa \gamma_3 - \alpha_6) s - \alpha_2 \eta \dot{a} + \alpha_3 \dot{s} + p^\star \tag{21a}$$

$$\dot{a} = -\theta(a^\star - a) \tag{21b}$$

It remains to substitute for the exchange rate target, $a^\star$ and the tax rate, s, in these equations.

Control of inflation by an exchange rate target

In this case we substitute for $a^\star$ from (18a), holding s constant, and so obtain in matrix form

$$\begin{bmatrix} \dot{p} \\ \dot{a} \end{bmatrix} = \begin{bmatrix} -\alpha_1 \varkappa \gamma_1 \theta k_1 + \alpha_2 \eta \theta k_1 & \alpha_1 \varkappa \gamma_1 \theta - \alpha_1 \varkappa \gamma_2 - \alpha_5 \eta - \alpha_2 \eta \theta \\ -\theta k_1 & \theta \end{bmatrix} \begin{bmatrix} p \\ a \end{bmatrix} + \text{constants} \tag{22}$$

For saddle-path stability we require a single unstable root. The determinant is $-\theta k_1(\alpha_1 \varkappa \gamma_2 + \alpha_5 \eta)$ and is negative if $k_1 > 0$. The

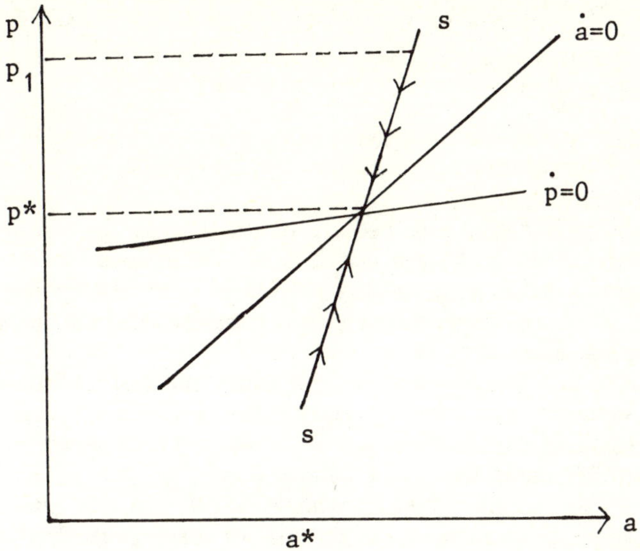

Chart 7.2 The price/real exchange rate phase diagram

system then has one unstable root. We assume that this unstable root is removed by a 'jump' in the nominal exchange rate which sets the system on a saddle path to the steady state. The condition $k_1 > 0$ implies that, although the nominal exchange rate target need not rise in order to rein in prices, the real exchange rate must be allowed to rise. The case of a fixed nominal exchange rate ($k_1 = 1$) is obviously consistent with saddle-path adjustment.

Chart 7.2 illustrates this. From (22) the $\dot{a} = 0$ line, along which $a = a^\star$, has a positive slope. The $\dot{p} = \varrho^\star$ line is flatter, and may have a negative slope (although for sufficiently high θ the slope is certainly positive). SS is the saddle path. When p is higher than $p^\star$ at p_1, then the following happens. $a^\star$ is raised, so r is raised, a jumps upwards (but not by as much as the change in $a^\star$) and we converge back to $p^\star$ along SS.

Thus our analytical investigation has shown in a stylised way how such a policy regime would work, and has not revealed any difficulties concerning potential instabilities.

Fiscal control of inflation by a tax rule

With fiscal control of inflation, and a fixed real exchange rate target, the system, after substituting for s from (19a) is

$$\begin{bmatrix} \dot{p} \\ \dot{a} \end{bmatrix} = \begin{bmatrix} \dfrac{-(\alpha_1 \varkappa \gamma_3 - \alpha_6)k_2}{1 - \alpha_3 k_2} & \dfrac{\alpha_1 \varkappa \gamma_1 \theta - (\alpha_1 \varkappa \gamma_2 + \alpha_5 \eta - \alpha_2 \eta \theta)}{1 - \alpha_3 k_2} \\ 0 & \theta \end{bmatrix} \begin{bmatrix} p \\ a \end{bmatrix}$$

$$+ \text{ constants} \qquad (23)$$

This system is degenerate, because of the zero in the transition matrix: the saddle path, if it exists, is vertical in $p - a$ space, and so if there is saddle-path stability a remains at $a^\star$. To investigate stability therefore, we need only consider the top left-hand element showing the effect of p on $\dot{p}$.

Consider first the (unlikely) case in which the positive long-run cost-push effects of a higher level of taxes dominate the negative demand-pull effects (that is, $\alpha_6 > \alpha_1 \varkappa \gamma_3$). Then inspection of equation (23) shows that stable control is possible with a perverse signed fiscal controller (that is, with $k_2 < 0$).[22] In this case if p begins above $p^\star$, then taxes are cut and we converge stably to the lower price level $p^\star$. But as already observed, our empirical work suggests that this case is not a relevant one.

Now consider the case when $\alpha_1 \gamma_3 \varkappa > \alpha_6$: that is, positive long-run cost-push effects of a high level of taxes are less strong than the negative demand-pull effects. Then equation (23) shows that for stability k_2 must be positive. But, as a consequence, we run into an immediate difficulty.

The larger is the short-run cost-push effect of a tax increase the smaller must be the strength, k_2, of the fiscal controller if we are to avoid an unstable spiral. For rising p will lead to increasing taxes, leading to more strongly rising p. That process is completely explosive if $k_2 \alpha_3 > 1$, and we must limit ourselves to values of k_2 small enough to avoid this. The problem is that this limits the ability of tax increases to control inflation. In fact our empirical work will suggest that the short-run cost-push effects of tax increases are likely to be large enough to prevent control of inflation by these means. In such circumstances monetary policy will have to be the major element of a policy designed to control inflation. To have shed light on this difficulty is a useful contribution made by the present analytical investigation.

We now check to see if our results survive the translation to regressive expectations.

Regressive expectations

With regressive expectations the two equations driving the system become

$$\dot{p} = \dot{\alpha} - \alpha_1 \varkappa \gamma_1 [r_f + \theta(a^\star - a)] - (\alpha_1 \varkappa \gamma_2 + \alpha_5 \eta) a - (\alpha_1 \varkappa \gamma_3 - \alpha_6) s$$
$$- \alpha_2 \eta \dot{a} + \alpha_3 \dot{s} + p \qquad (24a)$$

$$\dot{a} = \theta(a^\star - a)/\phi_1 \qquad (24b)$$

Control of inflation through an exchange rate target
Where monetary policy is used via a target exchange rate, we substitute for $a^\star$ by means of (18a) and the system becomes in matrix form

$$\begin{bmatrix} \dot{p} \\ \dot{a} \end{bmatrix} = \begin{bmatrix} -\alpha_1 \varkappa \gamma_1 \theta k_1 - \alpha_2 \eta \theta k_1/\phi_1 & \alpha_1 \varkappa \gamma_1 \theta - (\alpha_1 \varkappa \gamma_2 + \alpha_5 \eta) + \alpha_2 \eta \theta/\phi_1 \\ \theta k_1/\phi_1 & -\theta/\phi_1 \end{bmatrix} \begin{bmatrix} p \\ a \end{bmatrix}$$

$$+ \text{ constants} \qquad (25)$$

With model-consistent expectations we required there to be one unstable root which would be cleared by a jump in the exchange rate. With regressive expectations it is assumed that variables do not jump and so there should be no unstable roots. This is assured if the trace is negative and the determinant is positive. The trace is $-\theta k_1(\alpha_1 \varkappa \gamma_1 + \alpha_2 \eta/\phi_1) - \theta/\phi_1$, which is negative with $k_1 > 0$ and the determinant is $\theta k_1(\alpha_1 \varkappa \gamma_2 + \alpha_5 \eta)/\phi_1$ which is positive with $k_1 > 0$. The system has no unstable roots, as required.

Fiscal control of inflation through a tax rate rule
With fiscal stabilisation the system is

$$\begin{bmatrix} \dot{p} \\ \dot{a} \end{bmatrix} = \begin{bmatrix} \dfrac{-(\alpha_1 \varkappa \gamma_3 - \alpha_6) k_2}{1 - \alpha_3 k_2} & \dfrac{\alpha_1 \varkappa \gamma_1 \theta - (\alpha_1 \varkappa \gamma_2 + \alpha_5 \eta) + \alpha_2 \eta \theta/\phi_1)}{1 - \alpha_3 k_2} \\ 0 & -\theta/\phi_1 \end{bmatrix} \begin{bmatrix} p \\ a \end{bmatrix}$$

$$+ \text{ constants} \qquad (26)$$

We require no unstable roots (that is, negative trace and positive determinant).

The problems previously found with fiscal management recur. The determinant is $k_2 \theta(\alpha_1 \varkappa \gamma_3 - \alpha_6)/\phi_1(1 - \alpha_3 k_2)$. It is apparent that a positive determinant will ensure a negative trace, and so stability. Consider the empirically relevant case where $\alpha_6 < \alpha_1 \varkappa \gamma_3$. It can be seen that the condition for the determinant to be positive is the same as that required for stability in the consistent expectations case. Once again, if $\alpha_6 > 0$, too powerful a fiscal policy will create instability. Thus our stability conditions do not depend on the way in which expectations are formed. This suggests that there is at least some chance of finding empirical control rules which work independently of the way in which expectations are formed.

The comparative advantage of fiscal and monetary policy

The relevance of comparative advantage for policy design

We now turn away from simple policy regimes in which particular instruments are assigned to the control of particular targets. Instead we ask the following more complex question: 'in cross-coupled regimes[23] which instrument should be mainly relied upon to control which target?'

In order to consider the question of whether reliance should be placed mainly on fiscal or mainly on monetary policy in order to damp inflation, it is helpful to introduce the concept of comparative advantage. Comparative advantage, *w*, may be defined as follows. If we consider the problem of controlling two variables, y_1 and y_2, by means of the instruments x_1 and x_2 in the system

$$y_1 = k_{11}x_1 + k_{12}x_2 + \text{other terms} \quad (27)$$

$$y_2 = k_{21}x_1 + k_{22}x_2 + \text{other terms}$$

We define a weighting index, ω as

$$\omega = (k_{11}/k_{21})/(k_{12}/k_{22}) \quad (28)$$

Then we may say that x_1 has a comparative advantage in controlling y_1 if $|\omega| > 1$.

We have found that short-term comparative advantage provides an indication of a good structure for the proportional component of control rules. If x_1 has a comparative advantage in controlling y_1, then the proportional component of a control rule designed to damp a disturbance in y_1 should rely mainly on x_1. Indeed relative instrument movements can differ from what is indicated by the parameter ω only to the extent that one or both of the targets are allowed to slip. The pattern of long-term comparative advantage indicates the relative magnitude of changes in the policy instruments which will have to be made in order to achieve particular target values in the steady state. We find that knowledge of this is also useful in helping to design good policy rules. Essentially this is because in any linear economic system, the values required, *ex post*, by the policy instruments in order to achieve particular values for both of the target variables depend on the structure of the model rather than on any choice made by the policymaker. This was demonstrated in the third section. The relevant aspect of that structure is usefully summarised by the pattern of long-term comparative advantage.

If fiscal policy has, in the long run, a comparative advantage in suppressing inflation, then the adjustments necessary to damp an inflationary disturbance will, in the long run, have to rely mainly on the use of fiscal policy, at least if the wealth target is not to be abandoned. If, on the other hand, the comparative advantage of monetary policy lies in fighting inflation, then price stabilisation will have to rely mainly on monetary instruments. In a dynamic model there is the possibility that the comparative advantage of one policy instrument will lie with fighting inflation in the short term, but with looking after wealth in the long term. This means that, although knowledge of comparative advantage is useful, there is no substitute for careful examination of the effects of policy rules on the model which they are intended to regulate. We have made such an examination in our empirical work.

Long-term comparative advantage

We consider first the question of long-term comparative advantage. This is simple, in that it is independent of the way in which expectations are formed (because with both our expectational rules, expectations are fulfilled in the steady state). In the short term the instrument of monetary policy is the real interest rate. However the long-term real interest rate is, at least in this model, constrained to equal that in the rest of the world. In studying long-term comparative advantage, it is necessary to regard the real exchange rate target as the instrument of monetary policy. Our required apparatus is already available from the third section.

We treat s and a as the first and second instruments respectively and $\dot{p}$ and i as the first and second targets respectively. Thus ω shows the relative weight of fiscal policy in the control of inflation and

$$\omega = \frac{\delta \dot{p}/\delta s}{\delta \dot{p}/\delta a} \Big/ \frac{\delta i/\delta s}{\delta i/\delta a} \tag{29}$$

Substitution from equations (16) yields.[24]

$$\omega = -\frac{(\alpha_1 \varkappa \gamma_3 - \alpha_6)}{(\alpha_1 \varkappa \gamma_2 + \alpha_5 \eta)} \Big/ \frac{\eta \varkappa \gamma_3}{\gamma_2 [1 - \eta \varkappa]} \tag{30}$$

Four cases are possible, corresponding to the four parts of Chart 7.1. The first case is $\omega < -1$. This is possible, but not necessarily the case, if the long-run cost-push effects of the tax increases α_6 are small. In this case taxes have a long-run comparative advantage in controlling inflation; and do so by demand-pull means. This case is depicted in section (a) of Chart 7.1, and appears to be the relevant case for our empirical model. For bigger values of the cost-push parameter α_6 — but still with $\alpha_6 < \alpha_1 \varkappa \gamma_3$ — we have $-1 < \omega < 0$: (case b). When $\alpha_6 > \alpha_1 \varkappa \gamma_3$ we have $0 < \omega < 1$ (case c). In both of these cases monetary policy has a comparative advantage in controlling inflation. In extreme circumstances $\omega > 1$ (case d): in this case taxes again have a comparative advantage in controlling inflation, but do so by cost-push means.

Short-term comparative advantage

The evaluation of short-term comparative advantage is more complicated. We take as our starting point equations (12) and (14). In order to consider short-term comparative advantage, we work in discrete time and consider the one-period effect of a change in the real interest rate and the tax rate. It is necessary to specify how the real exchange rate changes in the short term. The response of the real exchange rate to a change in the real interest rate depends on the way in which expectations are formed and, if expectations are forward looking, on the expected future level of the real interest rate. However we shall see that it is possible to come to reasonably firm qualitative conclusions about the pattern of short-term comparative advantage merely by assuming that an increase in the real interest rate causes some increase in the real exchange rate in the short term. The magnitude of this increase turns out to be relatively unimportant. Thus we put $\Delta a = \sigma \Delta r$. Then, using (12) and (14), we may show that

$$\omega = -\frac{(1 - (\alpha_6 + \alpha_3)/\alpha_1 \varkappa \gamma_3)}{1 + \dfrac{\sigma\eta}{\varkappa}\left(\dfrac{\alpha_5}{\alpha_1} + \dfrac{\alpha_2}{\alpha_1}\right)/(\gamma_1 + \sigma\gamma_2)} \cdot \frac{(1 - \varkappa\eta)}{\varkappa\eta} \quad (31)$$

We may analyse this expression in stages.

First consider the effects of σ on comparative advantage. A positive σ unambiguously tends to reduce the absolute magnitude of ω and increases the comparative advantage of monetary policy in fighting inflation. This is partly the familiar effect of higher interest rates appreciating the exchange rate and lowering costs directly. But there is also an effect of exchange rate appreciation in curtailing inflation through lower demand.

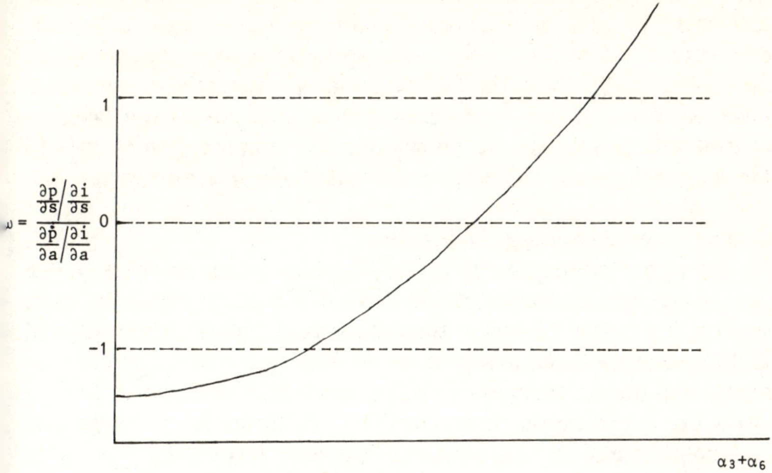

Chart 7.3 Short-run comparative advantage in the analytical model

Now ignore all cost-push effects of taxes (that is, set $\alpha_3 = \alpha_6 = 0$), supposing that taxes only have an effect on inflation through demand. Then the only other influence on comparative advantage is the term $(1 - \varkappa\eta)/\varkappa\eta$, and this says that the bigger is the import leakage the more monetary policy has an influence in fighting inflation. This is because fiscal policy works on investment only through effects on imports, $\gamma_3\varkappa\eta$, which result from the effect, γ_3 on demand, whereas the interest rate works directly on investment, γ_1, and this is offset by the induced changes in imports $\varkappa\eta\gamma_1$. Fiscal policy might thus not be relatively powerful in influencing i if η is small.

We may conclude that, in the absence of any cost-push effects from taxation, monetary policy certainly has a comparative advantage compared with demand-pull effects of taxes, in fighting inflation – that is, ω is certainly between minus one and zero – providing only that the import leakage η is not too small. This condition holds in our empirical model.

Finally consider the influence of the cost-push terms α_3 and α_6. Their effect is clearly to increase ω towards zero and, if they are large enough, to make ω positive or even greater than unity.

In fact we may plot ω against $(\alpha_3 + \alpha_6)$ as in Chart 7.3. This is exactly what the graphs of comparative advantage look like in our empirical work[25] and they show that for significant values of α_3

and α_6 tax cuts will have a comparative advantage, through their cost-push effects, in fighting inflation. These figures are of considerable significance for our work on policy design. They express in another way the fact that with significant short-run cost-push pressures of tax increases it will be difficult to use taxes to control inflation (since we know from our empirical work that in the long run taxes will have to be raised for this purpose).

Comparative advantage in practice

In order to consider the structure of policy rules empirically, we have developed a model of the United Kingdom economy from version 7 of the National Institute model, which the National Institute kindly made available to us. We have made a number of highly significant changes to this model which have an important effect on the response of the model to disturbances in exogenous and policy variables. In particular we have introduced models of the main capital markets which are capable of being solved with either regressive or with model-consistent expectations. We have also modified the consumption and investment functions so that these aggregates too are capable of being determined by either regressive or by model-consistent expectations. In particular, with model-consistent expectations, consumption depends partly on the capitalised value of future labour income or human capital. Investment depends on the stock-exchange valuation ratio, which may itself be determined by either regressive or by model-consistent expectations. The changes we have made are described by Christodoulakis, Meade, Vines and Weale (1986). We use our model here to illustrate consequences of wage indexation to which the analytical results of this chapter have drawn attention.

The wage equation in version 7 of the National Institute model, which we take as our starting point is

$$\begin{aligned}\Delta \ln WAGERATE_t = 0.307 - 0.138 RTT_{t-3} + 0.759 \Delta \ln P^e_t \\ - 0.00651 \Delta AVHMF_t - 0.00268 AVHMF - 2.72 \Delta^2 UPC_{-1} \\ - 2.43 \Delta UPC_{-3} - 0.262 UPC_{-4} \qquad (32)\end{aligned}$$

where *WAGERATE* – wage rate; *AVHMF* – average hours in manufacturing; *UPC* – unemployed/labour force; *RTT* – real earnings aspiration gap defined as $RTT = \ln AVEARN/(P \times 0.976 \times (1.00554)^t)$; *AVEARN* – average earnings; *P* – consumer price index; $\Delta \ln P^e_t$ – expected rate of inflation, determined regressively with $\Delta \ln P^e_t = 0.75 \Delta \ln P_{t-1} + 0.15 \Delta \ln P_{t-2} + 0.10 \Delta \ln P_{t-3}$. Equation (32) implies a target rate of growth in the real wage of 2.2 per cent a year; we assume that long-run productive capacity per head also grows at this rate, and so that it does not present inflation problems. The effect of the terms in manufacturing hours is small. We neglect it. The equation as it stands suggests that only 76 per cent of expected price increases are reflected in wage demands. More recent work (Layard and Nickell, 1986) tends to impose the restriction that wage increases are fully represented in price increases. However we wish to consider the effects of different degrees of indexation. Accordingly we modify the NIESR equation to give an equation more like that used in our analytic work above:

$$\begin{aligned} \Delta \ln WAGERATE_t &= 0.307 - 0.138 RTT_{t-3} + \zeta \Delta \ln P_t^e \\ - 2.72\Delta^2 UPC_{-1} - 2.43\Delta UPC_{-3} &- 0.262 UPC_{-4} + (1-\zeta)p^\star \quad (33) \end{aligned}$$

where $p^\star$ is the core target rate of inflation. We can allow the parameter, ζ, to take values between 0 and 1.

If the model is to be solved with model-consistent expectations we assume that $\Delta \ln P_t^e = (\Delta \ln P_t + \Delta \ln P_{t-1})/2$, a simplifying assumption that wages are set at the beginning of the current period on the basis of the average of the past and the correctly-foreseen current inflation rate. This assumption avoids the need to use Taylor's (1979) overlapping contracts framework at the cost of assuming that wage contracts only last one period and that actual prices are not distinguished from expected prices. This expression is open to the criticism that it gives a strong instantaneous wage-price loop which makes inflation easy to control.

If the model is solved with regressive expectations we use the expression in the original NIESR equation, shown above. It implies a slower adjustment of wages to inflation than in the previous case, but is not otherwise very different. In the notation of this chapter, the wage equation has $\beta_2 = \zeta$ and $\beta_4 = 1-\zeta$. We now allow the parameter, ζ, to vary between 0 and 1 and plot ω against this, where ω is the relative weight of fiscal policy in the control of inflation as defined in equation (29).

We first consider the case where the fiscal instrument is a tax variable. Previous research (Vines *et al.*, 1983) suggested that VAT and employees' national insurance contributions were feasible fiscal instruments which could be used for fine-tuning on a quarterly basis. A compound fiscal variable consisting of equal percentage point movements in the VAT rate and the rate of employees' contributions seems to be the most broadly-based fiscal instrument available. It may be the case that our wage equation understates the cost-push effect of such an instrument, since it does not show any cost-push effect arising from the changes in employee's contributions. We also show the relative weight of fiscal policy if government consumption rather than taxes is used as the instrument of fiscal control. We only present pictures for the economy with regressive expectations, because the plots for model-consistent expectations are at present creating computational problems.[26] We present graphs of relative weight for a range of values of ζ between 0 and 1 for different time periods.

It may be seen that the pattern of relative weight depends crucially on the choice of fiscal instrument and on the degree of wage indexation in the economy. Furthermore the changing pattern of relative weight over time has the implication that the stability of dynamic policy rules must be carefully investigated. It is not possible to consider issues of financial policy without being aware of this.

The following graphs do suggest that, when taxes are the only fiscal instrument available, and if the economy is cost-push, much greater short-term weight will need to be placed on monetary policy rather than fiscal policy for price stabilisation. Only if there were the possibility of a rapid response with government spending could fiscal policy be used for fighting inflation. Since we have no reason to believe that this possibility exists, we have, in the subsequent section on policy rules, limited ourselves to the use of taxes as the fiscal instrument.

Macroeconomic policy rules for economic stabilisation

We have argued here that the design of policy rules has to reflect the structure of the economy. In particular if the economy has cost-push linkages in the wage equation, then it is likely that reliance will have to be placed on monetary policy as a means of fighting inflation, while, if these linkages are weak, fiscal policy may be more appropriate. However, as Chart 7.4 demonstrates, the pattern of comparative advantage does change over time and it is necessary to investigate any proposed policy rules carefully so as to ensure that they are asymptotically stable and have a satisfactory ability to damp disturbances.[27] This investigation has proceeded as follows. Starting with our non-linear model of the United Kingdom economy, we then produce an efficient linear representation of the model, using the technique described by Maciejowski and Vines (1984). (The structure of this linear model depends on whether expectations are regressive or model-consistent). This linear model serves two purposes. First, it allows the policy rules to be tested for desirable dynamic policies such as stability, performance and robustness (*op. cit.* and Vines *et al.*, 1983), Part IV). Secondly, if

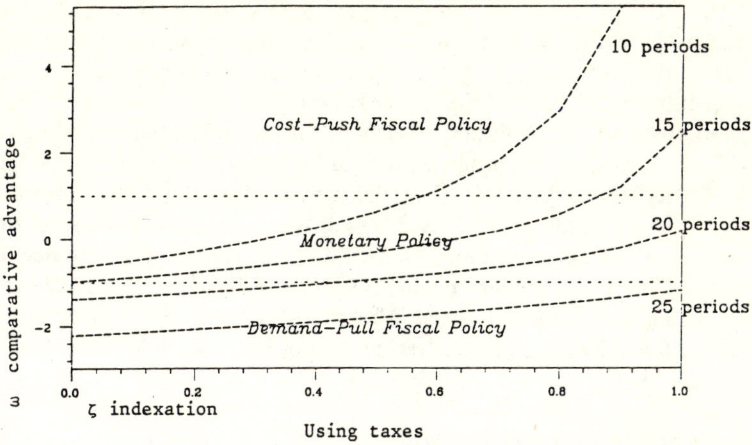

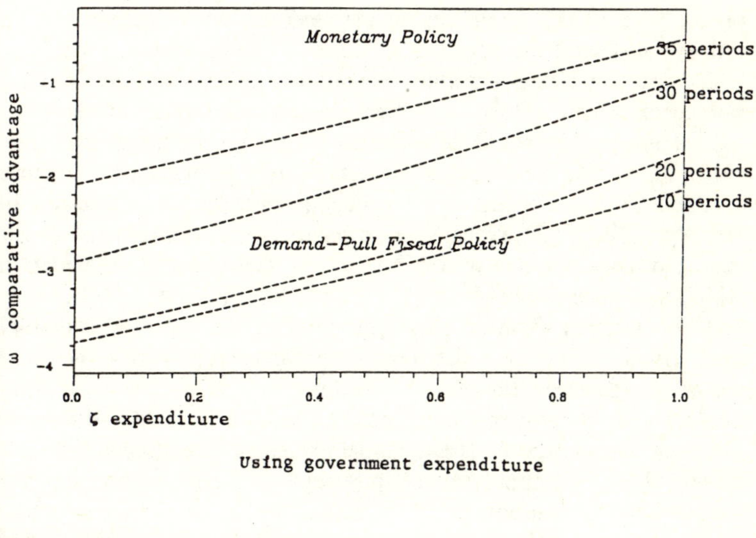

Chart 7.4 Relative weight of fiscal policy (ω)

the model is to be solved with model-consistent expectations, it allows the solution method presented by Blanchard and Kahn (1980) to be adopted. If this were not done, and rules were designed on the assumption of model-consistent expectations using the non-linear model, then firstly the results would depend on arbitrary terminal conditions and secondly there would be no guarantee that the solution trajectory was a stable path at all.

Policy rules can be designed on the linear reduction of the model – for both the regressive or model-consistent expectations cases — using the techniques developed by Christodoulakis (forthcoming in Weale, Blake, Christodoulakis, Meade and Vines). The approach adopted is very similar to that used by Edison *et al.* (1987) in designing simple policy rules. We have done this using the Simple Interactive Design package[28] so as to produce the rules which we present here.

Simultaneous rules and lagged rules

Our analytical model was set out in continuous time. It did not, therefore, allow us to distinguish policy rules which respond simultaneously with current events from those which can only respond with a lag. For example, the rate of interest can be adjusted on a day-to-day basis while fiscal policy cannot be adjusted so frequently. Daily information accrues on the exchange rate and on the level of the foreign exchange reserves, while information on money GDP and on national wealth only accrues with a lag.[29]

In our analytical model, economic policy would respond immediately new information became available about the state of the economy; this would be reflected at once in the target exchange rate. In a discrete time model in which information becomes available with a lag the target exchange rate cannot be treated in this way. If a target exchange rate regime were adopted, the target rate and fiscal policy would be set on the basis of information which becomes available only infrequently (for example, money GDP or national wealth). Until new information becomes available, both fiscal policy and the target exchange rate would be held constant. However the target exchange rate would be used as a guide for short-term monetary policy (the interest rate and foreign exchange intervention). If the actual exchange rate strayed from its target value, then appropriate adjustments to the short-term interest rate and to intervention could be made very quickly, that is, effectively simultaneously. This approach may be contrasted with one in which the interest rate was set directly on the basis of lagged information about the level of money GDP and the level of national wealth. In such a framework the exchange rate could move to an inappropriate level for quite a long time building up future difficulties for economic management. These difficulties can be avoided if the exchange rate is held close to an appropriate target value by means of short-term monetary policy.[30]

The basic structure for our policy rules is therefore to set the fiscal variable and the target real exchange rate on the basis of past values of money GDP and national wealth, while the interest rate and intervention is set on the basis of the deviation of the actual real exchange rate and the foreign exchange reserves from their current and past target values. The rules for short-term monetary policy can be described as simultaneous rules, while the rules for setting fiscal policy and the target exchange rate are lagged rules. In principle any lag structure would be possible. However, the simplest specification includes proportional and integral components only, giving rules in the following form

$$\Delta s_t = a_{11}\Delta(g_{t-1} - g^\star_{t-1}) + a_{12}(g_{t-1} - g^\star_{t-1}) + b_{11}\Delta(w_{t-1} - w_{t-1}{}^\star) + b_{12}(w_{t-1} - w_{t-1}{}^\star) \quad (34a)$$

$$\Delta a^\star_t = a_{21}\Delta(g_{t-1} - g^\star_{t-1}) + a_{22}(g_{t-1} - g^\star_{t-1}) + b_{21}\Delta(w_{t-1} - w_{t-1}{}^\star) + b_{22}(w_{t-1} - w_{t-1}{}^\star) \quad (34b)$$

$$\Delta r_t = c_{11}\Delta(a_t - a^\star_t) + c_{12}(a_t - a^\star_t) + d_{11}(f_t - f^\star_t) \quad (34c)$$

$$z_t = c_{21}\Delta(a_t - a^\star_t) + c_{22}(a_t - a^\star_t) + d_{21}(f_t - f^\star_t) \quad (34d)$$

where g_t = log money GDP at end of period t; w_t = log national wealth at end of period t; f_t = log foreign exchange reserve at end of period t; s_t = fiscal variable in period t; a_t = log actual real exchange rate in period t; z_t = foreign exchange intervention in period t; r_t = nominal interest rate; $\star$ indicates a target value. The proportional component of a rule of this type ensures a rapid response to any disturbance, while the integral component guarantees that, provided the system is stable, the final targets are actually met. The proportional component is not essential to ensure stability, but its absence would mean that any disturbance would persist for a long time before offsetting action was taken. Without the proportional component the response of the controlled economy would be slow and possibly cyclical.

One of our aims is then to produce simple policy rules. A second aim is to try to produce rules which are robust across a range of model specifications. The analysis of the fifth and sixth sections suggests that the way in which expectations are formed might not have a major effect on model stability, whilst the structure of the wage equation is likely to have an important impact on both stability and pattern of comparative advantage in the model, greatly affecting the structure of well-designed policy rules. This suggests that it may well be possible to find a simple rule which is robust to the way in which expectations are formed, but that it may well not be possible to find a rule which works for all values of the indexation parameter (ζ in equation 33) between 0 and 1. In practice, just as we are not able to consider all possible types of expectations formation, so too we cannot consider all possible values of ζ. We now proceeded to present policy rules for the two extreme cases. The 'unreformed' case has $\zeta=1$, while the 'reformed' wage case has $\zeta=0$.

Policy rules for an unreformed wage equation

We are able to design the following rule for the economy with $\zeta=1$.

$$\Delta s_t = -0.2\Delta(g_{t-1}-g^{\star}_{t-1}) - 0.1(g_{t-1}-g^{\star}_{t-1}) - 0.2\Delta(w_{t-1}-w^{\star}_{t-1}) - 0.1(w_{t-1}-w^{\star}_{t-1}) \quad (35a)$$

$$\Delta a^{\star}_t = 3\Delta(g_{t-1}-g^{\star}_{t-1}) + 0.2(g_{t-1}-g^{\star}_{t-1}) \quad (35b)$$

$$\Delta r_t = -0.6\Delta(a_t-a^{\star}_t) - 0.03(a_t-a^{\star}_t) \quad (35c)$$

This rule has the following four features. First, it is not diagonal: one instrument (taxes) responds to both targets. Second, the real exchange rate target exercises the major control over inflation.[31] A 1 per cent rise of money GDP above its target causes a 3 per cent appreciation of the real target exchange rate.[32] Third, fiscal policy controls wealth (slowly), and a rise of money GDP above its target leads to a cut in taxes, and fourth, the interest rate rule is strong: a 1 per cent fall of the real exchange rate below target causes a 0.6 per cent rise in the (nominal) interest rate. Notice that there are integral components to the rules for the fiscal variable, the target exchange rate and the interest rate. Also, the model has a high degree of capital mobility and it is found that intervention is unnecessary as a means of keeping the actual exchange rate close to its target value.

Chart 7.5 shows the outcome of using a rule of this type to reduce money GDP by 1 per cent. Expectations are assumed to be model-consistent.[33] Time is measured in quarters. Even with

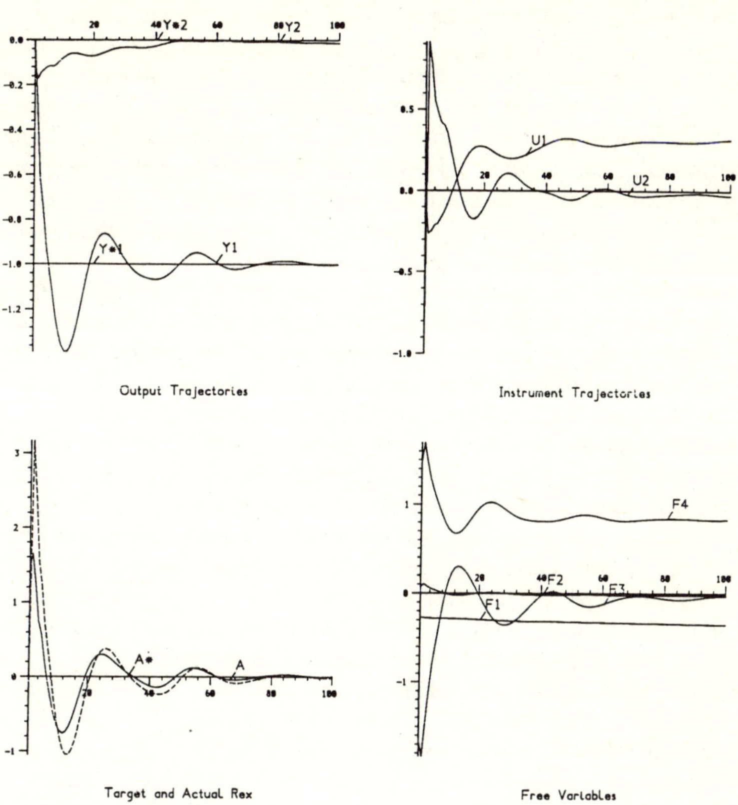

Key:

Y_1 Money GDP (% deviation)

Y_2 National wealth (% deviation)

A Real exchange rate (% deviation)

A* Target real exchange rate (% deviation)

U_1 Tax variable (deviation)

F_1 Nominal exchange rate (% deviation)

F_2 Valuation ratio (% deviation)

F_3 Consol rate (% deviation)

F_4 Human capital (% deviation)

U_2 Treasury bill rate (deviation)

Chart 7.5 Money GDP – 1 per cent with model-consistent expectations and unreformed wages

model-consistent expectations the response is considerably slower than that described by Vines, Maciejowski and Meade (1983).[34] We can identify two reasons for this. The first, and probably most important, is that they treated wages as a control variable while we have relied on an estimated equation only slightly modified. The second reason is that the modifications we have made to the consumption function have the effect of making demand less sensitive to current income than it was in their model.

The target real exchange rate appreciates (the nominal rate overshoots its long-run value) and the tax rate is decreased so as to curb inflation. (The actual real exchange rate moves rather less with model-consistent than with regressive expectations because it reflects not only current but also future interest rate differentials.) The reduction initially reduces profits and this, together with the rise in interest rates, leads to a slump on the stock exchange. GDP overshoots its target value. (This is deliberate: we have found this to be a useful feature when rules are applied to stabilise a simulation of the trajectory of a historical economy.) The cyclical behaviour of the economy after the first twenty periods or so of course depends on the way in which expectations are formed. However, by simulating both the model with adaptive expectations and the model with consistent expectations for 100 additional periods we are able to establish that the steady states are very similar in both cases.

We find that the interest rate settles back at its original value. The tax rate does show a steady-state offset and we attribute this to the fact that, although national wealth is returned to its original value, nevertheless the composition of this will have been permanently changed in the adjustment process. The production function implicit in the model does not imply a constant marginal productivity of domestic capital, while the marginal return on foreign assets is constant. So any change in the mix of wealth between home and foreign assets will lead to steady-state changes in real national income and thus to the steady-state tax rate.[35] This offset is reflected in a downward jump in the value of human capital in the case of the model-consistent expectations model. As a consequence consumption will have fallen. (The regressive expectations model does not show any value for human capital, but here too consumption will have fallen by the time the model reaches its steady state.)

With both types of expectations formation the short-term monetary policy rule is found to be effective at keeping the actual exchange rate reasonably close to its target value. The rule is in fact more effective with regressive than with model-consistent expectations since, as noted above, in the latter case the value of the exchange rate depends on expected future as well as current interest rates.

Chart 7.6 shows the consequences of using the same rules to raise

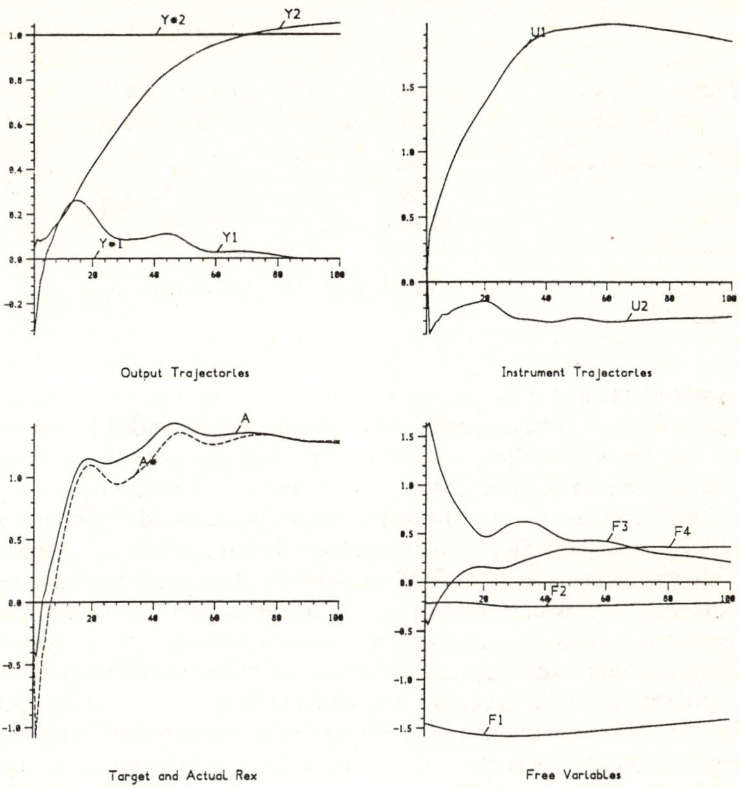

Key:

Y_1 Money GDP (% deviation)	F_1 Nominal exchange rate (% deviation)
Y_2 National wealth (% deviation)	F_2 Valuation ratio (% deviation)
A Real exchange rate (% deviation)	F_3 Consol rate (% deviation)
A* Target real exchange rate (% deviation)	F_4 Human capital (% deviation)
U_1 Tax variable (deviation)	U_2 Treasury bill rate (deviation)

Chart 7.6 National wealth plus 1 per cent with model-consistent expectations and unreformed wages

national wealth by 1 per cent of its value. The adjustment of national wealth is, with both types of expectations, much slower than was the adjustment of nominal national income. This is not very surprising. Changes in national wealth can only be achieved by

Table 7.1 Welfare losses with unreformed wages

		Total	GDP	Wealth
Model-consistent expectations	Money GDP	1.609	1.475	0.134
	Nat. wealth	7.854	0.550	7.304
Adaptive expectations	Money GDP	3.676	2.976	0.800
	Nat. wealth	11.563	0.964	10.599

Note: The welfare function is $W = \Sigma_{t=1}^{100} 0.9975^t[(g_t - g_t^{\star})^2 + (w_t - w_t^{\star})^2]$, implying an (annual) discount rate of little over 1 per cent.

means of variations in the rate of national saving (apart from valuation effects on foreign assets). Money GDP can be varied by means of policies which affect the price level, and this can be modified without requiring large changes in people's real behaviour.

The direct mechanism by which wealth is increased is through a reduction in the budget deficit promoted by an increase in taxation. This tax increase reduces GDP in the very short term but once its inflationary pressures are felt GDP increases. So the target real exchange rate is first reduced and then increased. The increased foreign saving (current account surplus) of the economy leads to an appreciation of the exchange rate and the interest rate can in fact be allowed to decline slightly. These lower interest rates raise the stock exchange valuation ratio giving a further impetus to saving, while the permanently higher taxes have a depressing effect on consumption.

The effects of the rules may be summarised by means of a table showing quadratic losses on money GDP and national wealth.

The rules we have presented are efficient at avoiding large interactions between money GDP and wealth. When money GDP is reduced, wealth is disturbed by no more than 0.4 per cent in the adaptive expectations case. Similarly policy-induced changes to wealth do not disturb money GDP by more than 0.4 per cent (again in the adaptive expectations case). This is reflected in the small quadratic welfare losses found in wealth when money GDP is being regulated and the small losses found in money GDP when wealth is being regulated (table 7.1). We also notice that regulation is easier with model-consistent expectations than with regressive expectations; this is because jumping variables speed up the convergence to equilibrium. As already noted the regulation of GDP is much easier than the regulation of wealth. This happens because changes in GDP can be achieved by means of changes in prices, while real wealth can (apart from valuation effects on foreign investment) only be varied by influencing national saving.

Policy rules for a reformed wage equation

The analysis of the sixth and eighth section above leads us to expect that if a reform of pay-bargaining were to lead to a value of $\zeta = 0$, then the pattern of comparative advantage of monetary and fiscal policy would be altered and, as a consequence, reliance could be placed mainly on fiscal policy for fighting inflation, with monetary policy being used predominantly for looking after national wealth. We find that the following policy rules are satisfactory, whether expectations are model-consistent or regressive

$$\Delta s_t = 2.5\Delta(g_{t-1} - g^{\star}_{t-1}) + 0.2(g_{t-1} - g^{\star}_{t-1}) \qquad \text{(36a)}$$

$$\Delta a^{\star}_t = 0.8\Delta(g_{t-1} - g^{\star}_{t-1}) + 0.3(g_{t-1} - g^{\star}_{t-1}) + 1.2\Delta(w_{t-1} - w^{\star}_{t-1}) + 0.25(w_{t-1} - w^{\star}_{t-1}) \qquad \text{(36b)}$$

and the rule for short-term monetary policy is as before

$$\Delta r_t = -0.6(\Delta(a_t - a^{\star}_t) - 0.03(a_t - a^{\star}_t) \qquad \text{(36c)}$$

Again note four features of this rule. First, it is not diagonal. Second, taxes only control money GDP (see Edison, Miller and Williamson, 1987). Third, the real exchange rate target mainly controls wealth and has a much smaller response to money GDP.[36] (This illustrates the tradeoff between wage reform and the exchange rate system.) Fourth, the interest rate rule is as before.

Chart 7.7 shows the results of using these rules to reduce money GDP by 1 per cent with model-consistent expectations. The time profile of money GDP is not very different from that which was found with unreformed wages. However, now the reduction is generated by an increase in taxes and much less use is made of interest rates. Nevertheless the real exchange rate is not constant in the adjustment process: it depreciates by about one third of the depreciation needed with unreformed wages. Indeed, it is difficult to see how an initial rise of 1 per cent in the real exchange rate could be avoided, since the nominal exchange rate jumps close to its new equilibrium (which is an appreciation of around 1 per cent) almost immediately. Control is rather more precise with model-consistent expectations than in the case with adaptive expectations (not shown). The main reason for this is that, in our model,

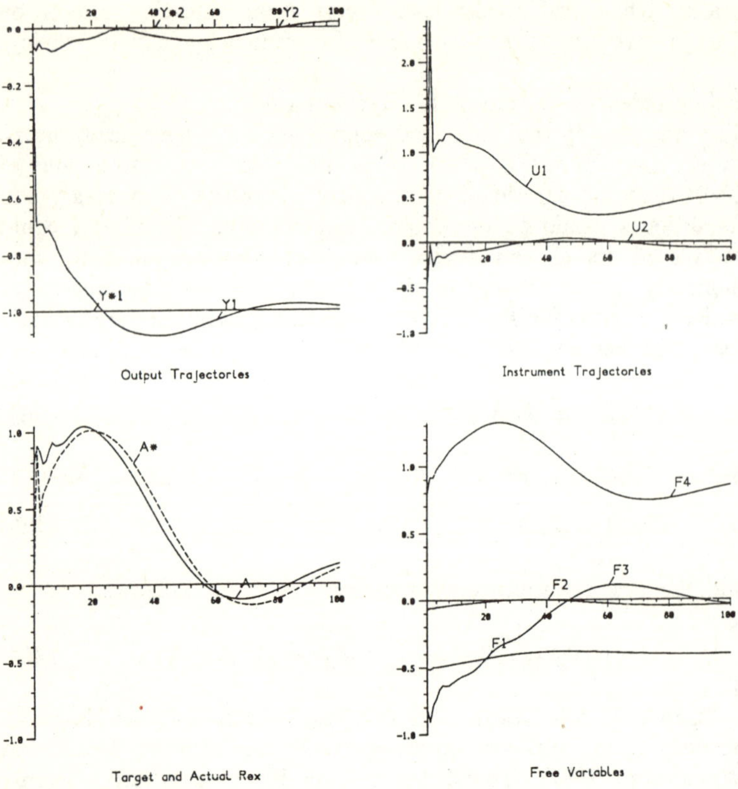

Key:

Y_1 Money GDP (% deviation)
Y_2 National wealth (% deviation)
A Real exchange rate (% deviation)
A* Target real exchange rate (% deviation)
U_1 Tax variable (deviation)

F_1 Nominal exchange rate (% deviation)
F_2 Valuation ratio (% deviation)
F_3 Consol rate (% deviation)
F_4 Human capital (% deviation)
U_2 Treasury bill rate (deviation)

Chart 7.7 Money GDP – 1 per cent with model-consistent expectations and reformed wages

consumption depends not only on current but also on expected future taxation. As a consequence, the effect on demand of the tax rule is much more sudden with model-consistent than with regressive expectations. This is reflected in the jump in human

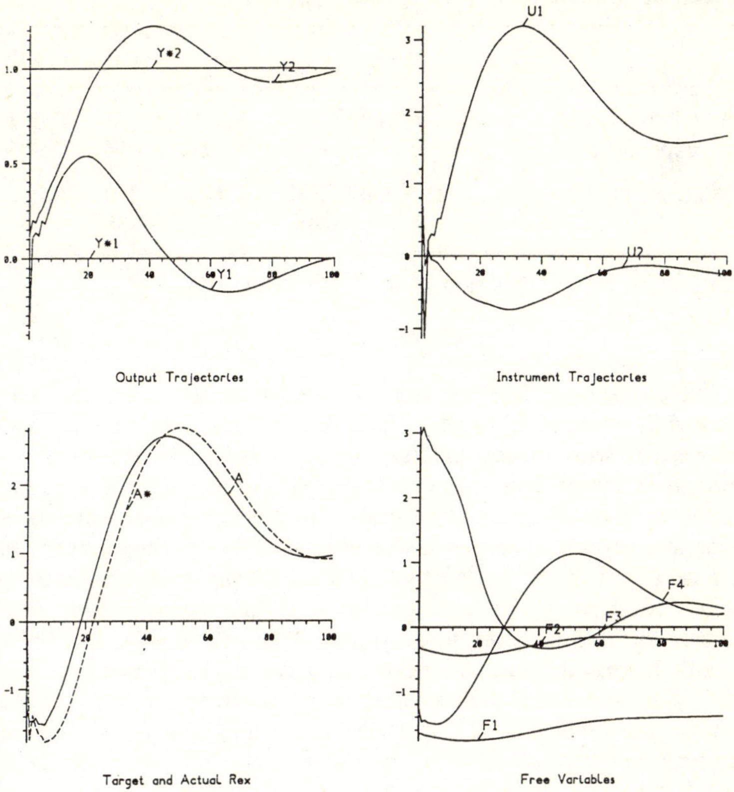

Key:

Y_1 Money GDP (% deviation)	F_1 Nominal exchange rate (% deviation)
Y_2 National wealth (% deviation)	F_2 Valuation ratio (% deviation)
A Real exchange rate (% deviation)	F_3 Consol rate (% deviation)
A* Target real exchange rate (% deviation)	F_4 Human capital (% deviation)
U_1 Tax variable (deviation)	U_2 Treasury bill rate (deviation)

Chart 7.8 National wealth plus 1 per cent with model-consistent expectations and reformed wages

capital. We also note that the deflationary conditions lead to a slump in the stock exchange (shown by the downward jump in the valuation ratio) which is, however, less serious than in the case of unreformed wages.

Table 7.2 Welfare losses with reformed wages

		Total	GDP	Wealth
Model-consistent expectations	Money GDP	0.935	0.873	0.062
	Nat. wealth	5.521	2.614	2.906
Adaptive expectations	Money GDP	2.687	1.840	0.847
	Nat. wealth	13.150	3.558	9.592

Note: The welfare function is $W = \Sigma_{t=1}^{100} 0.9975^t[(g_t - g_t^{\star})^2 + (w_t - w_t^{\star})^2]$.

These rules regulate the stock of wealth rather more promptly than with unreformed wages. Chart 7.8 shows a 1 per cent increase in wealth, with model-consistent expectations. The accumulation process is triggered by means of a decline in the real exchange rate. However taxes have to rise because of the inflationary pressures generated by the increase in domestic and foreign investment. In the later part of the period the simulation bears some similarity to chart 7.6 showing the same change with unreformed wages. The reason for this is quite straightforward: in the steady state with wealth increased there will be no increase in prices in either case and so it does not matter whether wages are indexed or not. (The steady states will only differ as between these cases on account of hysteresis effects arising from the fact that the different trajectories which have been followed may have influenced the split of national wealth between domestic and net foreign assets.) Also note that even though the exchange rate is 'assigned' to regulating wealth, in the steady state taxes are increased and the real exchange rate is appreciated. The results are summarised in table 7.2.

These values again show that the economy is easier to regulate with model-consistent expectations than with regressive expectations. Also, except in the last case, the economy appears easier to regulate with reformed wages than it was with unreformed wages. This result, too, is not a surprise. However a final point to note is that, in regulating wealth, considerable disturbances are produced in money GDP. It may well be possible to reduce these by refining the policy rule.

Conclusions

In this chapter we have shown how the joint use of monetary and fiscal policy allows the authorities to achieve an investment or wealth target as well as of a target level of money GDP (or target price level). At the same time we have demonstrated that monetary policy can be guided by means of an exchange rate target, with the short-term interest rate being set with reference to the deviation of the actual exchange rate from its target. If mainly monetary policy is used to control inflation, the exchange rate target can be varied in response to the deviation of money GDP (or prices) from its target. If mainly fiscal policy is used to control inflation, the exchange rate target must be used so as to achieve the desired level of national wealth.

The analytical exposition has made clear that the use of a target exchange rate is quite compatible with conventional models of the actual exchange rate, although it does mean that the interest rate needs to be used as the policy variable, and the money stock becomes demand-determined. The models show the normal saddle path property if solved with model-consistent expectations (and no unstable roots if solved with regressive expectations). The analytic model is a great simplification of reality. It has, however, drawn our attention to the fact that the use of instruments to achieve targets (when there are the same number of each), gives an outcome which in the steady state is independent of the policy rules used.[37] Secondly it has shown that strong wage–price interactions may make fiscal control of inflation difficult to achieve.

When we analysed these issues using a more complex empirical model we observed that for high degrees of wage indexation and using taxes as the fiscal instrument, the comparative advantage lies with monetary policy, or even cost-push fiscal policy, for fighting inflation. It is only in the long run that demand-pull fiscal policy appears to be effective for this purpose. Only if government consumption could be used as the fiscal instrument, which we regard as unlikely, could fiscal control of inflation by demand-pull means become possible. Our simulations suggest that it is the degree of wage indexation, rather than the type of expectations formation in financial markets, which is crucial for the design of monetary and fiscal policy.

Notes

1 A theoretically more appropriate variable is probably the present discounted value of future consumption, but it is difficult to imagine that being used as a formal aim of economic policy. A target for national wealth offers a more useable alternative.

It is important to note that the procedure of including real GDP in an intertemporal maxim and is in no way equivalent to this. Debt service payments can make a very marked inroad into permanent national income, but they have no effect on real GDP.

2 This second set of objections is derived from the ideas of Poole (1970): in the

presence of a fixed money supply velocity shifts and foreign capital market disturbances cause disturbances to final objectives through changes in the interest rate and the exchange rate.

3 The reason for this assumption is that we think that the only form of government spending which could be fine-tuned is transfer payments, but that we consider fine-tuning of transfer payments to be politically impossible.

4 This section sets out in greater detail the model described by Blake and Weale (1988). The main differences from that model are that the monetary policy is represented by the real interest rate, and that a core rate of inflation is assumed to be present.

5 Since the analytic model does not cumulate stocks we are obliged to limit ourselves to a target expressed in terms of the flow of investment.

6 This definition follows the conventional measurement of the exchange rate in the United Kingdom.

7 A range of learning processes could be postulated but they would add a further differential equation to our analytical model.

8 The presence of the core rate of inflation in equation (1) can be explained in one of two ways. There may be two groups of workers, one of which has model-consistent expectations, while the other uses the core rate or norm as the basis for their expectations. Or workers may use a Bayesian process to form a view about current inflation, both on the basis of available information and on the basis of their view of normalcy. It makes good sense, in fact, to simplify by supposing that the workers view of normalcy is determined by the government's inflation target, $p^{\star}$.

9 See footnote 14 below.

10 See footnote 14 below.

11 It does not embody forward-looking expectations of the type stressed by Taylor (1979).

12 In discussion at the conference Steven Nickell drew attention to the importance of hysteresis effects in the empirical wage equation used below. These are demand-pull pressures which are caused by an increase of y. For simplicity we ignore these in our analytical models.

13 Notice that setting the real interest rate and real exchange rate terms in equation (8) equal to γ_1 and γ_2 respectively implies that, in equation (6), (i) we ignore the effects of the real interest rate on domestic consumption, and (ii) we ignore the Laursen-Metzler effect which makes the 'impact' effect of the real exchange rate on aggregate demand different from that on the trade balance. Setting the coefficient on output equal to η in equation (8) also implies that the import content of investment is equal to that of consumption.

14 Notice the absence of any time trend in this equation. If there were a time trend in l^s in the labour supply equation – due to the growth in workers' aspirations – and a time trend in labour productivity $\bar{l}^d$ (see equation 4), then prices would rise or fall without limit unless the effects of these terms were brought into equality. One would then need to study the process by which that happened, but modelling that would introduce an extra dynamic equation into our system. We abstract from all of this.

15 Notice that, because we treat the real interest rate rather than the nominal interest rate as the instrument of monetary policy, this equation does not display the potential for instability of the price level in the open loop economy noted by Cagan (1956). If, by contrast, the nominal interest rate is exogenous, then when inflation increases (i) this reduces the real rate of interest which increases investment which raises the rate of inflation and (ii) this increases wage pressure which increases inflation. If the sum of these two feedbacks is large enough then there will be an explosion. See Blake and Weale (1988) for an alternative specification of our policy problem in which this is a possibility.

16 See p. 196.

17 The results are explained using chart 7.1. The reader can verify them from equation (17).

18 In our empirical work $a \rightarrow a_\infty$ only as a result of 'integral control' in the policy feedback rules rather than as a result of setting a directly with reference to a_∞. But to add integral control would add another differential equation to our analytical model, which would not be helpful.

19 In our empirical work $s \rightarrow s_\infty$ only as a result of integral control. See the remark in the previous footnote.

20 Vines *et al.* (1983) found, in particular, that expenditure taxes (VAT and employees' national insurance contributions) could be varied on a quarterly basis.

21 This is possible because the evolution of investment does not affect the dynamics of our system, given that stock effects are neglected and given our simplifying assumption that no policy instrument feeds back on investment. It is not possible in our empirical work.

22 This is true however large the short-run cost-push effect of α_3 of a tax increase.

23 That is, regimes in which both instruments are used to look after both targets.

24 In the steady state this analysis is valid even when $p = p$. In such circumstances the pattern of comparative advantage tells us about the adjustments to monetary and fiscal policy which are needed in response to a shock in the exogenous variables or constants of equations (16), so as to restore steady-state inflation. When the system is homogeneous of degree 1 in core inflation, the pattern of comparative advantage does not tell us anything about the adjustments needed to move from one steady-state rate of inflation to another.

25 At least with regressive expectations. We have had technical problems, noted below in producing such plots for the model-consistent case.

26 With model-consistent expectations the behaviour of the economy depends not only on the current values taken by the policy instruments, but also on their expected future values. As a consequence it is not possible to define comparative advantage unambiguously.

27 It is often argued that policy rules should be designed using the techniques of optimal control. This approach has much to commend it, particularly if a target trajectory for the economy is being chosen at the same time as a disturbance is being damped. By contrast, we consider that it is helpful to present policy rules with a very simple structure which aim to do no more than return the economy to a preset trajectory after a disturbance. As an analogy, if a rocket is sent to the moon, an optimum trajectory will be calculated so as to economise on fuel. If the rocket veers slightly off course the trajectory will not be recalculated. Instead simple rules will be used to return it to its original trajectory. In the same way our policy rules are designed to return the economy to a target trajectory after some disturbance. They take this target trajectory as given, although its design might involve a great deal of careful optimisation.

28 This package has been written by Andrew Blake.

29 McKay (1987) has investigated ways in which timely estimates of money GDP can be produced. We have assumed, in setting out our policy rules here, that his preliminary estimates of money GDP are available immediately after the end of the quarter to which they relate and that similar preliminary estimates of national wealth exist.

30 This argument has two parts. First it relies on the assumption that a 'correct' exchange rate with 'inappropriate' interest rate is much less damaging to the economy than an 'incorrect' interest rate with an 'appropriate' exchange rate. We are confident that this is true for a country such as the United Kingdom, although do not necessarily claim that it is universally true. Secondly, it supposes that the effects of an incorrect exchange rate on money GDP or wealth are lagged, so that setting the interest rate with respect only to those targets would

not call forth immediate corrective action in response to an incorrect rate.

31 For the record, we have found that even under rational expectations, fixed nominal exchange rates do not provide adequate anti inflation discipline.

32 With an import content of roughly one third this rule almost completely cancels domestic inflationary pressure by the effect of cheaper imports ($3 \times 1/3 = 1$).

33 The case of adaptive expectations is depicted by Weale *et al.* (forthcoming).

34 It is far slower with adaptive expectations.

35 Of course this raises the question of whether the assumption that home assets and foreign assets are, in social welfare terms, perfect substitutes. An investigation of this question is a major project on which we hope to work in the near future. However we do not regard our present model to be an appropriate tool for investigating this issue.

36 The reason that the target real exchange rate still pays some attention to money GDP is partly as a result of the adjustment to the exchange rate which would become necessary as a consequence of changing taxes to control inflation. If taxes were increased so as to reduce money GDP, the current account of the balance of payments would go into surplus and it would then become necessary to appreciate the real exchange rate to bring wealth back to its target value. This cross-linkage can then be seen as a means of reducing the interaction between money GDP and wealth.

37 Recall that our analytical model has no hysteresis effects.

Comment on Chapter 7

Stephen Hall

This chapter is, in many ways, the most ambitious of those presented in this book. It may be considered at many levels; for example, one might consider the details of the models under discussion or the analytical tools which have been applied. Its most important aspect, however, is that the authors are actively setting out a framework for macroeconomic policy formulation. The detailed modelling work may then be seen simply as an illustration of this general policymaking framework. It is their general approach to policy formulation on which this comment will focus.

Implicitly at least, the proposed procedure works through four stages; the first stage considers a general non-linear stochastic model which is believed to provide a valid description of the real world. The second stage involves deriving a time path for target values of nominal GDP and real wealth; these target values must be obtainable and they must represent what the authorities would like to happen. The third stage involves producing a small linear deterministic version of the large non-linear model. Finally, the fourth stage involves using this linearised model to calculate feedback rules which allow the economy to be kept on the target paths for nominal income and real wealth.

Most of the discussion undertaken by Blake *et al.* focuses on the last two of these four stages, the linearisation of the model and derivation of the feedback rules. The authors argue that the use of simple feedback rules is particularly appropriate as these rules are simple to understand and explain and it is claimed that they are also robust.

In many ways this framework for policy analysis is a very appealing one, particularly as it seems to avoid many of the formal problems which have received a great deal of recent attention when standard optimal control techniques are applied to large models. In particular, the time-inconsistency and credibility questions are not raised here and the computationally difficult problem of optimal control of a non-linear stochastic model appears to be avoided. This, however, is not really the case. These problems are inherent in the first two stages of the procedure and they only disappear once the target paths for nominal GDP and real wealth have been fixed. These paths must be obtainable and they should, if they are to be used in actual policy setting, also be in some sense 'best'. It is therefore very hard to avoid the conclusion that they should be the solution path from a full optimal control exercise on the non-linear stochastic model. As such they will be subject to all the well-known problems from the time-inconsistency and credibility literature. They will also be subject to the problem of calculating the optimal solution to a stochastic non-linear model and all the well-known difficulties of optimal control, such as the importance of the choice of control variables and objective functions.

Even assuming these problems can be overcome, the advantages of the final two stages of the procedure are not without cost. Using small linearised versions of large models clearly considerably simplifies the computational work involved. But the cost of this is that the linearised model is, at best, only a local approximation to the large model. In devising feedback rules this approximation may not be important but the use of feedback rules are themselves not costless. When the authors talk about feedback rules they do not mean the full optimal feedback rule but rather a simple rule which contains only a small set of feedback terms. The advantage of such rules is that they are easily understood but the cost is that the economic performance may be considerably impaired relative to the full optimal solution. So one wonders just how many unemployed can be justified in order to use a simple rule rather than a more complex one, or even direct open-loop control.

Finally, let us consider one of the features of the simple feedback rules which is often attributed to them by their proponents, robustness. The concept of robustness is not an unambiguous one in this context and there is no precise definition or criteria for measuring robustness. Nonetheless, we know that the full optimal feedback rule is not invariant to changes in the model's specification so, in general, the only way in which a simple rule can be invariant to changes in the model structure is if it is so inferior to the optimal rule that changes in the model have no effect on its performance. The more closely a rule approaches the optimal rule the less likely it is to be robust. Robustness then tends in practice to mean that a rule is equally inefficient under varying model structures. In fact robustness, even of this form, is not easy to attain; this is illustrated by the rules the authors give in equations 38a and b and 39a and b, which vary considerably even though they are based on models which differ by only one parameter value.

8 Conflict and Cooperation in International Macroeconomic Policymaking: Past Performance and Future Prospects*

David Currie and Simon Wren-Lewis

Introduction

The past decade of floating exchange rates has seen periods of prolonged exchange rate misalignments and the emergence of persistent and large current account imbalances amongst the major OECD countries. These have, in turn, given rise to considerable uncertainties in financial markets and costly and not easily reversible adjustments in goods and factor markets. This experience has led to growing dissatisfaction with the performance of floating exchange rates when combined with uncoordinated macroeconomic policies among the major OECD countries.

In consequence the recent years have seen a renewed interest in issues in international macroeconomic policy coordination, and in forms of exchange rate targets or zones. This is reflected in the growing research literature on international policy coordination (see, for example, Buiter and Marston, 1985, Bryant and Portes, 1987, and Cooper, 1985, for an excellent survey of the earlier literature). It has also been reflected in recent policy initiatives. The Plaza Accord of September 1985 saw the first practical step in this direction, with agreement on coordinated exchange market intervention. This was followed by the Tokyo summit of May 1986, the Louvre Accord of February 1987, and the Venice summit of June 1987. These initiatives continued the agreement on coordinated action on exchange rates, but also increasingly emphasised the need for adjustments in monetary and fiscal policy in each of the G7 countries. The Tokyo and Venice summits approved the

* This research was undertaken while David Currie was Visiting Scholar in the Research Department of the International Monetary Fund and has benefited from helpful discussions in that period with the IMF Research Staff, particularly Jim Bougton, as well as with John Williamson and Marcus Miller. The development of the National Institute's Global Econometric Model is supported by finance from the Economic and Social Research Council. The views expressed are solely those of the authors.

concept of using a set of 'indicators' as a framework for coordinating policy, but did not articulate how such an indicators system might operate in practice.

The state of the policy discussion therefore makes it timely to consider possible schemes for more effective policy coordination among the G7 countries. Prominent among such schemes has been Williamson's (1983), target zone proposal, which argues for greater stability of real exchange rates, aimed at achieving external current account equilibrium. This proposal may be contrasted with the view which emphasises the need for adjustments of underlying monetary and fiscal policies in a coordinated manner (see Boughton, 1987, Frenkel, 1987, and IMF, 1987). This distinction should not be over-emphasised: those like Williamson who argue for greater stability of exchange rates fully recognise the need for adjustment of underlying policies, and argue further that a commitment to exchange rate targets may be helpful in bringing this adjustment about: while those who argue for adjustment of underlying policies see this as bringing in its wake greater stability in foreign exchange markets. But a possible danger of the former approach is that it may result, in practice, in firm policy commitments with respect to exchange rates and rather less precise understandings on the adjustment of underlying monetary and fiscal policies. If underlying policies do not adjust to support the exchange rate objectives, the consequent loss of credibility may add to instability in foreign exchange markets, as well as eroding confidence in subsequent attempts at international coordination. The experience of the Louvre Accord may well illustrate these dangers.

It is therefore helpful that the most recent statement of the target zone proposal by Williamson and Miller (1987) has extended it to include explicit rules for the adjustment of both monetary and fiscal policy. These rules envisage the use of monetary policy to pursue a set of mutually consistent target zones for real exchange rates, with nominal domestic demand targets pursued primarily by fiscal policy. An aim of this chapter is to examine this proposal in detail using the National Institute Global Econometric Model (GEM), in order to assess how macroeconomic policy in the G3 countries would have performed, relative to history, under these rules.

In the next section we review briefly the recent literature on international policy coordination. Its purpose is to motivate the quest for a simple, rule-based framework for macroeconomic policy coordination of the type advocated by Williamson and Miller. The third section then reviews alternative types of rules, focusing particularly on the Williamson/Miller proposal and an alternative where fiscal policy is focussed on ensuring external balance while monetary policy assumes primary responsibility for domestic nominal demand growth. The fourth section uses GEM to investigate the Williamson/Miller proposals and briefly reviews how the international economy might have evolved under these rules. Finally, we present our main conclusions.

International policy coordination and simple rules

The case for the international coordination of macroeconomic policy is based on the presence of significant policy spillover between countries, so that individual, non-cooperative decision-making by governments will result in an inefficient Nash outcome. These policy spillovers may take a variety of forms. Governments may be reluctant unilaterally to expand, or to offset a contractionary tendency, because of the resulting balance of payments deficit and downward pressure on the exchange rate; the consequence may be a deflationary bias in the world economy. Governments may tend to tackle inflationary pressures by a combination of tight money and an appreciating exchange rate, coupled with expansionary fiscal policy to offset the output consequences of the resulting loss of competitiveness; the consequences at the world level may be unduly high real interest rates and a wrong monetary-fiscal policy mix. Governments may reasonably treat commodity prices as determined in world markets, and neglect any effect of demand expansion on commodity prices; but if generalised, such demand expansion may prove over-inflationary because of the consequences for the commodity terms of trade. Governments may have inconsistent objectives concerning their desired current account position, and non-cooperative policy initiatives to try to secure these objectives may prove disruptive to the international economy. These, and other spillovers, have been an important aspect of the international economy over the past decade. The biases that these spillovers induce with non-cooperative policymaking are often in different directions, and may therefore in part cancel each other. (For example, the deflationary bias for balance of payments considerations may be offset by the expansionary bias for neglecting effects on commodity prices.)

In view of these arguments, it is perhaps surprising that much of the literature on international policy coordination gives a rather negative view of the benefits to be expected. (For a helpful recent survey, see Kenen, 1987.) The pioneering study by Oudiz and Sachs (1984) suggests rather minor gains, equivalent to less than ½ per cent of GDP, from complete and perfect coordination of monetary and fiscal policy among the G3 for the period 1984–6.

Such calculations provide an upper bound for the realisable gains from the actual policy process of coordination, with its imperfections and delays, so these results give little support to the advocates of coordination. Some later work gives still less encouragement. Rogoff (1985) points out that international policy coordination may actually be welfare-decreasing, if the coordination process eases the constraints on governments to engage in inflationary monetary expansions. In this example, governments without reputation are deterred by the prospect of a depreciating exchange rate from springing monetary surprises on their private sectors with a view to raising output; coordination to peg the exchange rate results in a greater incentive to spring monetary surprises, so that the equilibrium rate of inflation rises, with an overall fall in welfare. Although the example is specific, it is a general point that coordination without reputation may be counterproductive (see Levine and Currie, 1987b and Currie, Levine and Vidalis, 1987). Frankel and Rockett (1987) investigate the consequences of the plausible assumption that governments differ about their view of the world. Using six of the international models participating in the recent Brookings model comparison exercise (Bryant *et al*, 1988) as representing possible views and states of the world, they examine all the possible combinations where the two governments (the United States and the rest of the world) can subscribe to any of the six models, and the true state of the world can in turn be any of the six models. Cooperation gives benefits only in just over 60 per cent of the possible cases; in more than one third of the cases, cooperation makes matters worse for at least one of the countries.

This rather pessimistic view of the benefits to be expected from international coordination has been questioned by more recent work. The Frankel/Rockett result concerning the negative consequences of model uncertainty for the benefits to be derived from international cooperation depends crucially on the assumption that policymakers are pigheaded, and takes no account of divergencies of model view in formulating their policies. Frankel (1987) shows that use of a compromise model in cases of disagreement increases appreciably the probability of benefits from coordination. Holtham and Hughes-Hallett show that ruling out 'weak' bargains, in which one party or the other expects the other party to be made worse off, greatly improves the success rate; they argue that governments would wish to rule out such bargains, because they will be liable to reneging and will jeopardise future coordination attempts. Ghosh and Masson (1987) show that the presence of model uncertainty may appreciably raise the benefits from cooperation, provided that governments design cooperative policies with explicit regard to the presence of model uncertainty. It may be objected that policy-makers are indeed pigheaded in recognising only one view of the world (though this is hardly consistent with the significant exchange of views on such matters in international fora), but this would point more to the need to educate policymakers on the dangers of this approach rather than to avoid international cooperation.

Recent work has also placed in context the Rogoff (1985) result that, in the absence of reputation, cooperation may be undesirable. Levine and Currie (1987b) and Currie, Levine and Vidalis (1987) show a related result, that, in the absence of cooperation, reputational policies may be undesirable. This points to the conclusion that the benefits from reputation and cooperation are joint, so that one without the other may well be counterproductive. Since governments have been increasingly concerned to establish a reputation in policy matters, this is a rather compelling argument for cooperation. They also show that cooperative reputational policies are sustainable in plausible circumstances.

Currie, Levine and Vidalis (1987) also use a two-bloc reduced version of the OECD Interlink model to estimate the potential benefits from cooperation with reputation. The benefits from cooperation with reputation in the place of purely temporary disturbances is found to be small, of the order of the equivalent of less than 0.1 per cent of GDP for disturbances to demand and supply. But the benefits from coordination are estimated to rise steeply as the persistence of the disturbance increases. Moreover, these benefits rise through time: non-cooperative non-reputational policies are more likely to push undesirable adjustments into the discounted future, so that their long-run consequences are dismal; while the alternative of reputational policies without cooperation is rather prone to instability. In the long run Currie, Levine and Vidalis find gains of the order of the equivalent of 15 per cent of GDP from coordination with reputation in the face of permanent supply and demand disturbances. This provides an upper bound for the benefits of cooperation, since in any historical episode, disturbances are likely to be a combination of shocks of different persistence. Thus, Holtham and Hughes-Hallett (1987) obtain estimates of the order of 4–6 per cent of GDP, using seven alternative models of the international economy drawn from the Brookings model comparison exercise. Interestingly, they find greater benefits from models with rational expectations, confirming the role of reputation in such benefits. In summary then, these results suggest that the benefits of coordination with reputation may be considerable, particularly if coordination focuses on how policy should adjust to persistent or permanent disturbances to the international economy.

A potential difficulty with all these studies is that the policies being coordinated are fully optimal ones and therefore highly complex. It is plausible to argue that policies that are to be implemented in practice should be relatively simple in formulation (even if complex calculations go into their design), though it is not straightforward to define simplicity (see Currie and Levine, 1985b). If this is so, then it applies with still greater force to cooperatively agreed international policies: it is hard to imagine politicians or senior officials agreeing in international form to anything other than rather simple operating rules for macropolicy. This argument suggests the need to search for simple policy designs that might guide international policymaking.

If such policies took the form of rules or guidelines, this may also provide a helpful way for policymakers to establish and maintain reputation vis-à-vis the private sector. Of course, simplicity imposes costs in terms of policy performance. (However, this cost may not be too great: Holtham and Hughes-Hallett, 1987, find that cooperative policies exhibit greater continuity and smoothness of final objectives than do non-cooperative ones.) This highlights the need for the careful design of systems of simple rules for international policy. The remainder of this chapter is concerned with evaluating the potential performance of certain sets of simple rules or blueprints for international macropolicy that have been advanced.

Blueprints for international cooperation

Dissatisfaction with the performance of floating exchange rates in a period of uncoordinated international policy has led a number of economists to propose blueprints for coordination of macroeconomic policies and the management of exchange rates. Prominent amongst these is the target exchange rate zone proposal of John Williamson (Williamson 1983), which envisages the targeting of real exchange rates at a level to ensure medium-term current-account equilibrium. This blueprint has recently been extended to include the targeting of the growth in domestic nominal demand, with rules for the conduct of both monetary and fiscal policy to achieve both sets of targets (see Williamson and Miller, 1987). This extended target zone proposal has much in common with the proposal of Meade (1984) for a new Bretton Woods, though the Williamson/Miller scheme envisages much wider bands of permissible exchange rate variation. McKinnon (1984, 1987) proposes a rather different move towards greater fixity of nominal, rather than real exchange rates, supported by careful coordination of monetary policy between central banks. Dornbusch and Frankel (1987) provide a review of these and other less tightly specified proposals for international monetary reform.

The principal argument for wishing to limit the scope for real exchange rate misalignments is that these have damaging effects on the efficiency of the international trading system. This occurs in part because of greater uncertainty in the traded goods sector, but also because prolonged misalignments generate costly adjustments in the tradeable goods sector that may not be easily reversed. More generally, misalignments may result in inefficiencies in the international allocation of capital, and can enormously increase the pressure for protection, with severe consequences, both actual and potential, for the efficiency of the international trading system.

The high degree of international capital mobility means that there is only limited scope for targeting exchange rates by means of sterilised intervention in foreign exchange markets (though intervention may have a role in day-to-day market operations). Thus proposals for exchange rate targets or zones envisage the use of other instruments of policy, notably monetary policy, to limit exchange rate variability. A potential objection is that excessively large movements in interest rates may be required to achieve stable exchange rates. But against this, a credible system of exchange rate targets, backed up by effective policy rules, can act to provide an anchor for market expectations, thereby limiting the scope for speculative exchange rate bubbles of the kind to which foreign exchange markets seem to have been prone in recent years. In addition, targets for the real exchange rate will limit the scope for governments to curb general inflationary pressures by an excessive appreciation of the exchange rate brought about by a switch in the monetary–fiscal mix.

A frequent objection to a system of real exchange rate targets is that they provide no anchor for domestic inflation, since a given real exchange rate is consistent, in principle, with any evolution of nominal variables. However, this is to assume wrongly that the proposal is intended as a comprehensive specification of macropolicy. There is no reason why proposals for rules to govern the international conduct of macropolicy need be comprehensive. What is desirable is that rules should be devised that limit the degree to which conflicts can arise between the policies of different countries. If this is done, other aspects of policy may be left to individual national policymakers to determine as they choose. Instead of seeking to lay down a fully comprehensive set of rules for countries to pursue cooperatively, a more limited set of cooperative rules may be specified, and then other aspects of policy may be left to national governments to determine independently or noncooperatively.

Considered in this way, target zones for real exchange rates have the virtue over other rules (including nominal exchange rate targets) of internalising a major potential externality in the international system. Countries that engage in expansionary policies may seek to limit the inflationary consequences of such policies by an associated appreciation of their real exchange rate. (Whether by design or accident, Reaganomics of this form has been the policy adopted by the United States since 1981). But the appreciation of the real exchange rate acts to export the inflation to the rest of the world, exerting an important policy spillover. There is therefore a danger that in a world of inflationary pressures the fiscal–monetary mix will be wrong, with high real interest rates resulting from a combination of tight money and lax fiscal policy. This may result in problems of debt sustainability and associated instabilities. Internationally agreed targets for real exchange rates may well act to limit the scope for such policies, and therefore help to reduce this potential bias.[1] By reducing the scope for exchange rate appreciation, individual countries will be faced directly with the inflationary consequences of their own policy actions.

There are, nonetheless, good reasons for supplementing the target exchange rate proposal with rules for the conduct of domestic macropolicy, as Williamson and Miller (1987) have done in the extended target zone proposal. This is partly because an understanding (or an evaluation, as made here) of how the proposal would work requires an appreciation and assessment of how domestic macropolicy should be conducted. But it is also because there may be other policy externalities at work in the international system. Thus it is not implausible to suggest that there is a bias towards contraction in the international system resulting either from incompatible and overambitious targets for current account surpluses or from the tendency for countries undertaking expansionary measures to experience a depreciating exchange rate and rising inflation. Real exchange rate targets may, in the absence of guidelines for domestic policy objectives, increase this contradictory bias in the international system by reducing the ability of governments to engage in non-inflationary expansionary measures. Supporting guidelines for the conduct of domestic macropolicy are therefore required.

It is therefore a combined set of rules for monetary and fiscal policy that have been proposed by Williamson and Miller. These rules may be summarised as follows. First, countries should determine a consistent set of real exchange rate targets, chosen so as to ensure medium to longer-run current account equilibrium. Second, countries should choose targets for the growth of nominal demand. These targets should take account of the need to reduce inflation towards zero, of the need to expand demand in the face of a fall in capacity utilisation, and of the need to adjust current account balances towards equilibrium. Third, differences in interest rates between countries should be varied to limit the deviation of currencies from their target levels, aiming to keep exchange rates within a given band around the target. Fourth, the average level of world interest rates should be varied to stabilise the aggregate growth of nominal demand around the sum of national targets for nominal demand growth. Finally, national fiscal policy should be varied with a view to achieving national targets for nominal demand growth.

It should be noted that excess nominal demand at the world level is influenced both by the average level of world interest rates (the fourth point above) and by fiscal policy, as the aggregate outcome of each country using fiscal policy to stabilise its growth in nominal demand. In effect, there is a spare degree of freedom in the scheme to determine the relative balance of monetary and fiscal policy at the world level, since for n countries there are $2n-1$ independent targets (n independent demand targets and $n-1$ independent exchange rate targets) and $2n$ instruments (the setting of monetary and fiscal policy in each country). The scheme assigns monetary policy (in the form of interest rate policy) to stabilise exchange rates at their equilibrium level; fiscal policy to stabilise domestic nominal demand trends; and some combination of aggregate monetary and fiscal policy to stabilise global nominal demand.

Since only monetary policy can be moved with sufficient flexibility to stabilise exchange rates in the short run, a target zone proposal naturally leads to this assignment of instruments. However, there are certain objections to it. The evidence from the empirical international models shows that the influence of monetary policy on the current account is quite small, whereas that of fiscal policy is more appreciable (see Bryant *et al*, 1988). This is in part because of the J-curve, but also because the income effects of expansionary monetary policy outweigh the substitution effects of the induced depreciation (see Edison, Miller and Williamson, 1987). The assignment may therefore assign instruments in the opposite way to that indicated by their comparative advantage. However, the instability that would usually arise with such an assignment need not arise with the Williamson/Miller proposals. This is because the exchange rate is set at, or near to, its medium-term equilibrium level rather than responding to the actual current balance position which could easily generate instability because of J-curve effects. Error in calculating the appropriate equilibrium exchange rate might still, however, lead to assignment instability problems, if such errors are perceived only *ex post* through a persistent current account disequilibrium. But this problem is less serious because the effects of monetary policy on the current account are stronger in the medium to longer run, and because of the use of domestic nominal demand, rather than nominal income, as the indicator of internal balance.

A rather different objection concerns the assignment of monetary policy to stabilise a real variable, namely the real exchange rate, and fiscal policy to stabilise the trend of nominal demand growth. In that class of models with perfectly flexible prices, fiscal policy influences only real variables, such as real interest rates and the real exchange rate, while the money supply influences only nominal magnitudes. This objection is not strictly applicable to the Williamson/Miller rules, since they take the instrument of monetary policy to be interest rates. Responding to an over-appreciated real exchange rate by monetary ease raises the growth of nominal demand, inducing a contraction in fiscal policy that lowers real interest rates and depreciates the real exchange rate. Too high a level of nominal demand growth induces a contraction of fiscal policy, and the resulting depreciation of the real exchange rate induces a tightening of monetary policy that slows the rate of nominal demand growth. These policy responses may seem curiously indirect in a new-classical world of perfectly flexible prices, but more direct and appropriate in the more relevant case where goods prices are slow to adjust.

A more substantial objection is that fiscal policy may be too blunt an instrument to be effective in stabilising nominal domestic demand growth. This may be because some contractionary fiscal actions (for example, increases in indirect taxes or payroll taxes) may tend to push up prices for a time, so that they are ineffective in restraining nominal demand growth except in the medium to long term (see Meade, 1987). This emphasises the need for a correct choice of fiscal instrument. Of greater importance is the presence of major political and institutional constraints on adjustment of fiscal policy. Such constraints are very severe in certain key countries: in the United States because of the independence, enshrined in the constitution, of the legislature from the executive; and in Germany because of a deep-seated aversion to fiscal deficits, however temporary. In the face of such constraints, the most that can be expected of fiscal policy may be that the structural deficit should be set in a manner consistent with medium-term trends, leaving automatic fiscal stabilisers to help stabilise demand growth in the shorter run. But fiscal policy operated in this way will not be very effective in stabilising nominal demand growth. In these circumstances, it is not evidently better to use monetary policy to target the real exchange rate, neglecting nominal demand fluctuations, rather than using monetary policy to stabilise nominal demand.

These arguments point to an alternative set of rules. (See Boughton, 1987, for a discussion of this alternative.) The structural fiscal position may be set to achieve the medium-term objectives of external balance (defined in terms of the sustainability of the external current account position). Nominal domestic demand growth would be stabilised in part by the operation of automatic fiscal stabilisers, but the primary responsibility would fall to monetary policy. This set of rules reverses the assignment inherent in the Williamson/Miller proposals, so that fiscal policy is primarily concerned with external balance and monetary policy with internal balance. As discussed above, this assignment corresponds to that indicated by the respective comparative advantage of monetary and fiscal policies with respect to the two objectives of internal and external balance.

It would be wrong to exaggerate the differences between these two approaches. The width of the proposed exchange rate zones under the Williamson/Miller proposals leaves considerable scope for the use of monetary policy to influence nominal demand growth within the zones. The efficient use of monetary policy to influence domestic nominal demand growth may well involve a response of monetary policy to nominal exchange rate movements, because of the feed-through onto domestic prices. And it seems likely that any scheme to avoid the severe fiscal imbalances that arose in the international economy in the 1980s would deliver a substantial benefit in terms of reduced exchange rate misalignments.

There is, however, one important difference between the two proposals. The Williamson/Miller rules require international cooperation over monetary policy, while leaving each government to use its fiscal policy to target its domestic nominal demand growth independently of demand growth in the rest of the world. The alternative assignment of fiscal policy to external balance requires international coordination of fiscal policy actions. At minimum, this coordination would take the form of agreement on mutually consistent targets for medium-term current account positions. A more ambitious objective would be to ensure that, in responding to disequilibrium, the fiscal policy adjustments in various countries are coordinated to prevent major global shifts in fiscal policy that destabilise world demand in the shorter run. Without any coordination of fiscal policy, an inappropriate mix of monetary and fiscal policy may easily arise, whether because of the pursuit of inconsistent current account objectives or because governments seek exchange rate appreciations as a beggar-my-neighbour resolution of domestic inflationary pressures.

At first sight, the fact that the mechanisms for monetary policy coordination are well established between the key central banks, whereas the mechanisms for fiscal policy coordination are almost non-existent, would seem to favour the Williamson/Miller proposals over the alternative. But this point cuts both ways. Since the major imbalances in the world economy at the current time arise from imbalances in fiscal policy, there is an advantage in schemes that highlight the need for fiscal policy coordination. To see this, one may note the highly undesirable consequences of a failure to adjust fiscal policy appropriately within the Williamson/Miller scheme. If fiscal policy is set at a level inconsistent with current account balance at the target real exchange rates, the commitment to target zones ties down monetary policy with potentially undesirable consequences for inflation. The Louvre Accord ran into difficulties on exactly this point, and may have set back, rather than advanced the scope for effective international policy coordination. Further cooperation may therefore be slow to develop, and one merit of the alternative assignment is that countries could pursue it in isolation. Thus, at the present time, it makes sense for the United States to cut its fiscal deficit with an eye to the external deficit, while using monetary policy to target nominal income growth. The consideration that this might lead to an undesirable shift in the monetary–fiscal mix at the world level is not important at the current time, since arguably the world economy would benefit from a shift in the monetary–fiscal mix towards tighter fiscal policy, with a view to bringing down real interest rates.

The upshot of all this is that there are merits in both schemes, and that it would be of interest to investigate in more detail the likely performance of both sets of rules. One means of doing this is to use the empirical international models to examine the counterfactual question of how the world economy would have performed under these two sets of rules during the last decade, both relative to the historical performance and relative to each other. The remainder of this chapter uses the National Institute Global Econometric Model (GEM) to investigate one half of this comparison. Specifically, we examine the performance of the Williamson/Miller rules relative to the historical record. This work represents an extension of that reported earlier (Currie and Wren-Lewis, 1988).

Later work will compare the performance of the alternative assignment, both relative to history and relative to the Williamson/Miller rules.

To investigate these rules, we follow Williamson and Miller (1987) in assuming that they take the form of proportional/integral controllers. These have the virtue of simplicity, but are also argued, more problematically, to have advantages of robustness. We may summarise these rules as follows:

$$y_i^\star = \Phi_{oi} + \Phi_1 p_i - \Phi_2 (CU_i - CU_i^\star) + \Phi_3 (b_i - b_i^\star) \quad (1)$$

$$\Delta r_i = \alpha_1 \Delta(y_a - y_a^\star) + \alpha_2(y_a - y_a^\star) + \alpha_3 \Delta(e_i - e_i^\star) + \alpha_4(e_i - e_i^\star) \quad (2)$$

$$g_i = \beta_{oi} - \beta_1 \Delta(y_i - y_i^\star) - \beta_2(y_i - y_i^\star) \quad (3)$$

where y is the growth in nominal income, p is the inflation rate, CU is capacity utilisation, b is the current balance as a ratio of nominal GNP, r is real interest rates, e is the real exchange rate, and g is the growth of government spending. Equation (1) represents the target for nominal income growth, depending on a country-specific constant term (representing productivity growth and inflation objectives), and terms on inflation, capacity utilisation and the deviation of the balance of payments from target. Equation (2) combines the third and fourth points above, containing a response to aggregate world income and a response to exchange rate deviations. Equation (3) requires government spending to respond to deviations of nominal income growth from its target at the national level. We assume that the parameters of the rule are the same for all countries, apart from country-specific constants, but this restriction could be relaxed. We have not followed Williamson and Miller in one respect that may be important. While we have assumed nominal GDP growth targets, they argue that nominal domestic demand growth targets would be preferable. This difference is unlikely to have a major influence on the results below, but later work will investigate this further.

The optimal design of the Williamson/Miller rules

We now apply optimal control techniques to determine the best design of monetary and fiscal feedback rules of the type advocated by Williamson and Miller. Thus optimisation methods are used to determine the best choice of parameter values in the feedback rules. For this purpose, we use the National Institute Global Econometric Model (GEM). This is a multi-country econometric model with some 200 behavioural equations, with detailed modelling of the main G7 countries. A fuller description of the model is provided in the appendix to this chapter.

The optimisation exercise was carried out over the period 1975–86. An earlier exercise (Currie and Wren-Lewis, 1988) along similar lines used the period 1975–84, and the additional two years 1985/6 in this exercise provide a useful test of the robustness of the earlier results. The Williamson/Miller rules were applied to the G3 countries: the United States, Japan and West Germany. However, since the exchange rates in other major European countries, except the United Kingdom, are closely related to the DM in the model, Germany acts in many ways as a proxy for continental Europe as a whole. Similarly, the Canadian economy is closely tied to the United States. The main economies not included in the policy cooperation exercise are therefore the non-OECD sectors and the United Kingdom, whose exchange rate over this historical period is estimated to have been only loosely related to the DM.

For simplicity, each country is assumed to have the same feedback rules, not simply with respect to the form of the rules but also with respect to the parameter values. As we observe, this simplification may be over-restrictive in certain respects, and future work may lift this restriction.

The objective function used to evaluate alternative rules is the discounted sum over the period of:

$$V = \sum_{i=1}^{3} w_i \{(\overline{CU}_i - CU_i)^2 + 5p_i^2 + 500/(R_i + 2.0)^4 + 0.25(g_i - \phi_{oi})^2\}$$

where variables are defined as above, and R_i is the nominal interest rate in each country. There is a non-linear trade-off between output and inflation. CU is set so that, at 'full' capacity utilisation and 5 per cent inflation, 1 per cent less output will be bought if inflation falls by more than 0.5 per cent. At 90 per cent utilisation and 5 per cent inflation the trade-off is 1 per cent/1 per cent while, if inflation was at 10 per cent it would be 1 per cent/½ per cent and, with no inflation, 1 per cent/3 per cent. A larger weight was also placed on deviations of capacity from its desired level in the final period of the optimisation, to avoid terminal date problems.

The term in nominal interest rates is designed to penalise negative or very small values. This term is negligible at interest rates above 2 percentage points. The final term penalises changes in government expenditure compared to trend. The weights, w_i, used to aggregate the values of the objective function for each country, are 0.4, 0.4, 0.2 for the United States, Germany and Japan. This roughly corresponds with GDP weights if Germany is regarded as 'representing' Europe as a whole. There is no explicit term in the distribution of activity between countries, so non-pareto changes are possible, although the quadratic nature of the function will discourage this outcome.

To calculate the optimal form of rules, the feedback rules for monetary and fiscal policy for the G3 are incorporated into the model, replacing the model's normal relationships for government expenditure and interest rates in these three countries. The parameters of the rules are chosen so as to minimise the objective function, V, defined above, evaluated over the period 1975–86. However, the feedback rules are over-parameterised. (Thus, substituting the rule for nominal demand into the other two rules, we can see this: a less-accommodating nominal GDP target is equivalent to faster adjustment towards the target.) As a result, one parameter can be fixed at an arbitrary value, and we have chosen to fix the coefficient on the inflation term at two thirds, implying that two thirds of inflation is accommodated. The constant term in the equation for the nominal GDP growth target can be viewed as the equilibrium real growth rate of the economy. These were set at 3, 4 and 3 per cent for the United States, Japan and Germany, respectively.

The target values for real exchange rates, $e^{\star}$, are set roughly equal to the average value of the actual real exchange rate over the 1970s, which also happens to be close to values recorded in 1980. This represents a significant simplification compared to the exchange rate zone proposals set out in Williamson and Miller, where target exchange rates are based on fundamental equilibrium exchange rates (FEERs). The difficulty with incorporating the FEERs is that their calculation inevitably involves a model, and the model used by Williamson and others could be quite different from GEM. Ideally we should use GEM itself to calculate values for $e^{\star}$, using the concept of underlying current account equilibrium, and later work could pursue this possibility. Needless to say, many serious problems remain, in particular regarding the concept of 'normal' capital flows. Our assumption of fixed $e^{\star}$ over this period may not in practice be a bad approximation to FEERs, which from the appendix to Williamson and Miller do not vary by very much. An important exception is Japan, where a significant increase in the FEER is calculated over the 1980s.

The desired value of the current balance ratio, $b^{\star}$, is set to zero for the United States and Germany, but to 1 per cent for Japan.

Table 8.1 Optimal parameter values

		Central rule	Variant A	Variant B
		(Optimisation over 1975/86)	(Optimisation over 1975/84)	(Optimisation over 1875/86 with increased inflation weight)
Nominal income rule				
Inflation	ϕ_1	0.66	0.66	0.66
Capacity utilisation	ϕ_2	0.55	0.20	0.16
Current account	ϕ_3	0.05	0.05	0.02
Interest rate rule				
World demand				
Proportional	α_1	1.08	0.20	2.73
Integral	α_2	0.03	0.01	0.05
Exchange rate disequilibrium				
Proportional	α_3	0.12	0.20	0.12
Integral	α_4	0.01	0.05	0.01
Fiscal rule				
Nominal income				
Proportional	β_1	0.91	1.50	1.75
Integral	β_2	0.45	0.37	1.23

We discuss below some of the difficulties involved with this. CU^* is approximately equal to the average level of capacity utilisation in each country.

The first column of table 8.1 reports the optimal parameters of the feedback rules for optimisation over the period 1975–86. The parameters of the nominal income growth target imply that a 1 per cent fall in capacity utilisation will raise the target for nominal income by just over ½ per cent, roughly the response suggested by Williamson and Miller. The paramenter on the current balance term implies a much smaller response, with a current balance surplus of 1 per cent of GDP leading to only a 0.05 per cent increase in the growth target, substantially smaller than that suggested by Williamson and Miller. However, this parameter might well be appreciably larger were we to adopt the Williamson/Miller scheme for a nominal growth target couched in terms of domestic demand rather than nominal income.

The optimal fiscal policy rule states that if nominal income is 1 per cent above target in any one quarter, real government expenditure will temporarily fall by just under 1 per cent, but permanently decline by ½ per cent. This represents a fairly high degree of fiscal activism. The response of monetary policy to deviations from the nominal GDP target is more modest. A sustained 1 per cent deviation of nominal income growth above target will immediately raise interest rates by just over 1 percentage point in the same quarter, with a very small subsequent response of 0.03 points in each succeeding quarter. The response to exchange rate disequilibria is much smaller: thus a substantial 1 per cent deviation of the real exchange rate from its target value leads to an immediate rise in interest rates of 0.1 percentage points, with 0.01 percentage points in each subsequent quarter. The response of interest differentials is twice as large, since the rules for the other G3 countries imply a roughly opposite adjustment, but nonetheless these responses remain small.

It is of interest to note the small responses of interest rates to world demand disequilibrium. Although the immediate, proportional response is quite appreciable, the subsequent integral control response is small. This is not because of the absence of significant effects of real interest rates on expenditures; for GEM has appreciable interest elasticities of expenditure. The problem arises because interest rates have effects of different magnitudes in each country. Thus, a general fall in interest rates will lead to changes in the distribution of activity, changes in current balances and therefore movements in exchange rates. This problem would not be avoided by allowing country-specific parameters on the monetary policy rules, because if interest rates responded differently in each country following global demand disequilibrium, this would produce undesirable fluctuations in exchange rates. However, it may be avoided if the fiscal rule is allowed to have different parameters across countries: thus countries with a high interest elasticity of expenditure might have a smaller fiscal response to excess demand, so that the combined thrust of monetary and fiscal policy is similar across countries with similar rises in real interest rates. However, this modification to the rule may have a cost in terms of less efficient stabilisation of nominal demand in the face of country-specific demand shocks. Subsequent work may investigate this possibility, but without it the optimal rule indicates that the principal burden of offsetting world demand disequilibria should fall on fiscal policy.

Table 8.1 also reports two alternative sets of parameter values derived under alternative assumptions concerning the optimisation. The second column reports the values derived in our earlier paper (Currie and Wren-Lewis, 1988), optimising over the shorter period 1975–84. (There were also some other minor differences between the runs, including some model development with respect to the LDC bloc of the model; these differences are unlikely to have a major impact on results.) Comparison of the first and second columns therefore gives some indication of the sensitivity of the results to the choice of time period. The third column reports the result of doubling the weight given to inflation in the objective function.

Inclusion of the years 1985/6 in the optimisation exercise makes some important differences. First, the weight, ϕ_2, on capacity utilisation in the nominal income target is greater for the longer period (column 1) compared with the shorter period (column 2). This may reflect the benefits for inflation of the 1986 oil price fall (implying less need to squeeze inflation), together with contractionary influences on German output in the mid-1980s. In addition, the interest rate rule changes significantly, with a reduced feedback on real exchange rate disequilibrium and a larger feedback on the growth of world nominal demand. These changes to the interest rate rule may reflect the fact that 1985/6 saw some large movements in exchange rates that GEM's exchange rate equations (along with other exchange rate equations) did not explain. (It is, indeed, unclear why the dollar continued to rise in 1985.) To offset these shocks would have required large shifts in real interest rates, with appreciable effects on domestic demand growth that would have been undesirable. Thus the optimal response to exchange rate disequilibrium falls with the addition of 1985/6. But it might be argued that these model runs exaggerate this difficulty, since the adoption of monetary rules to limit exchange rate disequilibria may help to dampen speculative bubbles in foreign exchange markets.

Increasing the weight on inflation in the objective function has the expected effects on the parameters of the feedback rules. The weight, ϕ_2, given to capacity utilisation in the nominal income rule drops sharply, while both fiscal and monetary policy become more active in their role of stabilising nominal demand growth.

Table 8.2 reports the values of the loss function, both in total and for each of the G3 countries separately. The first three columns relate to the standard objective function with the weight discussed above. Under the central rule, optimised over the 1975/86 period, the loss function is appreciably below that in history, the gain representing the equivalent of around 2 per cent of GDP per quarter or a fall of around 1 per cent in the average inflation rate.

However, the gains are unevenly distributed amongst the G3 members. In the historical base, the United States was able to obtain benefits, at the expense of the rest of the world, from a non-inflationary expansion brought about by a tight money/expansionary fiscal policy mix that appreciated the dollar sharply. The Williamson/Miller policy rules limit the freedom of the United States to engage in such policies, to the benefit of world economic performance as a whole, but especially in the rest of the world. Germany also benefits significantly from a more expansionary overall stance of policy. If rules of this kind were implemented in a cooperative manner, one might well expect that the bargaining process would lead to a more equal division of benefits, perhaps by means of different burdens of adjustment (that is, allowing for country-specific parameters in the feedback rules) or by means of variation in the form of rules (though this may depend on whether history appropriately reflects the relevant non-cooperative alternative).

The third column reports the effects of using the rule with the parameter values designed in our earlier paper (Currie and Wren-Lewis, 1988) over the period 1975/84. This rule also gives an appreciable, though smaller, gain representing the equivalent of some 1 per cent of GDP per quarter or a reduction of 0.5 per cent in inflation. However, under this rule, the United States is made worse off, so that this rule does not represent a Pareto improvement. This is because the rule incorporates a stronger reaction of monetary policy to exchange rate disequilibrium, so that United States interest rates react strongly to the movements in the dollar in the 1985/6 period. The sharper fluctuations in American interest rates have adverse consequences for American output that more than erode the small benefits that would otherwise accrue to the United States. A Pareto improvement would, however, arise if some asymmetries in the rules had allowed a more equal division of the gains from cooperation.

The remaining five columns in table 8.2 report the consequences of varying the objective function, providing some further indication of robustness. (Our earlier paper examines the implications for the objective function of specific changes in feedback parameters from their optimal values.) In columns four to six, the weight on inflation is doubled. If the policy rule is optimised taking account of this increased weight on inflation, the overall benefits from the policy rule are considerable measured relative to history (about the equivalent of 1.5 per cent of GDP per quarter, or 0.5 per cent off inflation). However, the benefits to Japan and the United States are quite small, and the principal gains accrue to Germany. If our

Table 8.2 Welfare losses

	Standard objective function		
	History	Central rule	Variant A
Welfare losses			
Total	20,139	16,727	18,208
United States	22,951	22,221	23,814
Germany	16,593	10,215	11,953
Japan	21,608	18,764	19,507

central rule (optimal with respect to the standard objective function, that is, with the lower weight on inflation) is used, the overall gains are halved while both the United States and Japan are made worse off. Once again, a Pareto improvement is likely to occur with rules that distribute the benefits of cooperation more equally in the central case.

The final two columns illustrate how our central rule performs relative to history if the penalty on changes in government spending is much higher, reflecting greater costs to the adjustment of fiscal policy. Because government spending is more variable in the historical base than under our central rules, this change increases the benefits for cooperation, which rise to over 2½ per cent of GDP or 1.2 per cent off inflation. Optimising the rule subject to this higher weight on government spending changes would lead to a still greater benefit from the rules.

These results suggest that the performance of the Williamson/Miller rules, suitably optimised, is fairly robust with respect to changes in time period and to some changes in the parameters of the objective function; and that these rules can deliver a significant improvement relative to history. However, the gains from the uniform rules analysed here which have identical responses in each country, do not accrue equally to each of the G3 members; and changes in the time period and objective function parameters may mean that the rule does not deliver a Pareto improvement. An asymmetric rule, which distributes the benefits more evenly, will almost certainly be more robust in this respect.

This conclusion is subject to three qualifications, each of which merit further consideration. First, the benefits to Germany occurring from the Williamson/Miller rules arise in part from a more

Increased inflation weight			Increased weight on government spending	
History	Central rule	Variant B	History	Central rule
30,044	28,500	26,616	22,027	16,841
36,965	38,226	35,921	23,015	22,354
21,903	15,553	13,975	16,672	10,286
32,483	34,941	33,288	21,758	18,923

expansionary stance of policy in the 1980s, which gives appreciable real output gains at some cost in terms of higher inflation. Thus capacity utilisation ends up 10 percentage points higher than in history, with capacity utilisation consistently higher from 1981 onwards, implying a massive cumulative gain in output; while inflation remains flat at around 5 per cent, instead of lower inflation historically, with negative inflation at the end of the period. It is appropriate to ask whether German policymaking was quite as misguided as these runs suggest, or whether actual policy did not simply reflect a very much greater aversion to inflation. Since results using alternative overall objective functions do not alter the results appreciably, it would appear that, to consider this, we need to try a variant in which German inflation is weighted more heavily relative to capacity utilisation, and to assess performance of the Williamson/Miller rules with respect to this reformulation of the objective function.

Secondly, one of the argued benefits of the target zone proposed is that, by reducing real exchange rate variability, it would give benefits by reducing the real adjustment costs associated with exchange rate volatility and misalignments. Such benefits may be captured to some degree in the present exercise to the extent that a smooth path for the real exchange rate implies a smoother path for the final objectives of total output and inflation. But to the extent that these resource costs relate to more detailed industry-level adjustments, because, for example, exchange rate changes shift the balance between tradable and nontradable sectors, those costs will not be captured in our objective function. This might suggest the inclusion in the objective function of additional terms penalising exchange rate variability or fluctuations in the size of the

Table 8.3 Exchange rate variation

Variance of effective real exchange rate		History	Central rule	Variant A	Variant B
United States	1975/86	0.83	0.48	0.17	0.50
	1975/84	0.57	0.33	0.13	0.33
Germany	1975/86	0.22	0.67	0.24	0.45
	1975/84	0.14	0.27	0.10	0.35
Japan	1975/86	0.35	1.09	0.45	1.13
	1975/84	0.25	1.04	0.37	1.10

traded goods sector. To the extent that the target zone proposals operate to dampen these fluctuations relative to history, this would improve the benefits from the Williamson/Miller proposals. Indeed, it could be argued that it is in this direction that the principal benefits of the proposals are to be expected.

However, table 8.3 shows that this argument is not straightforward. The central rule and other variants certainly dampen the variability of the dollar effective real exchange rate, so that additional benefits may be attributed to the United States. (This therefore qualifies the impression derived from table 8.2 that the United States benefits only marginally from the Williamson/Miller rules.) But for Germany and Japan the variance of real exchange rate actually rises relative to history, under the central rule. (In part, this increase in variance is attributable to a steeper trend, which to the extent that it is anticipated may have less serious resource costs; but variability around the trend does nonetheless increase.) This arises in part because the rules for monetary and fiscal policy assumed for EMS countries in the simulation lead to marked current account imbalances for non-German EMS participants, particularly at the end of the simulation period; and this distorts exchange rate movements in the last two years of the run. But it also arises because of the very weak nature of the monetary rule, as indicated by the optimised parameters in table 8.1. For the earlier analysis over the period 1975/84, the optimised rule (Variant A) gives lower exchange rate variability for Germany, but exchange rate variability for Japan is larger. These results occur because, in the face of general exchange rate disturbances in 1985/6 and in earlier episodes for Japan (in 1975 and 1979), the optimal rule is suggesting a less vigorous response of monetary policy to the exchange rate than that which occurred historically. In effect, the rule represents a very weak form of exchange rate targeting. This is because sharper movements of interest rates would have a deleterious effect on domestic output performance. If exchange rate variability entered directly into the objective function, this would lead to a more vigorous use of monetary policy in response to exchange rate fluctuations, but it is less clear that the resulting optimal rule would outperform history. Against this, however, there is the argument that, by neglecting the effects of a target zone arrangement on expectations in foreign exchange markets, the model overstates the problems associated with using monetary policy to stabilise the exchange rate.

Finally, it should be noted that, because the monetary policy rule is quite weak, most of the measured benefits of the Williamson/Miller rule arise from the better use of fiscal policy. (This is not to deny the point made above that there may be other benefits not captured in the simulations.) Thus, improved performance arises mainly from the more flexible use of fiscal policy, not from the targeting of the real exchange rate by monetary policy. (This is probably also the case for the results presented in our earlier paper (Currie and Wren-Lewis, 1988).) But there are other schemes for the improved coordination of fiscal policy, including the use of fiscal policy to avoid disequilibrium on the current account. Our results do support the argument that the extended target zone proposal of Williamson and Miller would have improved on historical performance, but leave open the question of whether its performance would have been superior to alternative proposals.

Historical paths

We now give a brief description of GEM's assessment of what history would have looked like if a form of the target zone cooperative strategy had been followed by the G3 over the period 1975–86. The feedback parameters we use come from column 2 in table 8.1, rather than the optimal set of parameters in column 1, because the former are closer in spirit to the target zone proposal. Tables 8.4 to 8.6 compare actual historical values of various variables (denoted by H) in each G3 country with their values in the model simulation embodying the cooperative feedback parameters (denoted by *TZ*). (Currie and Wren-Lewis, 1988, contains a fuller account of a similar simulation ending in 1984.)

The most noticeable characteristic of the simulation is the absence of the large rise in United States real interest rates around 1980. The increase in American interest rates over this period can be viewed as a classic example of an attempt to avoid deflationary action at home by exporting inflation overseas. This type of policy

Table 8.4 United States

Q4 values	Inflation (annual %)		Utilisation		Real exchange rate (1980=100)		Real interest rates (%)	
	H	*TZ*	*H*	*TZ*	*H*	*TZ*	*H*	*TZ*
1975	7.0	7.4	0.93	0.91	101	104	−0.8	−0.1
1976	5.1	4.7	0.98	0.95	101	104	−0.2	0.8
1977	6.7	6.0	1.01	0.96	101	105	−0.1	1.8
1978	7.5	5.6	1.06	0.99	109	104	2.6	3.2
1979	9.7	7.7	1.03	1.01	104	95	4.0	1.3
1980	10.1	9.5	0.99	1.01	98	91	5.6	−1.1
1981	7.8	9.2	0.95	1.00	89	95	5.5	−2.1
1982	4.8	8.6	0.85	0.93	81	100	4.2	−2.5
1983	3.7	7.3	0.94	0.98	80	98	5.7	−2.2
1984	3.4	6.2	0.98	1.01	74	93	6.1	−3.6
1985	3.6	6.3	0.96	0.99	81	100	4.3	−3.6
1986	1.7	5.2	0.94	0.94	96	112	4.1	−0.9

Q4 values	Government expenditure (1982 dollars)		Nominal GDP growth gap (% actual less target)	Current account (billion)	
	H	*TZ*	*TZ*	*H*	*TZ*
1975	587	586	−0.2	4.8	4.5
1976	579	573	1.7	0.2	1.0
1977	594	574	1.2	−5.9	−4.6
1978	611	543	4.3	−1.3	4.4
1979	612	549	1.8	−1.1	2.9
1980	618	558	1.3	1.5	−0.6
1981	636	538	2.3	1.2	−9.4
1982	660	590	−2.2	−6.2	−1.6
1983	642	554	4.0	−18.4	−1.5
1984	693	530	3.8	−30.1	−1.6
1985	754	537	1.5	−33.7	−2.0
1986	772	571	−2.2	−36.8	−2.6

Table 8.5 Germany

Q4 values	Inflation (annual %)		Utilisation		Real exchange rate (1980 = 100)		Real interest rates (%)	
	H	*TZ*	*H*	*TZ*	*H*	*TZ*	*H*	*TZ*
1975	5.5	5.2	1.03	1.03	106	104	−1.4	3.6
1976	3.7	2.7	1.06	1.03	100	95	1.1	2.5
1977	3.1	1.3	1.04	1.02	97	93	1.0	0.6
1978	2.6	1.5	1.03	1.01	95	93	1.4	−0.1
1979	5.0	5.2	1.04	1.03	96	101	4.4	0.6
1980	5.5	6.8	0.97	1.01	104	105	4.0	1.5
1981	6.4	7.6	0.94	1.01	106	101	4.8	2.3
1982	3.9	3.7	0.85	0.93	106	94	3.2	−0.5
1983	2.8	3.8	0.88	0.94	108	101	3.5	0.7
1984	2.1	3.0	0.88	0.93	114	109	3.9	2.7
1985	1.5	3.8	0.89	0.95	110	110	3.3	5.6
1986	−0.7	3.1	0.86	0.92	101	118	5.4	8.7

Q4 values	Government expenditure (1982 dollars)		Nominal GDP growth gap (% actual less target)	Current account (billion)	
	H	*TZ*	*TZ*	*H*	*TZ*
1975	66.3	68.6	−0.1	0.3	0.3
1976	67.1	67.0	2.2	0.4	2.0
1977	69.0	69.2	−1.4	2.0	2.2
1978	71.6	69.4	2.3	2.5	1.8
1979	73.3	69.1	2.8	−3.7	−5.3
1980	74.2	70.9	1.1	−4.7	−5.7
1981	74.9	73.7	0.9	1.9	2.5
1982	74.2	81.1	−2.7	1.9	1.2
1983	75.8	83.8	−0.6	0.6	−4.8
1984	78.3	89.2	−1.2	3.7	−2.6
1985	80.1	92.9	0.0	5.4	−3.5
1986	80.8	93.9	1.0	10.4	−3.5

Table 8.4 Japan

Q4 values	Inflation (annual %)		Utilisation		Real exchange rate (1980 = 100)		Real interest rates (%)	
	H	*TZ*	*H*	*TZ*	*H*	*TZ*	*H*	*TZ*
1975	7.6	9.7	0.95	0.97	110	125	1.0	0.5
1976	8.6	7.5	1.01	1.01	107	109	−1.3	0.8
1977	5.6	5.4	0.98	0.94	95	103	0.0	0.8
1978	4.0	2.6	1.00	0.96	84	92	0.6	−1.6
1979	4.6	3.1	1.02	0.99	109	111	2.8	2.8
1980	6.5	6.9	0.97	0.98	94	97	3.4	0.3
1981	4.0	4.4	0.96	1.00	102	88	3.0	−2.4
1982	1.9	4.5	0.88	0.97	115	101	5.0	−1.6
1983	1.3	5.3	0.91	1.02	104	96	5.1	−2.2
1984	2.3	7.2	0.95	1.06	107	109	4.0	0.8
1985	1.8	5.7	0.91	1.03	99	103	5.2	2.0
1986	−0.2	5.9	0.85	0.96	89	112	4.7	3.2

Q4 values	Government expenditure (1982 dollars)		Nominal GDP growth gap (% actual less target)	Current account (billion)	
	H	*TZ*	*TZ*	*H*	*TZ*
1975	4868	4763	−0.5	−0.6	−1.0
1976	5058	4768	0.7	0.7	1.8
1977	5320	5123	−1.8	3.2	3.8
1978	5596	5080	1.1	1.7	3.1
1979	5710	5245	0.1	−4.3	−1.4
1980	5975	5262	0.4	−0.1	0.4
1981	6250	5252	2.4	1.3	1.6
1982	6291	5401	0.9	0.9	−3.2
1983	6493	5348	2.3	3.2	−1.6
1984	6700	5280	2.8	11.3	7.0
1985	6843	5218	3.2	15.9	16.9
1986	8016	5747	−3.2	15.6	14.8

is ruled out of court by the form of cooperative rules examined here.

It is important to note that this simulation, or more generally the optimisation results described above, do not *prove* that this policy was suboptimal, either for the United States or for the world economy as a whole. Given the form of the cooperative interest rate feedback rules that we have looked at, it is simply not possible for one country to appreciate its real exchange rate against others in order to reduce its inflation rate. That such a policy would be suboptimal seems fairly self-evident if we are starting from a position in which the distribution of activity and inflation between countries is fairly equal. However, by the end of 1979, inflation in the United States was nearly twice the level of Germany and Japan, even though all three countries were at or near full capacity utilisation. In these circumstances, it is possible that some, probably temporary, appeciation in the dollar could have formed part of an optimal strategy designed to equalise inflation rates. This possibility could be explored by adding terms in inflation differentials to the interest rate feedback rule. However, it seems likely that at best only a small part of the United States appreciation that actually took place could be justified in this way.

According to GEM, a large part of the rise in the dollar over the 1980/82 period can be explained by the rise in American interest rate differentials. In the *TZ* simulation, therefore, the absence of this tightening of monetary policy substantially reduces the United States real appreciation over this period. However, a significant part of this appreciation is not explained by GEM's equations. We can conjecture that this unexplained and sustained positive shock to the dollar is associated with the large flows of foreign, and particularly Japanese, capital that entered the United States over this period, which are thought to reflect shifts in portfolio preferences rather than normal reactions to interest rate differentials. In an attempt to counteract this shock, American real interest rates become negative from 1980 onwards in the *TZ* simulation. If some of the dollar's appreciation over this period was due to changes in international portfolio preferences, then an interesting issue is whether the target value of the dollar should be adjusted in these circumstances, so that it becomes unnecessary to reduce American real interest rates to the extent shown in the simulation.

The rise in United States real interest rates forced other countries to tighten their own monetary policy to avoid even larger currency misalignments. As a result, this period saw a substantial and fairly abrupt tightening in global monetary policy. In the *TZ* simulation, this tight monetary policy is replaced by a tighter global fiscal policy, which is applied more gradually throughout the simulation period. Tables 8.4 and 8.5 indicate that fiscal policy in the *TZ* simulation is substantially more restrictive by the end of the period in both the United States and Japan. (The historical 1986Q4 figure for Japan is a little misleading, as it includes a substantial one-off advancing of expenditure into that quarter.) An interesting exception is Germany, where fiscal policy is actually more expansionary in the *TZ* simulation, suggesting that policy has been too contractionary in that country in the 1980s. (The actual figures for government expenditure in the simulation are a little misleading, because of our assumption that tax rates remain unchanged. In GEM, increases in direct taxes could be substituted for cuts in expenditure with no direct consequences for inflation.)

The *TZ* simulation therefore involves a substantial change in the global fiscal–monetary policy mix, with a tight monetary policy being replaced by a contractionary fiscal policy. (We can observe that policy is generally contractionary from the fact that actual nominal GDP growth exceeds target growth in most periods in all three countries.) The reasons for this have been discussed in the previous section, and relate to differences across countries in the effects of interest rates on demand compared with more uniform fiscal multipliers. For the world economy as a whole, both output and inflation are slightly higher in the simulation compared to history. However the global welfare gains in *TZ* do not primarily come from shifting the inflation–output mix, but instead reflect a more even distribution of activity and inflation both over time and between countries.

The more equal distribution of activity between countries comes about partly through the change in the fiscal–monetary mix, but also as a result of the operation of real exchange rate targets. We have already noted the much reduced dollar appreciation in the 1980/82 period, and the extent of the yen and DM depreciation is correspondingly reduced. One particularly interesting result is that the gradual rise in the American current account deficit since 1980 is all but eliminated in the *TZ* simulation. Equally interesting is the fact that the United States Federal budget deficit also remains fairly constant over this period, due to lower government expenditure, lower interest payments and a higher level of domestic activity.

As far as the non-G3 countries are concerned, we have assumed unchanged fiscal policies compared to history, but that changes in monetary policy in these countries follow changes in German real interest rates. This effectively eliminates changes in *real* EMS parities due to changes in real interest rates. Real exchange rates can still respond, however, to changes in current account positions. These assumptions work reasonably well until the last two or three years. A problem arises in France and Italy at the end of the simulation period as a result of the higher level of activity in Germany. This boosts these countries' exports, leading to current account surpluses. In contrast, Germany is in deficit over this period. As a result, both the franc and the lira appreciate, and these countries lose competitiveness. The consequences of this can be observed in tables 8.4–8.6 where, over the 1984–6 period the G3 all become more competitive. This difficulty may stem from our assumption that fiscal policy in France and Italy remains invariant to changes in policy and activity outside these countries, and later work could explore an alternative which linked both monetary *and* fiscal policies in the EMS.

Finally, it may be worth briefly describing how a simulation under the 'optimal rule' shown in column 1 of table 8.1 would compare with the *TZ* simulation. The smaller parameters on exchange rate disequilibrium in the interest rate feedback rule imply that rather less of the dollar's appreciation over the 1980/82 period is avoided. This in turn means that the United States current account does move into substantial deficit, although its size is smaller than actual historical values. A stronger effect from capacity utilisation to fiscal policy raises output and inflation in Germany, and counteracts the effects of the appreciation on American GNP. Two important features of the *TZ* simulation remain, however. The first is that global deflation takes place through a tight fiscal rather than a tight monetary policy, and secondly that this deflationary policy is applied consistently throughout the period, so that the extent of the 1980/82 recession is greatly diminished.

Conclusions

International policy cooperation based on exchange rate target zones has been widely discussed recently, but little systematic appraisal using empirical macromodels has been undertaken. In this chapter we have examined a proposal for policy coordination similar to that recently advocated by Williamson and Miller (1987) using the National Institute's Global Econometric Model over the period 1975–86. The parameters on the proposed feedback rules were determined using optimal control over that period.

Our results suggest that policy cooperation using the optimal feedback rules leads to a substantial Pareto welfare improvement compared to history. Within the rules themselves, our optimisation results suggest that fiscal rather than monetary policy should play the major role in stabilising global output and inflation, with monetary policy concentrating on exchange rate stabilisation. This result is due to the fact that interest rates have widely differing effects on demand between countries in the model, so that a general tightening of monetary policy due to global excess demand could lead to disequilibrium in the distribution of activity between countries. Our results also suggest little independent role for the current account as an additional intermediate target.

If policymakers had followed these optimal feedback rules over this historical period, the main difference would have been the absence of an interest rate hike by the United States around 1980. At a global level, monetary policy would have been easier but fiscal policy would have been more restrictive. However, our results leave open the possibility that some rise in interest rates and associated dollar appreciation (though less than in history) may have been appropriate to deal with the higher United States inflation rate relative to other OECD countries. This suggests exploring a possible modification to the Williamson/Miller rules, that monetary policy might respond to relative inflation rates. This policy response is allowed for within the wide target exchange rate zones, but may merit explicit recognition.

These results give general, if qualified, support to the extended target zone scheme of Williamson and Miller. However, the principal benefits may arise from the differences in fiscal stance, relative to history, implied by the fiscal policy rule, rather than from the use of monetary policy to stabilise the real exchange rate. Indeed, the results suggest that the latter part of the scheme might have been counterproductive if pursued too hard in the 1985/6 period, since very sharp movements in interest rates would have been required to stabilise exchange rates in the face of foreign exchange market disturbances, and this would have had destabilising domestic effects. It may be that, by neglecting reputational and expectational effects of the kind discussed above in the second section, the model overstates the problems of stabilising exchange rates by means of the Williamson/Miller policy rules. It is also the case that, as discussed in the fourth section, our results take no account of possible additional benefits of greater real exchange stability. It also remains an open question as to whether the principal benefits accrue from more flexible fiscal adjustments, so that appreciable benefits would also accrue from alternative rules for fiscal policy. In particular, the scheme discussed in the third section, whereby fiscal policy ensures medium-term external balance while monetary policy stabilises domestic nominal trends, may also perform well, and possibly even better than the extended target zone proposal. This question will be investigated in subsequent work.

Appendix: The structure of GEM

The National Institute's quarterly Global Econometric Model (GEM) consists of sixteen countries or sector blocs. The G7 economies are modelled in some detail, with each country bloc containing at least 25 behavioural equations and over 30 identities. The Netherlands, Belgium and the rest of OECD Europe are modelled in much smaller blocs. The version (3.0) of the model we use here also contains six other sectors, including OPEC, four LDC sectors, and the Centrally Planned economies. These blocs consist largely of trade equations, which in turn are heavily dependent on equations covering five commodity price indices.

The theoretical structure of the G7 country blocs is Keynesian in the sense that output is determined by aggregate demand. However in most countries, including the United States, interest rates play an important role in influencing individual components of aggregate demand. The disaggregation of aggregate demand, and the specification of these components, mirrors that of conventional Keynesian macromodels.

Each G7 bloc contains equations determining a number of price indices; the key variables are determined by import costs, earnings, productivity trends, non-wage labour costs, and some measure of capacity utilisation or demand. For most countries earnings are determined by real wage equations in which either output or unemployment plays an important role.

The exchange rate system in the model is described in Wren-Lewis (1987). At its heart are bilateral exchange rate equations determining the dollar, yen, DM and sterling. Although exchange rates are expressed in terms of dollars, the system is set up such that the choice of numeraire is irrelevant. (Thus, for example, the UK/US interest rate differential can influence the yen/dollar rate.) Explanatory variables are interest rate and inflation differentials, current balances expressed in real terms, and real oil prices. In the long run the system relates changes in *real* exchange rates to *real* interest rate differentials and real current accounts. This implies a 'flow' view of the capital account, although the estimated dynamics are such that initial responses to interest rate changes generally exceed long-run effects, implying portfolio adjustment. Subsidiary equations exist for the EMS currencies, where the DM plays a leading role.

Apart from exchange rates, interaction between countries takes place through trade volumes and prices. Import volumes depend on expenditure or production, relative prices or costs, and in some cases a measure of relative capacity utilisation. A trade matrix then weights together these import volumes to form an export market variable, and each country's exports depend on this, together with measures of relative prices or costs in third markets, and relative capacity utilisation. Manufacturing export prices are determined by behavioural equations in which domestic prices and competitors prices are the main arguments. A trade matrix is again used to weight these prices, together with the commodity price indices, to estimate import prices for each country.

The main limitation of the model at its current stage of development is the absence of wealth terms in expenditure equations. Money demand functions exist, but neither they nor the consumption equation have wealth as an argument. This in turn reflects the fact that the government's budget deficit is not modelled. Research is currently under way in this area, and the version of GEM used here does include equations that endogenise the United States public sector and Federal budget deficits.

Although the model as a whole contains around 600 variables, the number of behavioural equations is nearer 200. As such it is rather more compact than most other major world econometric models currently operational, such as the OECD's Interlink, the Japanese Economic Planning Agency's model or the United States Federal Reserve's MCM. Bryant and Holtham (1987) compare the United States current account sectors of six world econometric models including GEM.

Note

1 Strictly speaking, only point targets eliminate this bias altogether. With target zones, governments may tighten monetary policy for anti-inflationary reasons, taking the exchange rate to the top of its band. A series of successive competitive tightening of monetary policy may lead to a similar overall tightening of monetary policy as would occur without exchange rate zones. What limits this tendency is the reluctance of governments to move the exchange rate towards its limit for fear of inducing speculation against the zones. It is evident that this limitation will be stronger the narrower are the target zones.

References

Aizeman, J. and Frenkel, J. (1985), 'Optimal wage indexation, foreign exchange intervention and monetary policy', *American Economic Review*, Vol. 75, pp. 402–23.

Anderton, R. and Henry, S.G.B. (1987), UK exports of manufactures, NIESR, mimeo.

Andrews, M.J., Bell, D.N.F., Fisher, P.G., Wallis, K.F. and Whitley, J.D. (1985), 'Models of the UK economy and the real-wage employment debate', *National Institute Economic Review*, no. 112, pp. 41–52.

Artis, M.J., Bladen-Hovell, R., Karakitsos, E. and Dwolatzky, B. (1984), 'The effects of economic policy 1979–82', *National Institute Economic Review*, no. 108, May, pp. 54–67.

Artis, M.J. and Miller, M.H. (1986), 'On joining the EMS', *Midland Bank Review*, Winter, pp. 11–20.

Backus, D. and Driffill, J. (1985a), 'Inflation and reputation', *American Economic Review*, no. 75, pp. 530–8.

Backus, D. and Driffill, J. (1985b), 'Rational expectations and policy credibility following a change in regime', *Review of Economic Studies*, no. 52, pp. 211–22.

Ball, R.H. and Burns, T. (1978), 'Stabilisation policy in Britain 1964–81' in Posner, M. (Ed.) 1978, *op cit*.

Ball, R.J., Burns, T. and Laury, J.S.E. (1977), 'The role of exchange rate changes in balance of payments adjustment: the United Kingdom case', *Economic Journal*, March.

Bank of England (1981), 'Factors underlying the recent recession', Papers presented to the Panel of Academic Consultants, No. 15.

Bank of England (1983), 'A note on real short-term interest rates', *Bank of England Quarterly Bulletin*, 23, pp. 471–6.

Bank of England (1986), 'North Sea oil and gas', *Bank of England Quarterly Bulletin*, 26, pp. 510–8.

Barker, T.S. (1979), 'Economic policy formulation in a large-scale model' in Holly, S., Rustem, B. and Zarrop, M.B., *Optimal Control for Econometric Models*, London, Macmillan.

Barro, R.J. (1986), 'Reputation in a model of monetary policy with incomplete information', *Journal of Monetary Economics*, no. 17, pp. 101–22.

Barro, R.J. and Gordon, D. (1983), 'Rules, discretion and reputation in a model of monetary policy', *Journal of Monetary Economics*, vol. XXII, pp. 101–21.

Baumol, W. (1961), 'Pitfalls in countercyclical policy: some tools and results', *Review of Economics and Statistics*, vol. LXIII.

Bean, C. (1987), Sterling misalignment and British trade performance, London School of Economics, Centre for Labour Economics, Discussion paper 288.

Blake, A. and Weale, M. (1988), 'Exchange-rate targets and wage formation', *National Institute Economic Review*, No. 123, February.

Blanchard, O.J. and Kahn, C.M. (1980), 'The solution of linear difference models under rational expectations', *Econometrica*, Vol. 48, pp. 1305–13.

Boughton, J. (1987), Eclectic approaches to policy coordination, paper presented to the CEPR Conference on Exchange Rate Regimes, Money GDP targets and Macroeconomic Policy, Cambridge, July.

Bray, J. (1975), 'Optimal control of a noisy economy with the UK as an example', *Journal of the Royal Statistical Society*, Series A, Vol. 138, Part 3, pp. 339–73.

Breedon, F., Levine, P. and Smith, P. (1987), The party manifestos: an evaluation of Labour and Alliance economic policies, LBS Forecast Release, May.

Britton, A. (1986), 'Can fiscal expansion cut unemployment?' *National Institute Economic Review*, no. 115, February.

Bryant, R. and Holtham, G. (1987), 'The external deficit: why? Where next? What remedy? *The Brookings Review*.

Bryant, R. and Portes, R. (1987), *Global Macroeconomics: Policy Conflict and Cooperation*, London, Macmillan.

Bryant, R. *et al.* (1988), *Empirical Macroeconomics for Interdependent Economics*, Washington, Brookings Institution.

Budd, A. (1981), 'The recession of 1980 and its causes', in Bank of England (1981), *op cit*.

Budd, A. and Burns, T. (1977), 'Why the exchange rate must be set free', *Economic Outlook*, April.

Budd, A., Dicks, G., Holly, S., Keating, G. and Robinson, B. (1984), 'The London Business School Econometric Model', *Economic Modelling* vol. 1, no. 4.

Budd, A., Levine, P. and Smith, P. (1986), Real wage adjustment and long-term unemployment, Centre for Economic Forecasting Discussion Paper no. 21–86.

Buiter, W.H. (1981), 'The superiority of contingent rules over fixed rules in models with rational expectations', *Economic Journal*, Vol. 91, September.

Buiter, W.H. (1985), Policy evaluation and design for continuous time linear rational expectations: some recent developments, Centre for Economic Policy Research Discussion Paper no. 15.

Buiter, W. and Marston, R. (1985), *International Economic Policy Coordination*, Cambridge University Press.

Buiter, W.H. and Miller, M.H. (1983), 'Changing the rules: economic consequences of the Thatcher regime', *Brookings Papers on Economic Activity*, no. 2, pp. 305–65.

Cagan, P. (1956), 'The monetary dynamics of hyperinflation', in Friedman, M. (Ed.), *Studies in the Quantity Theory of Money*, University of Chicago Press.

Choe, Y. (1987), The indeterminacy of short-run exchange rates in a managed float regime, mimeo.

Chow, G.C. (1975), *Analysis and Control of Dynamic Economic Systems*, John Wiley and Sons Inc.

Christodoulakis, N. (1984), Robust controller design for macroeconomic models, Ph.D. Thesis, Darwin College, Cambridge.

Christodoulakis, N. (1987), Reduced-form linear approximations of large economic models with rational expectations, London Business School, CEF Discussion Paper No. 17–87.

Christodoulakis, N. and Levine, P. (1987), 'Linear rational expectations models: a frequency domain versus optimal control approach to policy design', in *Proceedings of 1986 IFAC/JEDC Conference*, Budapest, North-Holland.

Christodoulakis, N., Meade, J.E., Vines, D.A. and Weale, M.R. (1986), Stagflation – Final Report, Cambridge, Department of Applied Economics, mimeo.

Cooper, R. (1985), 'Economic interdependence and coordination of economic policies' in Jones, R.W. and Kennan, P.B. (Eds), *Handbook of International Economics*, Vol. 2, Amsterdam, North-Holland.

Currie, D.A. (1985), 'Macroeconomic policy design and control theory – a failed partnership?' *Economic Journal*, 95, pp. 285–306.

Currie, D. and Hall, S.G. (1986a), 'The exchange rate and the balance of payments', *National Institute Economic Review*, no. 115, February.

Currie, D. and Hall, S.G. (1986b), A stock-flow model of the determination of UK effective exchange rate, National Institute of Economic and Social Research, Discussion paper no. 124.

Currie, D.A. and Levine, P. (1985a), 'Simple macroeconomic policy rules in an open economy', *Economic Journal*, 85, pp. 60–70.

Currie, D.A. and Levine, P. (1985b), 'Macroeconomic policy design in an international world' in Buiter and Marston (1985), *op cit*.

Currie, D.A. and Levine, P.L. (1987), 'Credibility and time

consistency in a stochastic world', *Journal of Economics* (New York), 47, No. 3, pp. 225–52.

Currie, D.A., Levine, P.L. and Vidalis, N. (1987), 'International cooperation and regulation in an empirical two-bloc model' in Bryant and Portes (1987), *op cit.*

Currie, D.A. and Wren-Lewis, S. (1988), 'Evaluating the extended target zone proposal for the G3, Centre for Economic Policy Research, Discussion Paper no. 221–88.

Davies, G. and Metcalf, D. (1985), *Generating Jobs – The Cost Effectiveness of Tax Cuts, Public Expenditure and Special Employment Measures in Creating Employment*, London, Simon and Coates.

Dornbusch, R. (1976), 'Expectations and exchange rate dynamics', *Journal of Political Economy*, Vol. 84.

Dornbusch, R. and Frankel, J. (1987), The flexible exchange rate system: experience and alternatives, mimeo.

Driffill, J. (1982), 'Optimal model and exchange rate policies', *Greek Economic Review*, 4, December, pp. 261–83.

Driffill, D. (1987), 'Macroeconomic policy games with incomplete information: a survey', Proceedings of the EEA Congress, 1987, Copenhagen.

Easton, B. and Patterson, K. (1987), 'Interest rates in five macroeconomic models of the UK: survey, analysis and simulation', *Economic Modelling*, 4, pp. 19–64.

Edison, H., Miller, M. and Williamson, J. (1987), 'On evaluating and extending the target zone proposal', *Journal of Policy Modelling*.

Flemming, J.S. (1987), 'Interest rates', Paper presented at a NEDO Conference on the 50th Anniversary of Keynes' *General Theory*.

Frankel, J.A. (1987), Obstacles to international macroeconomic policy coordination, Discussion paper 8737, University of California at Berkeley.

Frankel, J.A. and Rockett, K. (1986), 'International macroeconomic policy coordination when policy-makers disagree on the model', NBER working paper no. 2059.

Frenkel, J.A. (1987), 'The international monetary system: should it be reformed?' *American Economic Review* (supplement).

Friedman, M. (1968), 'The role of monetary policy', *American Economic Review*, vol. LVIII.

Friedman, M. and Schwartz, A. (1963), *A Monetary History of the United States, 1867–1960*, Princeton, Princeton University Press.

Gale, D. (1983), *Money in Disequilibrium*, Cambridge University Press.

Ghosh, A.R. and Masson, P.R. (1987), International policy coordination in a world with model uncertainty, mimeo.

HM Treasury (1978), Report of the Committee on Policy Optimisation, Chairman Professor R.J. Ball, *Cmnd* 7148, March.

HM Treasury (1981), Third Report from the Treasury and Civil Service Committee on Monetary Policy, III, London, HMSO.

HM Treasury (1985), *The Relationship between Employment and Wages*, London, HM Treasury.

Hall, S.G. (1983), 'The exchange rate', in Britton, A.J.C. (Ed.), *Employment, Output and Inflation*, London, Heinemann.

Hall, S.G. (1985a), 'On the solution of large economic models with consistent expectations', *Bulletin of Economic Research*, May.

Hall, S.G. (1985b), An investigation of time inconsistency and optimal policy formation in the presence of rational expectations using the National Institute model 7, National Institute Discussion Paper no. 71.

Hall, S.G. (1987a), 'A forward looking model of the exchange rate', *Journal of Applied Econometrics*, vol. 2, no. 1.

Hall, S.G. (1987b), 'Analysing economic behaviour 1975–85 with a model incorporating consistent expectations', *National Institute Economic Review*, no. 120, pp. 75–80.

Hall, S.G. and Henry, S.G.B. (1988), *Macroeconomic Modelling*, Amsterdam, North-Holland.

Harvey, A.C., Henry, S.G.B., Peters, S. and Wren-Lewis, S. (1986), 'Stochastic trends in dynamic regression models: an application to the employment-output equation', *Economic Journal*, no. 96, pp. 975–85.

Hilton, K. and Heathfield, D. (Eds) (1970), *The Econometric Study of the United Kingdom*, London, Macmillan.

Holly, S. and Corker, B. (1984), 'Optimal feedback and feedforward stabilisation of exchange rates, money, prices and output under rational expectations', in Hughes-Hallett (Ed.), *Applied Decision Analysis*, Klywer and Nijhoff.

Holly, S. and Hughes-Hallett, A.J. (1988), *Control, Expectations and Uncertainty*, Cambridge University Press.

Holly, S. and Markose, S. (1986), Disaggregated inventories in manufacturing, Centre for Economic Forecasting Discussion Paper No. 25–86.

Holly, S. and Smith, P. (1987), 'A two-sector analysis of the UK labour market', *Oxford Bulletin of Economics and Statistics*, vol. 49, no. 1, February.

Holly, S., Rustem, B., Westcott, J.H., Zarrop, M.B. and Becker, R. (1979), 'Control exercise with a small linear model of the UK economy' in Holly, S., Rustem, B. and Zarrop, M.B. (Eds),

Optimal Control for Econometric Models: An Approach to Economic Policy Formulation, London, Macmillan.

Holly, S. and Wade, K. (1986), 'A supply and demand of UK exports of manufactures', London Business School, Centre for Economic Forecasting, Discussion paper no. 24–86.

Holly, S. and Zarrop, M.B. (1979), Calculating optimal economic policies when expectations are rational, PROPE Discussion Paper No. 30.

Holly, S. and Zarrop, M.B. (1983), 'On optimality and time consistency when expectations are rational', *European Economic Review*, February.

Holly, S., Zarrop, M.B. and Westcott, J.H. (1978), Near-optimal stabilisation policies with large nonlinear econometric models, PREM Discussion Paper No. 23, Imperial College.

Holtham, G. and Hughes-Hallet, A. (1987), 'International policy cooperation and model uncertainty', in Bryant and Portes (1987), *op cit.*

IMF (1987), *World Economic Outlook*, April and October.

Keating, G. (1985), Estimation and simulation of the LBS financial model, Centre for Economic Forecasting Discussion Paper, No. 148.

Kenen, P.B. (1987), 'Exchange rates and policy coordination', Brookings Discussion Paper no. 61.

Kydland, F.E. and Prescott, E.C. (1977), 'Rules rather than discretion: the inconsistency of optimal plans', *Journal of Political Economy*, pp. 473–92.

Lawson, T. (1981), Incomes policy and the real wage resistance hypothesis: econometric evidence for the UK, Cambridge Growth Project Paper no. 509.

Layard, P.R.G. and Nickell, S.J. (1985), 'Unemployment, real wages and aggregate demand in Europe, Japan and the United States' in Brunner and Meltzer (Eds), *The New Monetary Economics, Fiscal Issues and Unemployment*, North Holland.

Layard, P.R.G. and Nickell, S.J. (1986), 'Unemployment in Britain', *Economica*, Supplement, Vol. 53, pp. 121–70.

Leigh Pemberton, R. (1987), 'The instruments of monetary policy', *Bank of England Quarterly Bulletin*, August, pp. 365–70.

Levine, P.L. (1987), Does time inconsistency matter? CEF Discussion Paper, 19–87.

Levine, P. and Currie, D. (1987a), 'The design of feedback rules in linear stochastic rational expectations models', *Journal of Economic Dynamics and Control*.

Levine, P. and Currie, D. (1987b), 'Does international macropolicy coordination pay and is it sustainable? A two-country analysis',

Oxford Economic Papers, vol. 39, no. 1, March.
Levine, P.L. and Holly, S. (1988), 'The time inconsistency issue in macroeconomics: a survey', *Journal of Economic Perspectives*.
Lucas, R.E. (1976), 'Econometric policy evaluation: a critique', in *The Phillips Curve and Labor Markets*, ed. K. Brunner and A.H. Meltzer, Amsterdam, North-Holland, pp. 19–46.
Maciejowski, J.M. and Vines, D. (1982), The design and performance of a multivariate macroeconomic regulator, Proceedings of the IEEE Conference on Applications and Multivariate Control, Hull, July.
Maciejowski, J.M. and Vines, D. (1984), 'Decoupled control of a macroeconomic model using frequency domain methods', *Journal of Economic Dynamics and Control*, Vol. 7, pp. 55–77.
McKay, A.D. (1987), Can estimates of UK National Income be made more timely? Paper presented to the European meeting of the Econometric Society, Lyngby, August.
Mackie, D.J. (1987), 'A three sector model of earnings behaviour', Bank of England Discussion Paper, Technical Series, no. 16.
McKinnon, R.I. (1984), *An International Standard for Monetary Stabilisation*, Washington, Institute for International Economics.
McKinnon, R.I. (1987), 'Monetary and exchange rate proposals for international financial stability: a proposal', *Journal of Economic Perspectives*.
Matthews, K. and Minford, P. (1987), 'Mrs Thatcher's economic policies, 1979–87', *Economic Policy*, no. 5, October, pp. 57–101.
Meade, J.E. (1984), 'A new Keynesian Bretton Woods', *Three Banks Review*, June.
Meade, J.E. (1978), 'The meaning of internal balance', *Economic Journal*, Vol. 88, pp. 423–35.
Meade, J.E. (1987), Monetary policy and fiscal policy: the assignment of weapons to targets, mimeo.
Meade, J.E. and Vines, D. (1987), 'Monetary policy and fiscal policy: impact effects with a new Keynesian "assignment" of weapons to targets', Cambridge, Department of Applied Economics, mimeo.
Meese, R. (1986), 'Testing for bubbles in exchange markets: a case of sparkling bubbles?' *Journal of Political Economy*, vol. 94, no. 2, April.
Meese, R. and Rogoff, K. (1985), 'Was it real? The exchange rate–interest differential relationship, 1973–1984', mimeo, Berkeley, University of California, May.
Miller, M. and Salmon, M. (1985), 'Dynamic games and the time inconsistency of optimal policy in open economies', *Economic Journal* Supplement, 124–35.

Minford, P. (1987), A political model of credibility, University of Liverpool, mimeo.

Minford, P., Ashton, P., Davies, D., Peel, M. and Sprague, A. (1985), *Unemployment — Cause and Cure*, 2nd edition, Oxford, Basil Blackwell.

Minford, P., Marwaha, S., Matthews, K. and Sprague, A. (1984), 'The Liverpool macroeconomic model of the UK', *Economic Modelling*, January, pp. 24–62.

Minford, P. and Peel, D. (1981), 'Is the government's economic strategy on course?', *Lloyds Bank Review*, April, pp. 1–19.

Muellbauer, J. (1986), 'Productivity and competitiveness in British manufacturing', *Oxford Review of Economic Policy*, no. 2, pp. i–xxv.

Muth, J. (1961), 'Rational expectations and the theory of price movements', *Econometrica*, 29.

National Institute of Economic and Social Research (1987a), 'Chapter I, The Home Economy', *National Institute Economic Review*, no. 120, pp. 6–20.

National Institute of Economic and Social Research (1987b), National Institute model 10.

Ormerod, P. (Ed.) (1979), *Economic Modelling*, London, Heinemann.

Oudiz, G. and Sachs, J. (1984), 'Macroeconomic policy coordination among the industrialised economies', *Brookings Papers on Economic Activity*.

Patterson, K., Harnett, I., Robinson, G. and Ryding, J. (1987), 'The Bank of England quarterly model of the UK economy', *Economic Modelling*, 4, pp. 348–529.

Peterson, W. and Turner, D. (1985), 'Prospects for job creation: an exploration using MDM'. Paper presented at the 1985 Cambridge Growth Project Conference on Industry and the Economy.

Phillips, A.W. (1954), 'Stabilisation policy is a closed economy', *Economic Journal*, vol. LXIV.

Phillips, A.W. (1957), 'Stabilisation policy and the time-form of lagged responses', *Economic Journal*, Vol. LXVII.

Poole, W. (1970), 'Optimal choice of monetary policy instruments in a simple stochastic quarterly model', *Quarterly Journal of Economics*, Vol. 84, pp. 197–216.

Powell, S., Horton, G. and Vernon, K. (1985), 'The economic effects of lower oil prices', Government Economic Working Paper no. 76.

Posner, M. (Ed.) (1978), *Demand Management*, London, Heinemann.

Renton, G.T. (Ed.) (1975), *Modelling the Economy*, London, Heinemann.

Rogoff, K. (1985), 'Can international monetary policy coordination be counterproductive?' *Journal of International Economics*, Vol. 18, pp. 199–217.

Rustem, B. and Zarrop, M.B. (1979), 'A Newton type method for the optimisation and control of nonlinear econometric models', *Journal of Economic Dynamics and Control*, Vol. 1, no. 3.

Sargent, T. (1979), *Macroeconomic Theory*, London, Academic Press.

Sargent, T. (1986), 'Stopping moderate inflations: the methods of Poincaré and Thatcher', in *Rational Expectations and Inflation*, New York, Harper and Row; earlier version appeared as 'The ends of four big inflations', in R.E. Hall (Ed.) *Inflation*, Chicago, Chicago University Press, 1982.

Sargent, T. and Wallace, N. (1975), 'Rational expectations, the optimal monetary instrument and the optimal money supply rule', *Journal of Political Economy*, 83.

Saville, I.D. and Gardiner, K.L. (1986), 'Stagflation in the UK since 1970: a model-based explanation', *National Institute Economic Review*, no. 117, August, pp. 52–69.

Sims, C.A. (1982), 'Policy analysis with econometric models', *Brookings Papers on Economic Activity*, no. 1.

Spencer, P. (1987), *Britain's Productivity Renaissance*, Credit Suisse First Boston Limited.

Surrey, M.J.C. and Ormerod, P.A. (1977), 'Demand management in Britain 1964–81', in *Demand Management*, ed. M. Posner, London, Heinemann, pp. 101–25.

Taylor, J.B. (1985), 'International coordination in the design of macroeconomic policy rules', *European Economic Review*, 28, pp. 53–82.

Taylor, J.N. (1979), 'Staggered wage setting in a macro model', *American Economic Review*, Vol. 69, no. 2, pp. 108–13.

Theil, H. (1964), *Optimal Decision Rules for Government and Industry*, Amsterdam, North-Holland.

Trinder, C. and Biswas, R. (1986), Unemployment and labour supply in the National Institute Model 8, National Institute Discussion Paper no. 112.

Vickers, J. (1985), 'Signalling in a model of monetary policy with incomplete information', *Oxford Economic Papers*, vol. 18, pp. 199–217.

Vines, D., Maciejowski, J.M. and Meade, J.E. (1983), *Stagflation, Volume 2: Demand Management*, London, Allen and Unwin.

Wadhwani, S. (1984), Are exchange rates 'excessively' volatile? London School of Economics, Centre for Labour Economics, Discussion Paper no. 198.

Wall, K.D. and Westcott, J.H. (1976), 'Policy optimisation

exercises with a simple control model of the UK economy', *Automatica*.

Wallis, K.F. (1980), 'Econometric implications of the rational expectations hypothesis', *Econometrica*, no. 48, pp. 49–73.

Wallis, K.F. (Ed.), Andrews, M.J., Bell, D.N.F., Fisher, P.G. and Whitley, J.D. (1984), *Models of the UK Economy: a Review by the ESRC Macroeconomic Modelling Bureau*, Oxford University Press.

Wallis, K.F. (Ed.), Andrews, M.J., Bell, D.N.F., Fisher, P.G. and Whitley, J.D. (1985), *Models of the UK Economy: a Second Review by the ESRC Macroeconomic Modelling Bureau*, Oxford University Press.

Wallis, K.F. (Ed.), Andrews, M.J., Fisher, P.G., Longbottom, J.A. and Whitley, J.D. (1986), *Models of the UK Economy: a Third Review by the ESRC Macroeconomic Modelling Bureau*, Oxford University Press.

Wallis, K.F. (Ed.), Fisher, P.G., Longbottom, J.A., Turner, D.S. and Whitley, J.D. (1987), *Models of the UK Economy: a Fourth Review by the ESRC Macroeconomic Modelling Bureau*, Oxford University Press.

Walters, A.A. (1985), *Britain's Economic Renaissance – Margaret Thatcher's Economic Reforms, 1979–84*, Oxford University Press for American Enterprise Institute.

Weale, M.R., Blake, A.P., Christodoulakis, N., Meade, J.E. and Vines, D.A. (forthcoming), *Exchange Rate Targets, Wage Behaviour and Macroeconomic Policy*.

Whitley, J.D. (1983), Incomes policy in the UK 1960–79: modelling and analysis, Ph.D. thesis, University of Warwick.

Whitley, J.D. (1986), 'A model of incomes policy in the UK, 1963--79', *Manchester School*, 54, pp. 31–64.

Williamson, J. (1983), *The Exchange Rate System*, Washington, Institute for International Economics.

Williamson, J. (1985), 'On the system in Bretton Woods', *American Economics Review*, vol. 75, no. 2 (supplement), pp. 74–9.

Williamson, J. (1986), 'Managing exchange rates', *Economic Review*, 4, pp. 31–4.

Williamson, J. and Miller, M. (1987), 'Targets and indicators: a blueprint for the international coordination of economic policy', Washington, Institute for International Economics.

Worswick, G.D.N. (1981), 'What caused the recession?', in Bank of England (1981), *op cit*.

Worswick, G.D.N. and Blackaby, F. (Eds) (1974), *The Medium Term*, London, Heinemann.

Wren-Lewis, S. (1987), 'Introducing exchange rate equations with a world econometric model', *National Institute Economic Review*, no. 119.

Zarrop, M.B., Holly, S., Rustem, B., Westcott, J.H. and O'Connell, M. (1979a), 'Control of the LBS econometric model via a control model' in Holly, S., Rustem, B. and Zarrop, M.B. (Eds), *Optimal Control for Econometric Models: An Approach to Economic Policy Formulation*, London, Macmillan.

Zarrop, M.B., Holly, S., Rustem, B. and Westcott, J.H. (1979b), 'The design of economic stabilisation policies with large nonlinear econometric models: two possible approaches' in Ormerod, P. (Ed.), *Economic Modelling*, London, Heinemann.

Recent publications

The National Institute of Economic and Social Research

publishes regularly

The National Institute Economic Review
A quarterly analysis of the general economic situation in the United Kingdom and the world overseas, with forecasts eighteen months ahead. The last issue each year contains an assessment of medium-term prospects. There are also in most issues special articles on subjects of interest to academic and business economists.

Annual subscriptions, £55.00 (home) and £75.00 (abroad), also single issues for the current year, £15.00 (home), and £22.00 (abroad), are available directly from NIESR, 2 Dean Trench Street, Smith Square, London, SW1P 3HE.

Subscriptions at the special reduced price of £22.00 p.a. are available to students in the United Kingdom and Irish Republic on application to the Secretary of the Institute.

Back issues and reprints of issues which have gone out of stock are obtainable from Wm Dawson & Sons Ltd, Cannon House, Park Farm Road, Folkestone, Kent. Microfiche copies for the years 1959–87 are available from EP Microform Ltd, Bradford Road, East Ardsley, Wakefield, West Yorkshire, WF3 2AT.

Published by Gower Publishing Company
Education and Economic Performance
Edited by GDN WORSWICK, 1984, pp. 152, £19.50 net.

Energy Self-Sufficiency for the UK
Edited by ROBERT BELGRAVE and MARGARET CORNELL, 1985, pp. 224, £21.50 net.

The Future of British Defence Policy
Edited by JOHN ROPER, 1985, pp. 214, £19.50 net.

Energy Management: Can We Learn From Others?
GEORGE F. RAY, 1985, pp. 131, £19.50 net.

Unemployment and Labour Market Policies
Edited by P.E. HART, 1986, pp. 230, £21.00, net.

New Priorities in Public Spending
Edited by M.S. LEVITT, 1987, pp. 136, £17.50 net.

Published by The Cambridge University Press

Economic and Social Studies

XIX *The Antitrust Laws of the USA: A Study of Competition Enforced by Law*, by A.D. NEALE and D.G. GOYDER. 3rd edn, 1980, pp. 548, £45.00 net.

XXI *Industrial Growth and World Trade: An Empirical Study of Trends in Production, Consumption and Trade in Manufactures from 1899–1959 with a Discussion of Probable Future Trends*, by ALFRED MAIZELS. Reprinted with corrections, 1971, pp. 563, £22.50 net.

XXV *Exports and Economic Growth of Developing Countries*, by ALFRED MAIZELS, assisted by L.F. CAMPBELL-BOROSS and P.B.W. RAYMENT, 1968, pp. 445, £20.00 net.

XXVII *The Framework of Regional Economics in the United Kingdom*, by A.J. BROWN, 1972, pp. 372, £22.50 net.

XXVIII *The Structure, Size and Costs of Urban Settlements*, by P.A. STONE, 1973, pp. 304, £18.50 net.

XXIX *The Diffusion of New Industrial Processes: An International Study*, edited by L. NABSETH and G.F. RAY, 1974, pp. 346, £22.50 net.

XXXI *British Economic Policy, 1960–74*, edited by F.T. BLACKABY, 1978, pp. 710, £40.00 net.

XXXII *Industrialisation and the Basis for Trade*, by R.A. BATCHELOR, R.L. MAJOR and A.D. MORGAN, 1980, pp. 380, £30.00 net.

XXXIII *Productivity and Industrial Structure*, by S.J. PRAIS, 1982, pp. 410, £32.50 net.

XXXIV *World Inflation since 1950. An International Comparative Study*, by A.J. BROWN assisted by JANE DARBY, 1985, pp. 428, £32.50 net.

Occasional Papers

XXXI *Diversification and Competition*, by M.A. UTTON, 1979, pp. 124, £13.50 net.

XXXII *Concentration in British Industry, 1935–75*, by P.E. HART and R. CLARKE, 1980, pp. 178, £19.50 net.

XXXIV *International Industrial Productivity*, by A.D. SMITH, D.M.W.N. HITCHENS and S.W. DAVIES, 1982, pp. 184, £22.50 net.

XXXV *Concentration and Foreign Trade*, by M.A. UTTON and A.D. MORGAN, 1983, pp. 150, £19.50 net.

XXXVI *The Diffusion of Mature Technologies*, by GEORGE F. RAY, 1984, pp. 96, £17.50 net.

XXXVII *Productivity in the Distributive Trades. A Comparison of Britain, America and Germany*, by A.D. SMITH and D.M.W.N. HITCHENS, 1985, pp. 160, £22.50 net.

XXXVIII *Profits and Stability of Monopoly*, by M.A. UTTON, 1986, pp. 102, £13.95 net.

XXXIX *The Trade Cycle in Britain, 1958–1982*, by ANDREW BRITTON, 1986, pp. 108, £13.95 net.

XL *Britain's Productivity Gap*, by STEPHEN DAVIES and RICHARD E. CAVES, 1987, pp. 149, £17.50 net.

XLI *The Growth and Efficiency of Public Spending*, by M.S. LEVITT and M.A.S. JOYCE, 1987, pp. 211, £22.50.

XLII *British Imports of Consumer Goods. A Study of Import Penetration 1974–85* by ANN D. MORGAN, 1988, pp. 140, £19.50 net.

XLIII *Youth Unemployment in Great Britain*, by P.E. HART, 1988, pp. 155, £19.50 net.

NIESR Students' Edition

2. *The Antitrust Laws of the U.S.A.* (3rd edition, unabridged), by A.D. NEALE and D.G. GOYDER, 1980, pp. 548, £15.00 net.
4. *British Economic Policy, 1960–74: Demand Management* (an abridged version of *British Economic Policy, 1960–74*), edited by F.T. BLACKABY, 1979, pp. 472, £11.95 net.
5. *The Evolution of Giant Firms in Britain* (2nd impression with a new preface), by S.J. PRAIS, 1981, pp. 344, £10.95 net.